THE
QUESTIONS
OF
JESUS

ALSO BY JOHN DEAR

Disarming the Heart

Our God Is Nonviolent

Seeds of Nonviolence

Jean Donovan and the Call to Discipleship

Oscar Romero and the Nonviolent Struggle for Justice

The Sacrament of Civil Disobedience

The God of Peace: Toward a Theology of Nonviolence

Peace Behind Bars: A Journal from Jail

Jesus the Rebel

The Sound of Listening

Living Peace

Mary of Nazareth, Prophet of Peace

EDITED BY JOHN DEAR

Mohandas Gandhi: Essential Writings

Apostle of Peace: Essays in Honor of Daniel Berrigan

It's a Sin to Build a Nuclear Weapon: Writings by Richard McSorley

Christ Is with the Poor: Stories and Sayings of Horace McKenna

The Road to Peace: Writings on Peace and Justice by Henri Nouwen

And the Risen Bread: Selected Poems of Daniel Berrigan, 1957–1997

The Vision of Peace: Writings of Mairead Corrigan Maguire

CHALLENGING OURSELVES
TO DISCOVER
LIFE'S GREAT ANSWERS

IMAGE BOOKS
DOUBLEDAY
New York London Toronto Sydney Auckland

JOHN DEAR

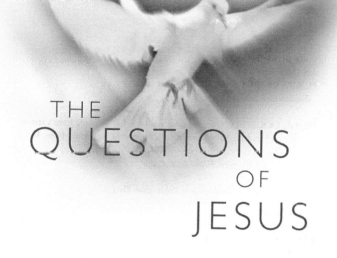

THE
QUESTIONS
OF
JESUS

AN IMAGE BOOK
PUBLISHED BY DOUBLEDAY
a division of Random House, Inc.

IMAGE, DOUBLEDAY, and the portrayal of a deer drinking from a stream
are registered trademarks of Doubleday, a division of Random House, Inc.

Book design by Judith Stagnitto Abbate/Abbate Design

Library of Congress Cataloging-in-Publication Data

Dear, John, 1959–
The questions of Jesus : challenging ourselves to discover life's great answers /
John Dear.—1st Image Books ed.
    p.   cm.
1. Jesus Christ—Conversations.   2. Questioning in the Bible.
3. Christian life—Biblical teaching.
4. Bible. N.T. Gospels—Criticism, interpretation, etc.   I. Title.

BT306.D43 2004
232.9'54—dc22   2004042134

ISBN 0-385-51007-1
PRINTED IN THE UNITED STATES OF AMERICA

December 2004
First Image Books Edition

10 9 8 7 6

FOR
BILL MCNICHOLS
AND
STEVE KELLY

FRIENDS AND BROTHERS
WHO LOVE THE QUESTIONS
AND THE ONE WHO ASKS THEM

We have to keep looking for the spiritual questions if we want spiritual answers.

—HENRI NOUWEN

Be patient with regard to all that in your heart is still unresolved and try to love the questions themselves like closed parts and books written in an extremely foreign language. Do not seek for the moment of the answer because you would not be able to live through it. Live the questions now. Perhaps you will live thereafter and gradually without realizing it, one day, live your way into the answer.

—RAINER MARIA RILKE

God, my God, with You it is always the same thing! Always the same question that nobody knows how to answer! While I am asking questions that You do not answer, You ask me a question that is so simple that I cannot answer it. I do not even understand the question.

—THOMAS MERTON

There have been times when, after long on my knees in a cold chancel, a stone has rolled from my mind, and I have looked in and seen the old questions lie folded and in a place by themselves, like the piled grave clothes of love's risen body.

—R. S. THOMAS

CONTENTS

15.   Obedience   201

16.   Discipleship   214

FOREWORD

BY RICHARD ROHR

In the realm of soul and spirit, there are not really answers as much as there are *answering persons*. The important thing is not to settle the dust and respond to the ego's need for closure and satisfaction, but in fact to lead one into a vital relationship. The ego so demands immediate satisfaction that it will almost always settle for satisfying falsehood rather than remain on the search for often unsatisfying truth. Jesus keeps us on the necessary search.

I am told, for example, that Jesus only directly answers 3 of the 183 questions that he himself is asked in the four Gospels! (I will let you find them.) This is totally surprising to people who have grown up assuming that the very job description of religion is to give people answers and to resolve people's dilemmas. Apparently this is not Jesus' understanding of the function of religion because he operates very differently. Jesus either keeps silent, as with Pilate (John 19:9), returns with another question, as with the coin of Caesar (Matthew 22:19), or gives an illustration, as with the Good Samaritan story (Luke 10:30 ff).

At other times he puts the question back inside the frame of reference of the inquirer, as if to make them critique it. He does so with the rich young man: "You know the commandments" (Mark 10:19). Sometimes he can only weep, sigh, or lament because of the seeming ill-will or hostility represented in the question, as when the Pharisees ask for a sign from him (Mark 8:12). Here he outrightly refuses to respond. He has painfully learned, no doubt, that any attempt to interact with an entrenched position of resentment or ego-fortified suspicion will normally only be used to dig the trench deeper and further fortify the argument. Many times silence, quiet prayer, and genuine love for the opponent are the only answers, even though you will be judged harshly in the moment and by any observers. It must have taken immense humility and groundedness on his part.

If we can understand this basic dynamic, perhaps we can see what Jesus is doing in asking his own questions instead. As John Dear brilliantly illustrates in this book, Jesus' questions are to reposition you, make you own your unconscious biases, break you out of your dualistic mind, challenge your image of God or the world, or present new creative possibilities. He himself does not usually wait for or expect specific answers. *He hopes to call forth an answering person.* He wants to be in relationship with a person, with the idea as it informs the person, and with the process of transformation itself. Thus his questions are worth examining because they, along with the parables, reveal his basic style of encounter with the soul, or what we would call today his style of "evangelization." One wonders why no one has written such a book as this before!

In general, we can see that Jesus' style is almost exactly the opposite of modern televangelism or even the mainline church approach of "Dear Abby" bits of inspiring advice and workable solutions for daily living. Jesus is too much the Jewish prophet to merely stabilize the status quo with platitudes or euphemisms. He much more destabilizes the false assumptions on which the entire question or one's world view is built. As Joseph Campbell said, speaking of the universal messages of myth, "In thinking, the majority is *always* wrong." Jesus knows that his hearers will soon return to the dominant consciousness, totally unprepared to deal with their own inner conflicts or the critique of others. The unspoken assumptions are embedded in every aspect of the culture, and the message will quickly evaporate as impossible or irrelevant. This is the normal pattern, in my experience. The shelf life of a sermon is about twenty minutes.

C. S. Lewis addresses this very issue in his essay on Christian Apologetics in *God in the Dock*. He says, "We can make people attend to the Christian point of view for half an hour or so, but the moment they have gone away from our lecture or laid down our article, they are plunged back into a world where the opposite position is taken for granted. As long as that situation exists, widespread success is simply impossible." This is the final anemia of any religion based primarily on sermons rather than relationships or lifestyle.

Instead, Jesus asks questions, good questions, unnerving questions, realigning questions, transforming questions. He leads us into liminal and therefore transformative space, much more than taking us into any moral high ground of immediate certitude or ego superiority. He subverts up front the cultural or theological assumptions that we are eventually going to have to face anyway. He leaves us betwixt and between, where God and grace can get at us, and where we are not at all in control. It probably does not work for a large majority of people, at least in my experience. They merely ignore you or fight you. Maybe this is why we have paid so little attention to Jesus' questions and emphasized instead his seeming answers. They give us more of a feeling of success and closure. We made of Jesus a systematic theologian, who walked around teaching dogmas, instead of a peripatetic and engaging transformer of the soul. Easy answers instead of hard questions allow us to try to change others instead of allowing God to change us. At least, I know that is true in my life.

Jesus always reminds us that "God alone is good" (Mark 10:18) and we had best not try to concoct our own goodness by providing ourselves with pat or immediate answers about great and intentionally unanswerable questions. Thus he merely lists the memorized commandments to a young inquiring man, while cleverly and compassionately slipping in "Do not defraud" second to last. He does not really answer the self-reassuring question "What must I do to inherit eternal life?" but instead quietly reveals the likely sin of this rich young man. Jesus knows *how* he got rich, and that is why he dares to tell him that he must give it all away. This would-be "thirteenth disciple" cannot bear the ego humiliation of this revelation. "His face fell and he went away" (Mark 10:22). He wanted to think of himself as good instead of rejoicing in the goodness of God. That is the problem with any religion based primarily on morality and satisfying answers instead of on questions. As a result, the young man missed the primary call, the moment of sheer relationship, the ultimate questioning of the soul—when "Jesus looked steadily at him and loved him." Nowhere else is there such a line in the whole New Testament.

The rich young man wanted satisfying answers instead of an answering person, and as a result he got neither. He wanted his question answered to reassure himself that he was in the in-crowd of the saved. Jesus told him personally—on the spot—that he was, but he did not have the freedom to hear any questions but his own.

RICHARD ROHR, O.F.M.
CENTER FOR ACTION AND CONTEMPLATION
ALBUQUERQUE, NEW MEXICO

ACKNOWLEDGMENTS

I would like to thank Helen Pratt for her great encouragement and assistance, Seamus Malarky for his helpful suggestions, Natalie Goldberg for friendship and encouragement, Trace Murphy for bringing this book to the light of day, Richard Rohr for his foreword and friendship, Ched Myers for his original inspiration and friendship, and, most of all, Kass Dotterweich for help editing the manuscript. Thanks also to my parents and my friends in New York and New Mexico.

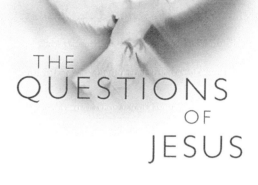

THE
QUESTIONS
OF
JESUS

INTRODUCTION

A few years ago I participated in a weekend retreat in the Nevada desert led by a friend of mine who is a Scripture scholar. As we discussed the Gospel of Mark and prepared to hold a peace vigil at the nuclear weapons test site, my friend said in passing that Jesus was, in the original Latin, "the great *Inter-rogator*," "the One who asks questions."

I was stunned. What an amazing way to look at Jesus! I always thought that Jesus was the one with all the answers. But my friend held the opposite view. Jesus was the one with all the questions.

Someday, I said to myself, I must write down those questions of Jesus and begin the process of finding the answers. I thought if I could learn to listen to the questions themselves, I might better understand the One who asks them.

Years went by. I moved to Derry, Northern Ireland, for a sabbatical year of prayer and reflection. One rainy day, I started writing my list of every question Jesus asked in the Gospels (except for the questions he asked within his parable stories).

The list went on and on. In the end, I found 307 questions.

I sat in my room and looked at the list. It was overwhelming. So many probing, difficult, unanswerable questions! Jesus is like a Zen master, offering unanswerable koans that can point us to the truth of reality. He is like Socrates, teaching the crowds by asking questions. He is like the prophets who rail against the ruling authorities with questions begging for justice, conversion, and peace.

Two thousand years after Jesus first appeared, these questions still hang in the air, awaiting our answers. Most of his questions were never answered. Indeed, most of them have been deliberately ignored.

I started to ponder the questions that touched me the most. One question that haunts me to this day comes at the end of John's Gospel. Jesus has been arrested and is being interrogated, when his best friend, Peter, publicly denies knowing him three times. Having predicted that Peter would deny him, Jesus turns and glances at Peter, as a cock crows in the distance. The next day, Jesus is tortured and executed. Three days later, he rises from the dead and appears to his friends along the Sea of Galilee. In a gesture of ultimate kindness and forgiveness, he builds a campfire and makes breakfast for them. After they eat, Jesus turns to Peter and asks him point-blank, "Do you love me?" Then, he asks Peter again, "Do you love me?" Finally, he asks a third time, "Do you truly love me?" In asking his question three times, Jesus mirrors Peter's three denials with three opportunities for Peter to restore their friendship.

But what a touching, heartbreaking question! Spiritual writer Henri Nouwen once said that this may be the most significant question of all time. God is crying out to each one of us, "Do you love me?" Jesus still waits for our answer.

For years I have sat with that question. As I imagine the sad, gentle, risen Jesus looking at me with love, asking that intimate question, my stubborn heart cracks open a little more to the love of God. That question, like all of Jesus' questions, has the power to melt our hearts and turn us back to our loving God.

The Gospels are filled with stories, actions, parables, miracles, commandments, declarations, imperatives, and incidents from the dramatic life of Jesus. But they also are filled with questions. Jesus has a question for everyone he meets, for every occasion, for every experience, for every potential disciple. From his first encounter with his future disciples to his last words before his ascension, Jesus looks at his friends and invites them deeper into the mystery of God by means of a probing question.

The disciples, scribes, Pharisees, Sadducees, political leaders, and crowds have many declarations for Jesus. They think they know all the answers. Jesus, on the other hand, asks questions in a spirit of love and truth. Like any great rabbi, he teaches his disciples using the technique of the question as a way to break open their stony hearts and their narrow minds to the meaning of life and the mystery of God.

Jesus' persistent questioning shows how compassionate he is. He does not hit us over the head with answers that we cannot comprehend. Rather, he gently invites us to discover for ourselves the truth about God and himself. His questions reveal his great love for the human race.

The most frequently asked question in all four Gospels is perhaps the most beautiful: "What do you want me to do for you?" With this question, we discover not so much a God who demands to be waited on, but a God who is eager to serve.

These tumultuous days of war and violence invite us to take another look at the questions of Jesus for clues about what we should do.

This book offers the questions of Jesus, each followed by a brief reflection about its context, its meaning for Jesus, and its meaning for us today. The text groups the questions under general themes. For your own further study and reflection, the appendix lists the questions according to the gospel in which they appear. After all, my reflections are mere starting points. The key in every instance is to hear what Jesus is asking, to feel the love with which he asks his question, to sit with his question and let it penetrate our hearts and minds. My hope is that you will let these great questions sink in, touch your heart, and lead you closer to God.

In *A Letter to a Young Poet*, Rainer Maria Rilke advises that the best way to deal with life's difficult questions is to sit with them for years and years. "Try to love the questions themselves," he writes. "Live the questions now." Someday, some way, without our knowing it, we may "live our way into the answer."

Sitting with the questions of Jesus may lead us to a renewed interest in the Scriptures and the story of Jesus. But even more, it may open up a new way to pray and reflect on the meaning of our lives, our world, and our God. Letting his questions touch us may lead us deeper into his heart and life, into the mystery of our own lives, and into the mystery of God.

May these reflections on the Great Questions help us on our journey to the Great Answer.

JOHN DEAR

ONE

INVITATION

What are you looking for?

(JOHN 1:38)

W hat are you looking for?"
        The first question Jesus asks does not address our sins, failures, or infidelity. It is not accusatory or hostile. Rather, it is a question rooted in compassion and love, calling upon our deepest desires, the best within us. It is a question full of hope.

"What are you looking for?"

John's Gospel begins when John the Baptist tells two of his disciples that Jesus is the Messiah. "Behold the Lamb of God who takes away the sins of the world," he says, pointing to Jesus. The two disciples immediately begin following Jesus. When he notices these two followers, Jesus turns around, looks them in the eye and asks, "What are you looking for?" He does not reject them. From the start, he is interested in them. He draws them out. He gets them to articulate their hopes and dreams. He is willing to listen to them. He shows them loving kindness.

Those first disciples are caught off guard by Jesus' disarming question. So they ask him a question. "Where are you staying?" Always inviting, Jesus welcomes them into his life. "Come and see," he says to them.

What is it we are looking for in our lives? A good place to begin our daily meditation is to sit in silent peace with the holy desires within us, and to imagine Jesus looking at us with loving kindness and asking, "What are you looking for?"

What would we say to Jesus? As we look at him, as we feel his sincerity and love, and as we notice his lack of judgment or anger, we can let those deep desires surface and be spoken. Seeing the love in his eyes, we know that he will not laugh at or reject us. We know that the best within us comes from God, that God has given us everything that is holy within us, and that he will affirm whatever holy desires we seek.

What is it we want? What do we truly desire? Life is short and precious. What are we most looking for in the remaining years we have left? If we can sit with his question for days and weeks, we will discover, perhaps to our astonishment, that we are not looking for money, power, fame, or control. We are really looking for love, goodness, truth, peace, happiness, justice, mercy, and joy. We are looking for meaning. We are looking for God. We are looking for Jesus.

St. Ignatius Loyola, the founder of the Jesuits, knew, even in the sixteenth century, the importance of holy desires. He taught that every time we pray we should ask God to give us "what it is we are looking for." The Buddhist monks of Tibet also recognize the spiritual wisdom of knowing what it is we seek. For thousands of years, their dharma was based on the understanding that the spiritual life begins by naming what we truly want.

Our deepest desires hold great power. If we can name them,

unleash their goodness, and channel those desires toward God, then our lives will be transformed. We will begin a journey toward God, into the mystery and peace of God, and become servants and friends of God.

If we listen to Jesus' question, name the pure, selfless, loving desires that lie buried in our hearts, and tell Jesus what we are looking for, he will listen and beckon us into a whole new life where those holy desires will be realized. If we dare say that we are looking for him, that we want to be with him, that we want to follow him, we can trust that he will invite us to join him on his journey and lead us to where he lives.

Why are you looking for me?

(LUKE 2:49)

According to Luke's Gospel, when Jesus is twelve years old, he goes with his parents on the annual pilgrimage to Jerusalem. Afterward, he stays behind without his parents knowing it. When they realize he is not in their caravan, they return to Jerusalem in a panic, searching everywhere for their boy.

After three days, they find Jesus in the Temple, where he sits "in the midst of the teachers, listening to them and asking them questions." Already at his young age, Jesus behaves like a rabbi, listening and asking questions. "All who heard him were astounded at his understanding and his answers," Luke reports.

"Son, why have you done this to us?" his mother asks. "Your father and I have been looking for you with great anxiety." The poor parents are worried, stressed out, and angry. They probably feared that something terrible had happened to Jesus, perhaps that he had been kidnapped or killed. But they do not respond with corporal punishment, verbal abuse, or humiliation. Rather, Jesus' mother asks a simple yet serious question.

But Jesus has just spent three days arguing the fine points of the Scriptures with the highest religious leaders in the holiest place on earth. Although he is just twelve, he has already become a spellbinding teacher, an extraordinary rabbi who listens, asks questions, and gives remarkable answers. So Jesus in return asks his parents a pointed question: "Why are you looking for me?"

Luke records that his parents do not understand what Jesus is saying, but that he returns home with them.

It's a good question. If we sit with it, we may hear Jesus' desire to know what motivates us—and we may find ourselves, likewise, unable to answer.

Over a billion people claim to be followers of Jesus. More books have been written about Jesus than any other person in history, and more books have appeared about Jesus in the past thirty years than ever before in history. In recent years, portraits of his face have appeared on the cover of nearly every major U.S. magazine.

Why are we looking for Jesus? Each one of us has a different answer. We look for Jesus because he is the most authentic person who ever lived. We look for Jesus because we feel his compassion for us. We look for Jesus because in his humility, suffering, forgiveness, and death, we see pure selfless love. We look for Jesus because deep down we believe he is alive, that the resurrection is true, and that he will help us through our personal brokenness and global catastrophes. We look for Jesus because we hunger and thirst for God and we believe that he embodies God.

In the end, we may say simply, "Jesus, we are looking for you because we love you, we need you, and we want to be with you."

What do you want me to do for you?
(MATTHEW 20:32; MARK 10:36 AND 10:51; LUKE 18:41)

The most frequently asked of Jesus' questions is also the most beautiful: "What do you want me to do for you?"

In Matthew's account (20:32), the mother of James and John approaches Jesus and bows down in homage before him. "What do you wish?" Jesus asks her. In Mark's version (10:35), James and John themselves approach Jesus and say boldly, "Teacher, we want you to do for us whatever we ask of you." Their selfishness does not faze Jesus. "What do you want me to do for you?" he asks them. In both cases, James and John want to sit by his side in heaven. They want to be in control, to dominate, to be God. But Jesus says that position is "not mine to give."

But Mark's Jesus keeps asking the question. In the next scene, Jesus hears a blind beggar named Bartimaeus call out to him, "Jesus, Son of David, have pity on me." Against the disciples' protests, Jesus calls him over. Immediately, the beggar throws aside his cloak—which would have held not only all the money he had collected but constituted his sole possession. He jumps up and runs to meet Jesus. Seeing this, Jesus places himself completely at the disposal of the poor man. "What do you want me to do for you?" he asks. "I want to see," Bartimaeus says. "Go your way; your faith has saved you," Jesus answers. His sight is restored, and Bartimaeus begins to follow Jesus "on the way." Luke tells almost the same story (18:41).

In both Mark and Luke, Jesus' question to the blind beggar occurs soon after Jesus is challenged by a rich official who wants to enter eternal life as his rightful inheritance. When Jesus invites him to sell what he has, give the money to the poor, and follow him, the rich man turns away sad. Mark even records that Jesus "looked on him and loved him" as he invited him on the discipleship journey.

But it is the blind beggar who wins Jesus over and gets what he wants. The blind beggar shows us our proper disposition before Christ and his question. We too are poor, blind beggars. We too need to come before God in our brokenness, helplessness, blindness, and poverty. We too need to call out to Christ to take pity on us. If we dare renounce our egos and selfishness and beg for God's help, we too will hear God ask, "What do you want me to do for you?"

The question is beautiful because it not only shows God's desire to help us, but it reveals the very nature of God. In Jesus, we have a God who is humble, loving, and generous, a God who longs to serve humanity, especially in its brokenness, poverty, and blindness. Jesus said he came "not to be served but to serve." With this question, we see once more how serious he is.

Like all the questions of Jesus, this one requires reflection, not a hasty response. Do we want to sit beside God in heaven in powerful domination over others, like the selfish male disciples did? Do we want eternal life as if it is our rightful inheritance, as if we deserve it, as if we are the great, worthy elite? Or do we recognize our poverty, brokenness, helplessness, and blindness—our need for God, our need for vision—and want simply to see again, to see God face-to-face?

If we come before God as the broken beggars we are, we can trust that Christ will restore our vision, and, like Bartimaeus, we will see God.

TWO

IDENTITY

Who do people say that I am?

(MARK 8:27; LUKE 9:18; MATTHEW 16:13)

A fter some quiet prayer in a secluded spot, Jesus turns to his friends and asks them what people are saying about him. He has been denounced by the religious authorities as possessed, by his family as crazy, by demoniacs as a torturer, and by the crowds as a blasphemer. But he wants to know if his followers have any clue who he is.

"Who do people say that I am?" Mark records the question. "Who do the crowds say that I am?" we read in Luke's version. "Who do people say that the Son of Humanity is?" Matthew's account says.

Jesus tries to share his identity with everyone, but he learns early on that he cannot come out and tell people who he is. People cannot handle it. They simply cannot accept it. In many ways, neither can we. Yet, Jesus wants to know what others are saying about him to see if they have understood who he is.

The people of Jesus' time were never able to grasp who Jesus was during his lifetime. They could not comprehend his heavenly origin, and, in the end, they brutally executed him as a fraud, a charlatan, a blasphemer.

But Jesus' question is asked from a heart of love, a heart that loves everyone. Even as the people respond to his healing miracles and preaching ministry with hostility and resentment, Jesus feels only compassion for them. He continues to reach out and speak the truth to them. He never stops inviting them into the grace and light of God's reign. He is interested in their lives—in helping them, in saving them.

"Some say you are John the Baptist," the disciples answer. "Others says Elijah. Still others say you are one of the prophets." The disciples have clearly been listening to the crowds and are impressed by some of the rumors. But they themselves do not point out that the crowds are wrong. Their answers belie their own uncertainty. They do not know who Jesus is either.

Jesus' question reveals a deep self-awareness, a searching spirit, someone used to reflecting on the meaning of his life and his own identity. Jesus surely must have put the question to himself first: "Who am I? Why am I here? What am I to do? What is God's will for me?" These are questions that Jesus would have spent time with, probably after his baptism, when he first heard the voice of God call him "my Beloved." He would have pondered these questions also during his forty-day fast in the desert.

At some point, Jesus decides on an answer. He accepts and realizes that he is, indeed, God's beloved. He understands that his special identity means that he will have to treat everyone else as his own beloved. His personal identity is rooted in his intimate relationship with his beloved God, but he knows that means he has to treat the whole human race as his beloved.

Throughout his brief public life, Jesus explores his identity. In John's Gospel, he announces who he is, not as God's Beloved, as the

Son of God, or as the Son of Humanity, but, in more poetic imagery, as the Light of the World, the Bread of Life, the Resurrection and the Life, the Way, the Truth, and the Life, the True Vine, the Good Shepherd, and the Gate. Such beautiful images could only emerge from deep self-reflection. Jesus must have constantly asked himself, "Who am I for others? What do they say about me?"

Jesus' search for self-understanding can inspire our own. "Who are we? What do others say about us? How does God identify me?" The more we ponder our identity and the purpose of our lives, the greater the inner peace and self-confidence we will know, and the greater the compassion and love we will be able to offer to others. Similar self-reflection will lead us to discover that we, too, are God's beloved, called to share that belovedness with every other human being and to help everyone else discover their own true identities as God's beloved sons and daughters.

But who do you say that I am?

(MARK 8:29; LUKE 9:20; MATTHEW 16:15)

Some say this question is *the* question of the whole gospel. After asking his friends who others say he is, Jesus asks them point-blank, "But who do you say that I am?" He asks this question with love, respect, and hope. The disciples have witnessed his miraculous healings, his liberating exorcisms, his dynamic preaching, and his warm presence. They know he is out-of-the-ordinary. At one point, they see him calm a violent storm at sea and literally silence the wind. But they do not know who he is. "Who is this that even wind and sea obey?" they ask each other in wonder and disbelief.

But now Jesus wants to know what they think. He wants to hear them name him, identify him, choose him. He puts them on the spot. "Who do you say that I am?"

At some point along our faith journey, Jesus turns to each one of us, as well, and asks us this same question. "Who do you say that I am?"

Each one of us needs to spend time with this question. We can imagine the gentle eyes of Jesus looking at us, smiling with his usual loving kindness, and hoping for our faith and loving affirmation. He knows who he is because he heard God call him "my Beloved." And he knows who we are, that God calls each one of us God's own beloved sons and daughters. But he knows too that we do not yet understand any of this, so he tries to draw us out, to lead us to the truth, to help us figure it out.

The identity of Jesus then is at the heart of his story and our lives. When Peter speaks up and says, "You are the Christ, the Son of God," Jesus tells him not to tell this to anyone. Why not? Because Peter, like all the disciples and all devout Jews, expects the Messiah to be a military leader who will seize control of Jerusalem, overthrow the Roman Empire, and restore Israel to sovereign power. Their Messiah will be part Che Guevara, part George Washington, indeed part Napoleon.

But Jesus knows who he is, and he is first and foremost not a violent Messiah. Rather, he is nonviolent. He is the embodiment of nonviolence, the incarnation of the God of love and compassion. Jesus will save humanity not through military might but through peaceful, loving means. He tells Peter that, contrary to an all-powerful, imperial, war-making Messiah, he will suffer. Soon, he will be betrayed, arrested, tortured, and brutally executed. He is the Suffering Servant described by the prophet Isaiah (in Isaiah 53). He will save humanity through his suffering and forgiving love on the cross. He will redeem the whole human race. He is the ransom paid to rescue us.

Peter will have none of it. "God forbid such a thing will happen to you," he says.

"Get behind me, Satan," Jesus answers. "You are thinking as men do, not as God does."

Like all of us, Peter cannot grasp the nonviolence of God, the way God thinks and acts. Jesus is the Messiah, the Son of God, but he is not a military, imperial leader. He cannot hurt or kill anyone. It is impossible for him! His innocent suffering will melt every human heart and win over the entire human race to himself, to the truth, to God's reign of nonviolence, to God.

In each Gospel, Jesus proceeds immediately to explain the cross to Peter and his friends. The cross is connected to our answer.

"Who do you say that I am?" Jesus asks us today. Do we answer like Peter, with rote affirmation, declaring that Jesus is the Son of God, yet missing the nonviolence that is at the core of his messiahship and is the key to our own discipleship? Dare we, instead, affirm his path of suffering love, his way of creative nonviolence, his willingness to risk martyrdom on the cross, as the way of God's redemption for us all, and so name Jesus as the God of love, the God of compassion, the God of nonviolence?

We need to look long and hard into the story of Jesus to begin to comprehend who he really is. Only then can we let our answer transform our lives and lead us in his footsteps toward that same paschal mystery: the cross and the resurrection.

Why do you ask me about what is good?

(MATTHEW 19:17)

Matthew's Gospel records the encounter between Jesus and a wealthy young man who asks Jesus, "What good must I do to gain eternal life?"

A good question, right? No. In every way, this is the wrong question to ask Jesus. The center of attention is not on Jesus' saving help, but on the wealthy young man's own initiative. According to the question, the wealthy young man thinks that he is in charge of eternal life, that eternal life is his rightful inheritance (just as his money and possessions are), that eternal life is something he deserves, that salvation is something he can earn. He does not understand that eternal life is a gift from God, that the proper attitude toward Jesus should be one of asking for help, as well as loving worship.

The Gospel invites us not to question Jesus about what we must do, but instead to beg Jesus and the Creator to have mercy on us and welcome us into the fullness of life here and now and later on in heaven.

Like every great teacher, from Socrates to Buddha, Jesus responds to the question by asking a question: "Why do you ask me about what is good?"

Jesus tries to draw out the wealthy young man, to help him recognize who Jesus really is. In a nonthreatening way, Jesus pushes him to go deeper: "Why are you turning to me? Why are you asking me? Do you think I might have an answer?"

And Jesus pushes us. He searches for our faith. Perhaps he wants to know if we trust him and need him, or if, because of our possessions, we have no need of God, since all our needs (supposedly, apparently) are met.

Jesus' question reveals a stunning modesty and humility. Here he is, the Son of God, the incarnation of the Creator, the embodiment of Goodness, and few if any recognize his true identity. Even today, we fail time and again to recognize who he is. Yet instead of lashing out at us, as we might do, Jesus simply raises questions. "Why do you ask me about what is good? Why do you call upon me? Do you think that I can tell you what is good? If I tell you, does that mean you will start to do the good?"

This exchange invites us to reflect upon our relationship with Christ. Why do we call upon Jesus and ask him about what is good? What do we expect of Jesus? Do we know that he really does have the answers, that he is full of goodness, that he is the ultimate judge of good and evil? More than that, do we understand our need for Christ, our total dependence on God, our total powerlessness and helplessness without God?

Jesus calls into question our understanding of life, the reality of death, our false reliance on money, our true dependence on God, and our need for salvation. At some level, Jesus wants to know if we really believe in him, if we are really going to listen to him tell us what is good—and if we are going to do the good.

This famous encounter contrasts with Jesus' meeting with the blind beggar, identified in Mark's Gospel as Bartimaeus. Bartimaeus has nothing, unlike the wealthy young man, and so he calls out, "Son of David, have pity on me." When Jesus responds, Bartimaeus throws aside his cloak and all the money he has begged, asks Jesus for vision, receives his sight, and then follows Jesus "on the way" to the cross.

In contrast, the wealthy young man is unable to surrender completely to Jesus. He does not realize his need for God. Rather, he clings to his possessions and his own feeble control of salvation.

"There is only One who is good," Jesus tells the wealthy young man. "If you wish to enter into life, keep the commandments." When the young man asks which ones, Jesus lists several of them, but adds a new one: "Do not defraud." When the young man presses for more, Jesus answers, "If you wish to be perfect, go, sell what you have and give to the poor, and you will have treasure in heaven. Then, come, follow me." At this clear invitation to discipleship and eternal life, the young man turns away, rejects Jesus, and walks away sad, we are told, "because he had many possessions."

Why do we ask Jesus about what is good? Do we want to hear Jesus tell us what is good and what is evil, and call us to renounce evil and do only good? If that is what we are looking for from Jesus, then we must be willing to change our lives, sell our possessions, give to the poor, and follow Jesus "on the way" to the cross.

Like the blind beggar, we need to call out to Jesus to take pity on us in our blindness and poverty. We need to ask for vision and respond to the gift of healing by following Jesus wherever he goes, come what may. Only then will we do what is good.

Why do you call me good?

(MARK 10:18; LUKE 18:19)

Most of us play little mind games to keep God under control. We try to trick ourselves into thinking that we can manage God, that we can keep God in a box, that we can keep God at bay. We pretend that we are doing God's will, that we are God's servants, that we worship God. We address God with glowing words, but within our own hearts, we are set on our own agenda. We spend our lives manipulating God and deceiving ourselves by thinking that, in fact, we have God right where we want him.

The shocking news of the gospel is that God cannot be tamed. God is not some pet that we can pat on the head periodically through the day, saying, "Isn't he nice?" Rather, God is out of our control. God is wild. God is way beyond us.

In Mark's and Luke's accounts, the rich young man addresses Jesus as "Good Teacher" and asks what he must do to inherit eternal life. In response, Jesus asks, "Why do you call me good? No one is good but God alone."

Is the rich young man trying to flatter Jesus? Does he really believe Jesus is good? Or is he trying to manipulate and control Jesus, like the rest of us?

Jesus' pointed answer to his own question not only indicts humanity's efforts to control God but actually describes the nature of God. We are evil, the Gospel implies. We do not do the good. God alone is good and does the good. God is goodness itself.

"Are you calling me God?" Jesus, in effect, asks the rich young man. "If so, then do you really want to question me? Shouldn't you stop trying to manipulate me and, instead, beg me to heal you and help you?"

Jesus is rarely called "good" by anyone. Rather, he is called all sorts of names, from troublemaking revolutionary to Satan himself. In the end, people denounce him as evil and execute him. The soldiers mock him. Pilate sarcastically calls him King of the Jews. Even as he dies in agony, the passersby on their way to the Temple for the holy days taunt him, saying, "If you are the son of God, come down from that cross."

Jesus sees right through our flattery. He looks into our hearts and knows our ulterior motives. He knows we do not really believe in him. He knows we do not want to do God's will. He realizes that we are determined to pursue our own selfish agendas.

But Jesus has compassion on us. His heart is "gentle and humble," and his questions spring from that depth of compassion. He looks for our faith, our love, our adoration, our sincere worship. He wants us to call him not only Good Teacher, Master, and Rabbi, but Lord, Savior of the World, Son of Humanity, Son of God. If we name him honestly as the Son of God, then he knows we will fall prostrate before him, beg for his saving help, worship him, thank him, and adore him for all eternity.

The Gospel invites us to reexamine our approach to the spiritual life. Instead of controlling and manipulating God, as if that were ever possible, the Gospel teaches us to let go of every effort to control God and to approach God humbly, sincerely, lovingly, for help. The Gospel questions our entire approach to Jesus.

What do we call Jesus? How do we name him? Why do we call him good? What are the ulterior motives behind our relationship to Christ? Once we figure out an honest, humble way to address him, he will answer us, help us, save us—and we will never be the same.

Did you not know that I must be in my
Father's house?

(LUKE 2:49)

When Jesus is discovered in the Jerusalem Temple after his parents search three days for him, he is surprised by their anxiety and worry. He has been debating with the rabbis, scribes, Pharisees, teachers of the law, and religious authorities. He feels at home in the Temple and speaks with an authority and wisdom that no one has ever seen. Indeed, he is not just their equal, but, at twelve years of age, he is already their superior.

Like every devout Jew, Jesus honors the Temple as the holiest site in all of Judaism. The faithful worship God there. Every Jew is required by Mosaic law to make an annual pilgrimage to the Temple at Passover, to change their idolatrous Roman money into Temple money, to purchase expensive doves or pigeons, to offer sacrifice and thus fulfill their religious obligations to God.

But Jesus sees beyond the law, the rules, the religious authorities, the annual pilgrimage, the banking system, the purchase of birds, the economic injustice, and the religious hypocrisy. He realizes that the Temple is indeed the house of God, a place of contemplative prayer. But he sees firsthand how it has become "a den of thieves," as he will later call it.

There in the Temple, for the first time, at the tender age of twelve, Jesus shatters centuries of religious misunderstanding and idolatry by calling the divine Creator of the universe Abba, or Daddy. He breaks through the cultural misconceptions of God and names God by the most honored and intimate relationship upheld in his culture, the relationship between a child and a father.

Mary and Joseph are doubly confused when Jesus asks, "Did you not know that I must be in my Father's house?" They do not understand their son's resistance to being with them, and they do not understand his insistence on being in the Temple. Calling the Temple "my Father's house" not only puts down Joseph and his Nazareth home with Mary, it also raises dangerous, perhaps blasphemous connotations. Joseph and Mary are probably shocked and appalled, but we are told simply that Jesus returns home with them to Nazareth and "was obedient to them," and that "his mother kept all these things in her heart, and Jesus advanced in wisdom and age and favor before God and people."

Years later, according to the same Gospel, Jesus one day announces that he is undertaking another pilgrimage to Jerusalem, more like a political campaign or a nonviolent crusade. When he finally arrives, this time at the age of thirty-three, he walks right into the Temple for the first time since he was twelve and declares, "My house shall be called a house of prayer, but you have turned it into a den of thieves." Then, in an act of peaceful, nonviolent civil disobedience, he turns over the tables of the money changers, leads the cattle outdoors, and stops people from buying and selling. This dramatic public action, like Gandhi's salt march or the sit-ins of the Civil Rights movement, leads almost immediately to his arrest, imprisonment, trial, condemnation, torture, and execution as a political revolutionary.

The seriousness of Jesus' questions can never be underestimated. One could say that Jesus gave his life for this early question. He would make God's house, his Father's house, a house of prayer, instead of the den of thieves it had become, and he would risk his life for that action. He would oppose religious collaboration with the Roman Empire, as well as the economic oppression of the poor, who were required to buy birds in order for their religious pilgrimage and public worship to be considered legitimate. Jesus would have none of it. He was determined to be in his Father's house, to make it a house of prayer, to do his Father's will, and to be faithful to his identity as the beloved son of God.

Jesus was serious about his intimate, loving relationship with God and accepted the consequences of his obedience to God his Father. He tried for three days to teach the religious authorities who God is, what worship of God is, and what the Temple should be like. Apparently, he got nowhere. When his parents arrived, he went home peacefully. We could conclude that he never really tried to teach the religious authorities again. Instead, he turned his attention to the poor and oppressed and gathered disciples and apostles from them.

If we dare embrace our loving God with the same steadfast, faithful, intimate love that Jesus did, we would find ourselves more and more turning back to God, living life in the presence of God, loving others equally as God's children, reconciling with all human beings as God's own children, transforming all places of worship and the entire planet from a den of thieves into a house of contemplative prayer. We would long to return one day to our true spiritual home, the house of Jesus' Father, which is our Father's house too. We would question our own relationship with God and discover what it means to be God's sons and daughters, and brothers and sisters of one another.

The spiritual life begins as we let go of our earthly attachments, turn to our loving God, and find our home in God. Once we discover our true home in the house of God, we begin to live as Jesus did, lov-

ing and serving everyone, leading others to God's house, and looking
forward to one day returning home.

Woman, how does your concern affect me?

(JOHN 2:4)

The first miracle Jesus performs is not the healing of a leper, the
recovery of sight to the blind, or the raising of the dead to life.
Rather, Jesus turns water into wine at a wedding banquet so that the
party can go on for days.

The details of the event shed light on not only Jesus' power but also
his personality and his lavish efforts to celebrate life. We are told that
there is a wedding in Cana in Galilee, that the mother of Jesus is there,
and that "Jesus and his disciples were also invited to the wedding." The
next thing we know, they run out of wine. I think that means Jesus and
his disciples make a spectacle of themselves. They drink all the wine!
That may be partly why Mary approaches Jesus to report, "They have
no wine." She also knows he can do something about it.

"Woman, how does your concern affect me?" he asks. In other
words, "What do you want me to do about it? What can I do?" This
is a reasonable question. What does his mother expect of him? Why
should he be bothered with a minor social crisis?

"My hour has not yet come," Jesus tells his mother. In fact,
throughout John's Gospel, "the hour" approaches gradually until at
last it arrives, and Jesus is betrayed, arrested, and executed. But here,
at the wedding, the story is just beginning. There is no hint of such a
disastrous outcome. We do not know what that hour might bring.

Jesus calls his mother "Woman," the normal, polite form of address for his time. His question is also a common Hebrew expression,
literally meaning, "What is this to me and to you?" But his question
does seem cold. He is not eager to help. He does not want to make a
spectacle of himself.

His mother knows, however, that Jesus is all heart. He will always
help. She does not want the host to be mortified or the wedding

party ruined. "Do whatever he tells you," she tells the servers. Jesus then obeys his mother and so instructs the servers to fill six empty stone water jars, usually used for Jewish ceremonial washings. Each jar can hold twenty to thirty gallons of water. He then tells the servers to draw out some wine and take it to the headwaiter. In the process, the water turns into the finest wine. With this, we are told, he "revealed his glory and his disciples began to believe in him."

Jesus creates not only the best wine but an enormous amount: 180 gallons! Although there may be a mere fifty people at the party, Jesus wants everyone to drink and celebrate. With one gesture, he wipes away the entire Jewish purification ritual. He abolishes the Jewish ceremonial washings by using those water jars for a party, foreshadowing the abundance of wine at the messianic banquet. He wants everyone to enjoy the fullness of life here and now. Jesus repeatedly describes heaven as a wedding banquet, a party that never ends, with enough wine for everyone. As his first public act, Jesus gets the party off to a great start.

"Woman, how does your concern affect me?" Notice, however, the question is never answered by Mary or Jesus. Rather, we are left to ponder the question and the outcome. Whenever we ask Jesus for help, even if only for more wine, he may question us, but he will never deny us. There will be wine enough for everyone in Jesus' reign. He is determined that everyone have life and "life to the full," that there be no more violence, no more suffering, no more death, only celebration, peace, and joy.

Mary knows this. We must know it, too, if we are to get on with the party, making sure that everyone has life to the full.

Who is my mother? Who are my brothers and sisters?

(MATTHEW 12:48; MARK 3:33)

Early in the Gospel of Mark, after he heals a man with a withered hand in the synagogue and starts calling disciples to himself, Jesus returns home to Nazareth, where enormous crowds gather to hear him. "When his relatives heard about this, they set out to seize him," Mark records, "for they said, 'He is out of his mind' " (3:21). Jesus' mother, as well as his brothers and sisters, think he is crazy. They come to take him away. They probably are not so much concerned about him as embarrassed by his actions and claims.

We hold Mary and Joseph in such admiration that we rarely talk about the struggles this family goes through as Jesus begins his public works. In the end, his mother stands by her son as he is crucified, thus becoming the model disciple. But, according to Mark, the early days of Jesus' public ministry are hard on the family. They do not want him making a scene and, in fact, they think he is "out of his mind."

Matthew records that Jesus' family members show up while he is speaking to the crowds. "They wanted to speak to him," so someone tells him, "Your mother and your brothers and sisters are standing outside, asking to speak with you." But instead of welcoming them, Jesus asks his question. Perhaps he is hurt by their earlier efforts to "seize him." He must feel deeply wounded knowing that his mother, brothers, and sisters think he is out of his mind.

After asking his question, Jesus turns to the confused crowd and gives the astonishing, shocking, liberating answer. "Here are my mother and brothers and sisters. Whoever does the will of my heavenly Father is my brother and sister and mother" (Matthew 12:49). Luke's version omits the question but offers a similar reply: "My mother and my brothers and sisters are those who hear the word of God and act on it" (8:21).

As Jesus begins to understand his mission to heal the broken, reconcile everyone, and save humanity, his heart widens to embrace the whole human race. Jesus loves everyone. He has compassion on everyone. He wants all of us to do God's will, to share that ever-widening compassion, to hear the word of God and act on it. He wants us to live as sisters and brothers, children of his loving Father.

If we do God's will, if we join Jesus on his mission of compassion, we become Jesus' own family. We become his faithful, trusting, loving relatives. We become his mother and brothers and sisters. We are that close to him, that intimate. It is an enormous responsibility, a tremendous calling, a great blessing. We are empowered not only to do God's will, to act on God's word, but to be Jesus' own intimate family. This vocation can transform the world, but, perhaps even more profoundly, it can lead us to spend eternity with our beloved brother.

> What is your opinion about the Messiah?
> Whose son is he?
>
> (MATTHEW 22:42)

Jesus is surrounded by the corrupt Pharisees, the vicious religious authorities who challenge him and seek to execute him. They have interrogated him and have done everything they can to destroy him except hand him over to die. But now the moment has come for Jesus to put a question to them. "What is your opinion about the Messiah? Whose son is he?"

The question can be taken in several different directions. "What do you think in general about the Messiah? What kind of person will the Messiah be? What will the Messiah do?"

The question can also lead us back to Jesus. Who do we think Jesus is? Whose son is he? Is he the child of Mary and Joseph, an heir of David, or the living God?

The Pharisees have an answer. "The Messiah is David's son."

This is Jesus' cue. "How, then, does David, inspired by the spirit, call him 'lord'? If David calls him 'lord,' how can he be his son?"

With that, the Pharisees are reduced to silence. "No one was able to answer him a word, nor from that day on did anyone dare to ask him any more questions." They can no longer question the Great Questioner.

It is easy for us now, at this safe distance, to put down the Pharisees. But how do we answer the question? Who do we say Jesus is? What is our opinion of the Messiah? What kind of savior do we want?

The long-expected Messiah was supposed to be sent by God to save us and redeem us. Jews look for the Messiah to liberate and restore them. But back then they expected the Messiah to be an imperial military figure who would wage war against the ungodly and use military might to install God's reign of global domination.

Few could imagine any other kind of Messiah. Nor can we. Deep down, people around the world look for messianic figures who will take over the world, kill their enemies, put some of us in charge, and lead those who are saved into the rapture. We do not want a Messiah who will stand with the poor and put down the sword. We do not want a meek, gentle, peaceful, powerless martyr for a Messiah. We do not want a failure, a victim of the death penalty, a bloodied torture victim who commands us to follow him on his way of the cross.

When we think of the Messiah, we too might answer that he is David's son or Abraham's son or Elijah's son, the child of our biblical lineage. But we try not to think too much about the nature of the Messiah or his true identity.

Nevertheless, the Gospel boldly announces that the Messiah has come, but he is not what we expected. Jesus of Nazareth is the Messiah, and he is perfectly nonviolent, unconditionally loving, consistently forgiving, infinitely compassionate, and at the same time he refuses to tolerate evil. The Messiah nonviolently resists systemic violence and institutionalized injustice. He gives his life in this campaign of active, disarming, transforming nonviolence and demands that we follow him. What's more, the Gospel declares that Jesus is none other than the Son of God, which means that God is a God of peace, love, and active nonviolence.

This question about the Messiah and his identity leads us into the nature and mystery not only of Jesus but of God and ourselves. As we meditate on Jesus' identity and the path he took to save us, we discover the nature of God and our own true identities. If Jesus is truly peaceful, loving, and nonviolent, and he is the Son of God, and

God is truly peaceful, loving, and nonviolent, and we are the sons and daughters of God, the brothers and sisters of Jesus, then we also are called to be peaceful, loving, and nonviolent. As we explore the true identity of Jesus and the nature of God, we discover what it means to be human and who we are, and, in the process, we are saved.

Can the wedding guests fast while the bridegroom is with them?

(MARK 2:19; LUKE 5:34)

When I think of the most joyful events shared in common by people around the planet, I think first of the birth of a child. And then I think of the wedding of loved ones, along with the reception and party afterward.

One of the most amazing statements in the Gospel is the declaration of Jesus that the reign of heaven is an eternal wedding banquet. Over and over he describes heaven as a never-ending wedding banquet, where everyone dances and drinks wine and eats the best food and celebrates with great joy—for all eternity! What a shocking and wonderful image. What would the world look like if we all grasped the truth that we are headed toward an eternal wedding banquet in heaven? Maybe we would start living life as if we were at a permanent wedding banquet right now. Maybe we would begin celebrating one another, celebrating every moment of life, celebrating our God who created us and invites us to an eternal party.

The disciples of John and the disciples of the Pharisees confront Jesus and ask him, "Why do our disciples fast but your disciples do not fast?" as if to say, "If you're so holy, why aren't you fasting all the time?"

In this early episode in Mark's Gospel, Jesus does not lash out at his critics. Rather, he simply returns their question with an even more provocative question: "Can the wedding guests fast while the bridegroom is with them?"

Of course not! We would not fast at a wedding banquet when we are celebrating a beloved bridegroom who is getting married to a beloved bride. We would want to toast the bridegroom with the best wine or the best champagne! We would want to serve the bride and groom the finest hors d'oeuvres, the best caviar, the most delicate escargot! We would want to make sure he and his beloved got the first and best plate of the feast! We would want them to have the first slice of the greatest cake ever made! And then we would want to toast them again!

The one place where we do not fast is at a wedding banquet. Jesus declares that life is a wedding banquet for everyone, and eternity is a never-ending, joyful wedding banquet in his reign. As long as he is around, there will be life and food and drink for everyone.

The day will come, of course, when our bridegroom will be taken away, when the Pharisees will get their way and kill him. When that happens, he avers, his disciples, including us, will fast.

The question opens a view into Jesus' perception of himself. Who does he think he is? How does he understand himself? We get a clue here when he calls himself a bridegroom, which is an unusual but wonderful self-image. We are not sure who the bride is, but the church teaches that the bride of Jesus is the whole human race, the Body of Christ, with whom he wants to live in perfect union for eternity. He thinks of himself as coming to a wedding, where he is about to have the greatest experience of his life.

The question reveals Jesus' attitude toward the human race, a disposition of affirmation, joy, unconditional love, and great expectation—the anticipation one feels as one prepares to go to a wedding banquet. If we can see ourselves as the friends of the bridegroom, whether we're fasting or feasting, we will be focused on him and do everything we can to please him, to assure his happiness, to take care of all the wedding details, to escort all his guests into the wedding celebration, to get the ring ready. We will do whatever he wants us to do so the wedding goes smoothly, thus ensuring that the wedding party is the most joyful in human history, first and foremost, for our beloved bridegroom.

Can the wedding guests mourn as long as
the bridegroom is with them?

(MATTHEW 9:15)

Over the years, I've known hundreds of people who have died.
Living in the New Mexico desert as the pastor of four
churches, I have presided at countless funerals and ministered to
thousands of mourning, weeping people. After September 11, 2001,
I worked as a chaplain in New York City and counseled over 1,500
grieving relatives who lost loved ones in the destruction of the World
Trade Towers. I have held people as they wept, consoled them as they
mourned, listened to their pain, and tried to speak to them healing
words of God's love.

Grief and mourning are deeply painful experiences, but in the
end they can become a great grace from God. They can lead us
deeper into faith, peace, and the presence of the risen Christ.
"Blessed are those who mourn," Jesus declares in the Sermon on the
Mount. In the midst of our sorrow, if we can go deep into our grief,
we may find there the consoling love of God, as we make the leap of
faith into the vision of resurrection and new life.

In the throes of grief, however, it is hard to envision anything.
Sometimes we even lose our reason to live. As hope vanishes, we do
not feel the presence of God anywhere.

Jesus again puts the question to us: "Can the wedding guests
mourn as long as the bridegroom is with them?" Again, he identifies
himself as the bridegroom and says that as long as he is here, the
wedding goes on, the party will happen.

The key to the spiritual life is simply to be with Jesus, to stay
with Jesus, and to remain with Jesus, now and forever. Heaven is eternal joy in the presence of his company. Wherever he is, there is peace,
joy, love, and life. While he was alive on earth, he brought life to
everyone. Those who touched the hem of his garment were healed.
Those he touched were healed. If he touched a dead person, that person was raised to life. In fact, he did not even have to touch the dead

body; he could simply call out the person's name, and the dead person would come to life again. Diseases vanished in his presence. Demons of death fled from him. In his presence, people felt whole and at peace, of sound mind, body, and heart. Everyone wanted to be like him, to love like him, to live like him, to be with him, to stand in his presence. Throughout his public life, he was mobbed, like the greatest celebrity in the world. Why? Because he is the fullness of life, the incarnation of the God of Life.

In the presence of Jesus, there is no more death. In his presence, we do not mourn. Rather, we live and love and celebrate. We walk with him and know the fullness of life. We are filled with peace and joy. If we live in his spirit, we are no longer about death. We no longer inflict death on others. We no longer cause anyone anywhere to mourn by killing their loved ones. We do not cause people to grieve. Instead, like Jesus, we console people, lead people to life, give people hope, and help people to celebrate joyfully the gift of life itself. We want everyone to taste the fullness of life which is his presence.

In the presence of the bridegroom, wedding guests do not mourn. They celebrate the wedding. As we work to share life, protect life, and defend life for all people, no matter what we go through, deep down we celebrate because we are with the risen bridegroom.

Friend, who appointed me as your judge and arbitrator?

(LUKE 12:14)

Jesus has just instructed his disciples to face without fear the inevitable persecution from the ruling authorities. Then, someone in the crowd says, "Teacher, tell my brother to share the inheritance with me." This bitter, resentful man wants what he thinks is rightfully his: the land and possessions that belonged to his late father.

The two of them—Jesus and the man in the crowd—are on entirely different wavelengths. Jesus does not want to get involved in our family feuds or divide up land and possessions. Rather, he is trying to get us to see beyond ourselves, our material goods, our brief lives. He wants to save our souls, to change the world, and to inspire us to lay down our lives on behalf of the human race as nonviolent martyrs for justice and peace.

Jesus has just instructed his disciples not to fear the first death but to fear the second death, where we can be thrown into an eternal hellfire. He wants us to give our lives in love for others, and to fear only the One who decides our eternal fate. Instead, the crowd is worried about money. This particular man is concerned only with his inheritance, not his soul, not eternal life, not his brother, not his dead father, not justice for the poor, and not the coming of God's reign.

This is true for so many of us; we are concerned only about money and possessions. Like the crowd, we are not interested in God but in how to make money, how to invest in the stock market, how to claim our inheritance, how to sue someone to get more money, how to win the lottery, how to get as many cars and televisions and houses as possible. Many of us are consumed with resentment toward our relatives over some material thing, some minor insult, some petty amount of money. We want what we think rightfully belongs to us, and we will bring in the lawyers to get our inheritance—even at the cost of never again speaking to our brothers and sisters. Instead of mourning the loss of our parents and focusing on God and the next life, which is what Jesus wants, we fight over who gets what. We ignore the needs of the poor and, in the process, lose our souls. Instead of joining a cause worth fighting for, the struggle for justice and peace, we waste our time, energy, and lives.

Jesus does not want us to spend the few decades we have left on earth chasing after money or arguing with our relatives about what is ours. Instead, he calls us to let go of everything, to live simply, to love one another, to seek God's reign, to serve the poor, and to take up the cross of nonviolent resistance to injustice. If we do these things, everything we need will be provided. We will have hundreds of houses and relatives—and eternal life.

Notice that Jesus does not get angry with the man in the crowd. Jesus is patient. He calls the man "friend," which is Jesus' basic attitude toward everybody. He sees us as his friends, and, as a friend, he looks at us as if to say, "Why are you wasting your time fighting over land and property? Let's enjoy life and live in peace with each other. Let others have what they want so that you can live simply, serve the poor, and seek God first." Only a friend would speak so honestly and tell us what we really need to hear.

When Jesus asks, "Who appointed me as your judge and arbitrator?," he points again to his identity. Who do we think he is? Is he our judge, our arbitrator? Does he decide about the inheritance of the rich? No. He wants us to give what we have to the poor and come follow him. He has a far more serious and significant agenda for us. Because he is our friend, he tells us the truth.

And yet, if we go deep into the question, we know that God the Creator has appointed Jesus as the Messiah. As Matthew 25 explains, Jesus is the judge who will "separate the sheep and the goats" and divide the nations of the world. Jesus will judge us according to our treatment of the poor, homeless, and hungry, those who inherit nothing. Did we give our inheritance to them? Did we feed them, house them, care for them, visit them? Our judgment will not be based on how we invested in the stock market but, as Dorothy Day said, on how we invested in the poor and marginalized. Jesus wants us to invest everything in the poor, including our very lives.

St. Vincent de Paul taught that we have stolen our possessions from the poor and that we must give away all that we own. Become meek, Jesus says, and you will inherit the earth, which is the only precious gift. Your eyes will be opened to the beauty of creation. You will learn to live in peace—to breathe, to love, to praise God, because you are at one with creation and the Creator.

What would it mean if we lived our lives and saw ourselves as friends of Jesus? For me, that is the most intriguing part of his question. Friendship, I am learning, is perhaps the greatest gift of life. As I ponder the Gospel, I think that Jesus wanted friends more than anything else. In the end, he calls his disciples not servants but friends. He wants to be their food, their drink, their very breath.

Jesus has a specific way of life, and he wants to share it with us.

His friends are not the rich. They have nothing to inherit. They walk away from their simple work as fishermen and tax collectors, leaving everything to be with their friend. Jesus wants us to do the same today, to see beyond our petty concerns, our materialism, and our greed, to become his friends.

And as his friends, we too will want to drop everything to be with our Friend.

O faithless generation, how long will I be with you? How long will I endure you?

(MARK 9:19; LUKE 9:41; MATTHEW 17:17)

Jesus has just been transfigured on the mountaintop, where Moses and Elijah appear to him and encourage him on his journey to the cross. God speaks from the heavens and says to Peter, James, and John, "This is my beloved son. Listen to him!"

As they descend the mountain, they find a large crowd and the remaining disciples engaged in a bitter public argument with the scribes. When Jesus asks what the problem is, a man comes forward to explain that he asked the disciples to heal his possessed son, but they could not cure him.

Jesus rarely loses his patience. He is like Buddha, like Gandhi, an icon of peace and serenity, even as all hell breaks loose around him. But today he cannot take it anymore. He is at his wit's end. For a brief moment, we hear the frustration of Jesus, the direct result not of the poor man or the possessed boy or the motley crowd or even the menacing scribes, but of the faithless disciples. They do not have enough faith to heal the boy, and Jesus, recently transfigured, is bitterly disappointed.

"O faithless generation, how long will I be with you? How long will I endure you?"

These questions appear in all three synoptic Gospels. Jesus sees the disciples, the scribes, and the crowd as a "faithless generation." According to Jesus, anyone with faith can heal the poor boy. Indeed,

as he tells the father, "All things are possible to those who believe."
Astonishing!

The father's answer immediately sets the proper disposition for
every generation to come: "Lord, I believe: help my unbelief." This
is the attitude of every disciple, indeed every human being before
Christ. Hearing these words, Jesus heals the boy.

Are we more faithful than that first generation? I doubt it. While
the majority of people in the United States profess faith in God and
in Jesus, when push comes to shove, they place their trust in weapons
of mass destruction. Their security is found not in God but in first-
strike nuclear weapons, in huge armies, in the Pentagon, in the flag.
There has never been such faithlessness in any previous generation.
Worst of all, the infidelity is found primarily among Christians. The
people who claim to be disciples, just like the gang at the foot of
Mount Tabor, are, more often than not, maintaining the nuclear arsenal, dropping the bombs, hoisting the flag, pledging allegiance not to
God but to some other idol. While they talk a good game, they do
not, in fact, trust Jesus. They do not reject the culture's idolatrous
weapons and begin the healing process.

"How long will I be with you?" The question can be taken three
ways. Part of Jesus can hardly bear to be with us anymore because of
our lack of faith. He wonders how long he will have to put up with
our nonsense. Alas, the answer is, not long. Like Moses and Elijah, he
knows full well that he is nearing his destination in Jerusalem, where
he will turn over the tables of the money changers in the Temple, an
act of nonviolent resistance that can only lead to his immediate execution at the hands of the ruling authorities.

And then there's the part of Jesus that asks the disciples to reflect
on how long they will have him. But again, the disciples cannot grasp
what lies in store for their friend Jesus, even though he has told them
three times already, even though three of them have just seen a vision of Moses and Elijah, who confirm his destiny as the Suffering
Servant.

If we dare take the question personally, however, the question
comes alive in a third way. How long will Jesus be with us? Do we

know? We do not. The prayer of the Christian is that we might always be with Jesus, that he might always be with us, that we might never leave him, that we might grow so rich in faith as to bring him joy, that he will take us to his side, that we may dwell in paradise with Christ forever.

But are we with Jesus right now? Do we want to be with Jesus today? Do we want to spend eternity with Jesus? If we answer yes to these questions, we need to plumb the depths of faith, like the disciples. We need to call out, like the father, "Lord, I believe: help my unbelief!" We need to put aside our infidelity, our complicity with this faithless generation, our false reliance on weapons of mass destruction, and place our security one hundred percent in the Christ and the Creator. We need to change our lives so that we are with Jesus and can be with him forever. Only then—when we ourselves are transformed—will we be able to hear Jesus calling us his friends, promising to welcome us into God's house, where we may dwell with him forever, beginning today.

> Lord, when did we see you hungry and feed you, or thirsty and give you drink? When did we see you a stranger and welcome you, or naked and clothe you? When did we see you ill or in prison and visit you? Lord, when did we see you hungry or thirsty or a stranger or naked or ill or in prison and not minister to your needs?
>
> (MATTHEW 25:37–39, 44)

The story is told about a prominent reporter who flew to Calcutta to interview Mother Teresa. He followed her on her usual rounds through the streets of Calcutta, where homeless people lie dying each day. Finding some desperate man covered in filth and vomit, she would bend down and greet him as if he were a king. With loving words and gentle hands, she and her sisters would start cleaning him right there on the street, before picking him up and bringing him to her home for the dying.

As Mother Teresa washed the vomit and vermin off the face, chest, and legs of a dying man, the reporter watched in horror, appalled that she would go near such filth. "I wouldn't do that for a million dollars," he said.

"Neither would I," Mother Teresa answered.

Jesus' questions, from the parable of the Last Judgment (at the conclusion of Matthew 25), are beautifully embodied in Mother Teresa's response to the reporter. Jesus says that when all the nations of the world finally stand before him, they will ask themselves, "Lord, when did we see you hungry and feed you, or thirsty and give you drink? When did we see you a stranger and welcome you, or naked and clothe you? When did we see you ill or in prison and visit you? Lord, when did we see you hungry or thirsty or a stranger or naked or ill or in prison and not minister to your needs?"

These questions point us toward the true identity of Jesus. Who is he? How does he understand himself? Where is he? What is he like? His questions lead us to a stunning, shocking realization. As we stand before him at that final judgment, we will suddenly realize with utter astonishment that Jesus was present in all those we rejected and ignored, that Jesus sided with the poor, the outcast, the marginalized, the oppressed, and the enemy. What we did to them, we did to Jesus. What we did not do for them, we did not do for Jesus. When we helped them, we helped him. When we did not help them, we did not help him. When we killed them, we crucified Christ all over again.

These questions will become our questions, Jesus says, as we stand before him. We will confess that we did not recognize him. We will realize our blindness, apathy, and stupidity. If we knew Jesus was sick and dying or poor and hungry or in prison, we would help him, we tell ourselves. If we knew Jesus was present in the poor, we would not turn our backs on them. Worse, we would not support the wars, weapons, corporate greed, and government systems that keep the poor and oppressed poor and oppressed. We would fight against this systemic injustice. If we ignore the poor, this is what we will regret.

The questions invite us to put on the glasses of faith, to see Christ in all those at the bottom or on the edge of society: the children of Iraq, the teenagers of Palestine, the tortured victims of U.S.-backed military death squads in Colombia, the men on death row, the homeless families in our city shelters, and the millions of Africans with HIV and AIDS. These people are Jesus, and from now on we know it. From now on, we have to try consciously, deliberately, and practically to serve Jesus in the poor.

"Our context today is characterized by a glaring disparity between the rich and the poor," Peruvian theologian Gustavo Gutierrez told *America* magazine (on February 3, 2003). "No serious Christian can quietly ignore this situation. It is no longer possible for someone to say, 'Well, I didn't know' about the suffering of the poor. Poverty has a visibility today that it did not have in the past. The faces of the poor must now be confronted. And we also understand the causes of poverty and the conditions that perpetuate it. There was a time when poverty was considered to be an unavoidable fate, but such a view is no longer possible or responsible. Now we know that poverty is not simply a misfortune; it is an injustice. What must we do in order to abolish poverty? Theology does not pretend to have all the technical solutions to poverty, but it reminds us never to forget the poor and also that God is at stake in our response to poverty. An active concern for the poor is not only an obligation for those who feel a political vocation; all Christians must take the Gospel message of justice and equality seriously. The preferential option for the poor is not optional, but incumbent upon every Christian. It is not something that a Christian can either take or leave. It involves standing in solidarity with the poor, but it also entails a stance against inhumane poverty."

The parable of the Last Judgment challenges us as individuals, but it also addresses the conduct of nations. It declares that God will judge the nations of the world and divide the nations into two groups, the sheep and the goats, the just and the unjust. The parable invites a national examination of conscience. What does the God of love and life think about our nation? Does God rejoice that we are doing God's will? Or does God grieve our violence and selfishness?

From God's perspective, looking down upon this beautiful planet, God sees that the United States of America is only 4.7 percent of the world's population, yet we hoard, dominate, and control over 60 percent of the world's resources. We take oil and other natural resources from the poorer nations and ignore their poverty and starvation. We sell weapons to all sides in all wars, instead of eradicating war and violence. We are the richest nation in the history of the world and are capable of doing so much good, yet over 2 billion people suffer in misery; 800 million people are chronically malnourished, and some 50,000 people die of starvation every day. God wants this nation to use its abundance to end world hunger, poverty, and war. If we share our wealth with the world's poor, we will cut the roots of terrorism, win everyone over with our compassionate love, and make war and weapons obsolete. Then God will call us blessed because we will have treated God humanly, Godly, lovingly. If our nation does not serve Christ in the poor and relieve their misery, God will judge us all harshly.

Our job, as mature Christians, is to love and serve Christ everywhere, regardless of what the world says. We will walk with Christ, serve Christ, and protect Christ in the least, most vulnerable, and most helpless people on the planet. We no longer limit our view of the world to the perspective of America. Rather, we see humanity from God's perspective. Everyone is our sister and brother. Everyone is Jesus.

We have to follow the logic of these Matthew 25 questions to Jesus' politically incorrect conclusion: "Whatever you do to the suffering people of Iraq, you do to me. Whatever you do to the people on death row, you do to me. Whatever you do to the billions of starving, impoverished people around the world, you do to me."

The Gospel invites us to ask these questions now, today—not at the moment of the Last Judgment. We will be blessed for all eternity by our answers to these questions today.

Have I been with you for so long a time
and you still do not know me?

(JOHN 14:9)

Jesus has just turned over the tables of the money changers in the
Temple, raised Lazarus from the dead, and washed his disciples'
feet and offered them his body and blood through bread and wine.
"Do not let your hearts be troubled," he tells them (John 14:1). "You
have faith in God; have faith also in me. In my Father's house there
are many dwelling places. And if I go and prepare a place for you, I
will come back again and take you to myself, so that where I am you
also may be. Where I am going, you know the way."

"How can we know the way?" Thomas asks him.

"I am the way and the truth and the life," Jesus explains. "If you
know me, then you will also know my Father. From now on you do
know him and have seen him."

Philip then speaks up. "Master, show us the Father and that will
be enough for us." In an hour or so, Jesus will be arrested and led
away to be interrogated, tortured, and executed. Philip, like all of us,
does not understand any of this. He does not grasp what is about to
happen or what Jesus has taught about God the Father. Philip wants
to see the Father, and "that will be enough."

"Have I been with you for so long a time and you still do not
know me?"

In this question, we can hear not just disappointment but a feeling of being crushed. Jesus is heartbroken. "What more can I say to
you, Philip?" he asks in effect. "You have not understood anything I
have said about myself or God."

But Philip's request leads Jesus to state a simple and profound
truth: "Whoever has seen me has seen the Father." There it is; it's that
simple. If we see Jesus, we see God.

I think this question can be asked of each one of us today. We
have heard and read about Jesus all our lives, yet in many ways we still
do not know him. We still do not believe. We still do not understand.

"Show us God, and that will be enough!" we think and whisper to Jesus, just like Philip.

But the consoling word is that Jesus wants us to know him! He wants us to understand everything about him and God. He wants us to see him and to see God in him!

As we sit with this question, we can get to know Jesus better and better. The way to know Jesus is simple: through daily contemplative prayer, regular Gospel reading, actively serving Christ in the poor, loving Christ in everyone, and joining the community of faith in authentic worship of our beloved God.

If we can take time each day to sit in intimate friendship with Jesus, we will get to know him. He will get to know us. And in the process, through Jesus, we will see God.

THREE

PURITY OF HEART

What are you thinking in your hearts?

(LUKE 5:22)

While Jesus is teaching in a crowded house, some people lower a stretcher bearing a paralyzed man through the straw roof right down in front of Jesus. When Jesus sees the faith of the man's friends, he says to him, "Your sins are forgiven." Jesus can see how loved the paralyzed man is. For Jesus, such forgiving love is not only moving and rare but the secret to life itself.

But the scribes and Pharisees who witness this beautiful declaration of forgiveness are appalled. They ask themselves, "Who is this who speaks such blasphemies? Who but God can forgive sins?" We are told that Jesus can see their resentment and knows what they are thinking. But instead of yelling at them for their hard-heartedness and hatred, he asks a question: "What are you thinking in your hearts?"

The scribes and Pharisees are too embarrassed to answer because the crowds will see the difference between Jesus' loving kindness and their bitter violence. While the crowds, however, hang on Jesus' every word and respect what he is saying, the religious authorities resent his authority and teaching and consider his interaction with the marginalized as illegal and unruly, if not outright blasphemous.

But Jesus is unperturbed. "That you may know that the Son of Humanity has authority on earth to forgive sins, I say to you, rise, pick up your stretcher and go home." With that the paralyzed man stands up, picks up his mat, and walks home "glorifying God."

The crowds are astonished, but the religious leaders are furious. Jesus has shown them up. They do not care that a sick person has been healed. They only know that their egos are bruised and their political authority is threatened.

Jesus can sense all of this. We might at first wonder why Jesus does not ask what we are thinking in our minds, but Jesus knows that what we think and feel in the recesses of our hearts energizes what we say and do. In fact, at various points throughout the Gospels, he explains to his disciples that the heart is the source of violence, injustice, war, greed, murder, cruelty, and sin. What we think in our hearts, what we value in our hearts, what we fuel in our hearts, determines our attitude and behavior toward others and, in the end, toward God.

We all have sinful, broken, violent hearts, but Jesus tells his friends that he is "gentle and humble of heart." He possesses neither violence nor pride. Rather, his heart is nonviolent and humble.

It is good for us to hear God ask us what we are thinking in our hearts. Instead of yelling at us because we harbor violence and resentment, God invites us to share the truth of our hearts with God, to humbly reveal to God our violence, resentment, and brokenness. Here lies the path to healing. If we can tell Jesus honestly what we are thinking in our hearts, he will respond by healing our hearts, which may ultimately be more important than even our ability to walk.

We need to expose to God the darkness and brokenness in our hearts, to let Jesus disarm our hearts, and to become gentle and humble of heart like him. This is the key not only to peace of heart but to the disarmament of the world. If we can allow God to disarm us and transform our hearts, then we too will begin to show forgiveness, compassion, and love to everyone, including the poor and the marginalized, as Jesus did.

One beautiful example of this journey of the heart is found in the witness of Etty Hillesum, a young Jewish woman who was killed in Auschwitz in November 1943, at the age of twenty-nine. Decades after her death, her diaries, entitled *An Interrupted Life*, were published to worldwide acclaim. Her writings reveal the gradual transformation of a searching soul who moved from worldly preoccupation to fear and anger and eventually to compassion and love for everyone, including Nazi police officers and soldiers.

In one of her last entries shortly before her death, Etty Hillesum wrote that she wanted to be "the thinking heart of the barracks." She showed how the spiritual search culminates in a heart of forgiveness, compassion, and nonviolence. This beautiful example offers the best answer to Jesus' probing question. Like Etty Hillesum, we need to become "the thinking heart of the world," to radiate forgiveness, compassion, and nonviolence as Jesus, the Sacred Heart, demonstrates.

Why do you harbor evil thoughts?

(MATTHEW 9:4)

When people bring Jesus a paralytic lying on a stretcher, he is so moved by their kindness to the paralytic and their faith in him that he says to the paralyzed man, "Courage, my child, your sins are forgiven." He speaks only words of kindness, encouragement, affirmation, consolation, and goodness. He is simply stating what has already happened. The paralyzed man's friends love him so much that they clearly forgive any of his faults, care for him, and go out of their way to carry him to the healer for help. Jesus just affirms what they have done: "You are already forgiven. See how much they love you. I love you too and I forgive you also."

Some of the scribes hear this and are appalled. They say to themselves, "This man is blaspheming. Who does he think he is? He thinks he's God." The scribes, religious leaders, and ruling authorities are always infuriated by Jesus, who is, in fact, God. Jesus hears what they are saying and asks simply, "Why do you harbor evil thoughts?"

Well, why do they? Why don't the scribes respond with love and gratitude for Jesus' affirming words? Why don't they care for the paralyzed man and his friends? Why don't they want us to forgive one another and reconcile with one another?

The religious leaders harbor evil thoughts at Jesus because they resent him. They want the attention, the adulation of the crowds, and the authority to speak about God. They think they are in control, in charge, the true agents of God. They want the power to decide who can forgive and who can heal, but suddenly Jesus is the one forgiving and healing and receiving the attentions of the crowd. The scribes do not care about God or the poor or anyone in need. Rather, they are concerned only about themselves. They are fundamentally power-hungry egomaniacs who cannot let go of their domination over others.

Matthew's word "harbor" is helpful. These scribes have spent their lives harboring evil thoughts against others. They are not just cynical. They cultivate sinister thoughts toward others, especially toward those who threaten their power and prestige. They are on the lookout to catch others in sin and blasphemy. They think they are God's police officers when, in fact, they are just the latest death squads of the Evil One.

It is easy to put down the scribes. It is not easy, however, to recognize the scribe within each one of us. We too harbor evil thoughts toward others. We too are resentful of others, jealous of others, seeking praise and trying to maintain power over others. We think we know God best, and we criticize others who do not worship God as we do. In our hearts, we name these people as blasphemers.

Unfortunately, our culture has trained us to be suspicious of others. In a militarized society that maintains thousands of nuclear weapons that can vaporize people in a flash, it is natural for us now to harbor evil thoughts toward other people. We have strayed a long way from Jesus. In fact, we have reached the point in our blind patriotism that some see anyone who criticizes America and its wars as unpatriotic, even blasphemous.

Jesus never harbors evil thoughts. He cultivates and holds good thoughts toward everyone. He lives and breathes the truth of compassion and love and is ready to forgive and heal others because he has incarnated goodness and prayerfully nurtured good thoughts toward all people. Even his question to the scribes shows his goodness. He does not yell at them or kill. He simply questions their love of evil.

Jesus wants us to cultivate good thoughts in our world today. From now on, we are to give others the benefit of the doubt, to presume the best in others, to forgive and call forth love from others, to respond instinctively with compassion toward anyone in need, to see Christ in others, to know only goodness. We are to tend our minds and hearts like a beautiful garden and grow goodness, love, kindness, and truth.

Mahatma Gandhi spent the last fifty years of his life deliberately cultivating truth. He pursued truth as if truth were God. He exemplified this attitude of Christ. After years of seeking truth, Gandhi began to trust everyone, forgive everyone, believe in the potential for goodness within everyone, and see God in everyone. He urged people to seek the truth as a way of life, to work at it daily, so that we move closer to truth and goodness and respond naturally to every encounter with loving kindness, truth, and goodness. Then, he taught, we will become like God and act more like Jesus because we harbor only good thoughts and do only good deeds.

Why do we harbor evil thoughts? In the end, it is not worth it. Evil is not worth our time and energy. Life is so much better if we renounce evil and focus only on goodness. Yes, goodness as a way of life is countercultural. Yes, we may be dismissed as naïve and stupid. But that does not matter. We are only concerned with how God sees

us. In the eyes of the God of goodness, the God who sees only goodness, we will be seen as wise and full of grace.

The life of goodness, in other words, is the only practical way to
live. It is the way people live in heaven, where they think only good
thoughts. It means that, from now on, we live as if we are already in
heaven.

Did not the Maker of the outside also make the inside?

(LUKE 11:40)

When Jesus dines at the house of a Pharisee, his host is
shocked that Jesus does not follow the Mosaic law. For example, the orthodox faithful are required to wash their hands and
their dishes before eating so that they might not be defiled by unclean
foods. If they do not wash their dishes or follow the other cleanliness
laws, they are unclean and could be excommunicated. They certainly
would no longer be considered holy or presentable to Yahweh.

In Jesus' time, the Jewish religious elite lived by those purification
laws, and followed them to the letter. At the same time, they supported the brutal Roman Empire, oppressed the poor, and kept tight
control over the population. They excommunicated and executed anyone they judged unfit for God or life.

Jesus, however, will have none of this hypocrisy, false piety, or injustice. Rather, he breaks those laws left and right and insists that we
become truly holy, that we turn back to God with all our souls, that
we serve God by serving one another. He practices divine obedience
and civil disobedience. In such a culture, under such oppressive rules,
his excommunication and execution are inevitable.

"O you Pharisees!" he exclaims. "Although you cleanse the outside of the cup and the dish, inside you are filled with plunder and
evil. You fools! Did not the Maker of the outside also make the inside?"

"Which is more important, clean hands or a clean heart," Jesus asks, "ritual piety and corrupt souls, or the true piety that springs from a humble, contrite, nonviolent heart?"

For Jesus, this question points to the meaning of the spiritual life, religious practice, authentic worship, the nature of God, and what it means to be human. He insists that people turn back to God with all their hearts, that they practice sincere and true worship, that they follow not the letter but the spirit of the law.

The Pharisees are concerned with the outside, with the appearance of piety, with the outward adherence to the law, with winning the approval of others and maintaining their religious domination over the culture. They want to be perceived as holy and righteous. But Jesus says that they are far from the reign of God. Inside, their hearts are full of violence, injustice, and evil.

Unlike the Pharisees, Jesus is concerned with the inside. He knows that what goes on inside us determines what we will do on the outside. He wants our hearts to be nonviolent, just, humble, devout, good, and loving. He wants our insides to be temples of the Holy Spirit. This inner work of purification and cleanliness is the first and most necessary task of the spiritual life. From a heart of prayer, devotion, and love, true worship of the living God flows naturally, as well as justice, love, and compassion toward others.

"Did not the Maker of the outside also make the inside?" The question points to the meaning of sin, the law, religious practice, the spiritual life, and the work of God. First of all, Jesus calls God "the Maker." God is the Creator of everything, from the expanse of our universe to material goods to our own bodies to what is inside our bodies—our heart, soul, and spirit. God makes both the inside and the outside.

The Pharisees teach that sin comes from unclean food, dishes, and people. The devout are to avoid anything and everything that is unclean. Jesus, on the other hand, teaches that sin comes from within, that the devout are to cleanse their hearts through prayer, penance, humility, nonviolence, forgiveness, and love. Jesus demands an inner purity of the heart. He follows the prophets who denounced the Hebrews because their hearts were far from God. Like the prophets,

Jesus insists that we turn our hearts back to God, that we cleanse our hearts for God, that we give our hearts to God. In the Beatitudes, he will bless those who are "pure in heart" and declare that "they shall see God."

"Did God not make your heart, your soul, your spirit as well?" Jesus asks the Pharisee. "Didn't the Maker create the real you, your inner, true self? Don't you think that preparing yourself for God means more than washing cups and dishes? Aren't we first of all to prepare our hearts and souls for God? Shouldn't we cleanse our hearts so that when we appear before God, we will be ready and welcomed into God's house to live forever?"

Though most of us do not wash cups and dishes as the central practice of our religious devotion, most of us do carry on a false outward piety while neglecting the rigorous purification of our own hearts. We may attend church on Sundays, sit in the front pew, and speak our prayers for all to hear, but in our hearts we resent our relatives, cheat our employers, inflate our egos, pursue selfish desires, and support war, the death penalty, racism, and nuclear weapons. As we parade around with our false outward piety, we may be very far from the reign of God.

But Jesus does not leave the Pharisees—or us—hanging in the lurch. Rather, he gives us a way out and points us in the direction of spiritual cleanliness. "As to what is within, give alms, and behold, everything will be clean for you!"

We can make up for a lifetime of false piety and inner impurity by giving contributions to the poor, by tithing our income and distributing it to those in need, and by financially supporting those organizations that serve the poorest of the poor. By giving alms, living simply, and not pursuing wealth, we will be purified.

FOUR

CONVERSION

Why do you notice the splinter in your
brother's eye, but do not perceive the
wooden beam in your own eye? How can
you say to your brother, "Let me remove
that splinter from your eye," while the
wooden beam is in your eye?

(MATTHEW 7:3–4; LUKE 6:41–42)

These questions get to the heart of the Gospel, the center of Jesus' teaching. He wants us to repent of our hypocrisy, sin, and
violence, and take up his way of truth, love, and nonviolence. He
wants to change the world, but he wants each one of us personally to

begin the process of global transformation through our own personal conversion, disarmament, and transformation right now.

"Why do you notice the splinter in your brother's eye," Jesus asks in the Sermon on the Mount, "but do not perceive the wooden beam in your own eye? How can you say to your brother, 'Let me remove that splinter from your eye,' while the wooden beam is in your eye?" Jesus wants us to help one another to see clearly, but he knows that we cannot help others when we ourselves are in a far worse condition.

He speaks of a splinter in the eye, something any carpenter would be familiar with. Getting a splinter in your finger can hurt, but getting a splinter in your eye would be terribly painful. Your eye turns red. It swells with tears. You cry. You panic. You fear blindness. You cannot do anything with a splinter in your eye. You have to stop what you are doing, try to pick it out, wash it out, have a friend remove it or go to the hospital.

A splinter in the eye is a serious injury, but a wooden beam in the eye would be far more painful, far more serious, far more deadly! We could not see at all. We would be completely incapacitated. The image of a wooden beam, a two-by-four, in our eye, sticking out five feet on either side of our head, is almost comical. But if we ponder this image which Jesus uses to describe the disciples and ourselves, we realize that he is trying to help us see how sick we are, how serious our condition has become, how close to death we are, how great our need for personal and global conversion has become. According to Jesus, we are blind and need to remove the wooden beam in our own eye before we can ever help anyone.

The problem is that we do not realize we have a wooden beam in our eye. We are blind and don't know it. We think we can see and insist that we alone can help others to see, but we are the blind leading the blind.

Jesus calls us to reflect upon our own condition, our own sinfulness, our own blindness. His questions can lead us from self-righteousness to humility, from judging others to apologizing to others, from domination to service, from condemnation to compassion, from sin to grace, from violence to nonviolence, from resentment to reconciliation, from blindness to vision.

If each one of us individually dedicated ourselves to reforming our lives, ending our violence, humbling our egos, apologizing for our mistakes, rooting out the social sin within us, disarming our own hearts and deepening our faith and love, the world would change for the better. If Christian communities started repenting and converting back to Gospel nonviolence instead of criticizing others, the world would change for the better. If we as a nation would convert to the ideals and principles we expect of others, if we disarmed; fed the world's poor; abolished war, executions, and injustice; and refused to exploit others or destroy the environment, we would carry far greater moral weight in the world and be truly blessed by God. Jesus is trying to convert his disciples and us, so that we can love as he loves, serve as he serves, see as he sees, think as he thinks, forgive as he forgives, and act publicly for justice and peace, as he does.

Jesus points the way out of our madness with the golden rule, found in nearly every religious scripture: "Do unto others what you would have them do unto you."

These questions are two of the most significant questions Jesus ever asked. They call us to conversion, to turn back to God, repent of our sins, and ask for healing. If we ask God to remove the wooden beam in our eyes—personally, communally, nationally, and globally—God will heal us, and we will learn, for the first time, to see with the eyes of Christ, with the vision of peace, love, and nonviolence, and we will recognize one another as equal children of our beloved God.

Do you think that because these Galileans suffered in this way they were greater sinners than all other Galileans? Or those eighteen people who were killed when the tower at Siloam fell on them, do you think

they were more guilty than everyone else
who lived in Jerusalem?

(LUKE 13:2,4)

On September 11, 2001, my visiting parents and I were having breakfast in a hotel room overlooking Central Park in New York City, when we heard that two airplanes had just crashed into the World Trade towers. My parents immediately left town, and I walked downtown toward the massive, stinking cloud to volunteer at St. Vincent's Hospital and the Red Cross emergency centers. Within days, the Red Cross asked me to help coordinate all the chaplains working with grieving relatives at the main Family Assistance Center. For three months, I worked full-time with over 500 chaplains of all religions and personally counseled thousands of grieving relatives and rescue workers, both at the center and at Ground Zero itself. Before, during, and after those days, I also spoke out publicly against U.S. warmaking, particularly the bombing of Afghanistan and Iraq.

When I eventually returned home to the West Side Jesuit Community late in the evening of September 11, I wanted a consoling word from God. I needed to know what Jesus would say after such a disaster. As I thumbed through my Bible, I came across this famous passage in Luke's Gospel (13:1–5), when some people tell Jesus "about the Galileans whose blood Pilate had mingled with the blood of their sacrifices." Jesus replies with these two questions: "Do you think that because these Galileans suffered in this way they were greater sinners than all other Galileans? Or those eighteen people who were killed when the tower at Siloam fell on them, do you think they were more guilty than everyone else who lived in Jerusalem?"

"By no means!" Jesus concludes. "But I tell you, if you do not repent, you will all perish as they did!"

I was stunned. I was looking for a consoling word from Jesus for myself and a message I could offer the grieving people of New York. Yet Jesus' response to his people about the collapse of the tower at Siloam seemed cold and harsh: "If you do not repent, you will all perish as they did!"

But truth often sounds harsh at first. If we do not repent of our violence, Jesus explains, we are doomed to suffer the consequences of violence. Violence in response to violence always—always—leads to further violence. Those who live by the sword—and the bomb and terrorism and nuclear weapons—will die by the sword—and the bomb and terrorism and nuclear weapons. What goes around, comes around. The means are the end. You reap what you sow.

Jesus' questions challenge us to recognize the terrible violence our country has reaped upon the world (especially toward Iraqis and Palestinians), to understand how we have pushed some people so far that they have resorted to the insanity of suicidal violence; to see that the only way to ensure that such terrorism never happens again is to renounce our own terrorism, to stop our own wars, to dismantle our own weapons, to stop hoarding the world's resources, to share our wealth, to feed the starving masses, and to win over humanity through our loving service to the world's poor, regardless of their race, class, religion, or nationality. If we—disciples of Jesus—are willing to respond to Jesus' call to global repentance, people will not want to fly airplanes into our buildings, mail us anthrax, or blow us up. Rather, they will love us.

But have we repented? No. Instead, we have mounted the warhorse and turned deeper into the downward spiral of revenge, retaliation, violence, and death. And if we choose to continue along this path of destruction, waging war and hoarding the world's resources, we are doomed to perish.

For Jesus, these questions are not about the guilt of the victims. The victims of these tragedies—or any tragedies—should not be considered outstanding sinners who were singled out for punishment, as so many of us assume even today. For Jesus, the challenge is not to die like them, as victims of the culture's violence, but to live in the light of God's grace, to walk in God's realm of nonviolence, to resist the culture's violence, and to be ready to enter God's house of peace.

Jesus' questions and his sobering answer are a great gift. They are the only way out of the world's madness of violence. They require prayerful reflection and immediate action on our part. For Jesus, it is never too late to repent of violence and convert to nonviolence. That is the lesson of the tortured Galileans, the victims of the Siloam tower, those who perished on September 11, 2001, and all those who continue to suffer the ravages of war, violence, and injustice.

FIVE

LOVE

If you love only those who love you, what credit is that to you? Do not the tax collectors do the same?

(MATTHEW 5:46; LUKE 6:32)

L ove is the center of Jesus' life and message. His teachings and actions can be summed up in his command to love—to love one another as we love ourselves, to love our neighbors, to love God, and to love our enemies. For Jesus, life makes sense only if we widen our hearts to embrace the whole human race, including those who hurt or would kill us. In doing so, we not only take the high road, we imitate God, who loves the whole human race. In his Sermon on the Mount, Jesus surpasses the ancient biblical commandment "Thou shall not kill." He calls us beyond anger, violence, murder, and war, to God's own unconditional, compassionate love.

"You have heard it said that you should love your neighbor and hate your enemies," he says, "but I say to you, love your enemies and pray for those who persecute you" (Matthew 5:43). With these words, Jesus outlaws every act and intent of violence, including war, revenge, retaliation, nuclear weapons, bombing raids, and the death penalty. He summons us to love every human being on earth, including those who hurt us, murder those we love, wage war against us, attack us, or would kill us.

If we claim to be followers of Jesus, we cannot be mere fans or admirers. Rather, we have to take him at his word and do what he says. Therefore, we will not participate in or support war ever again. Because we try to love our enemies, we will oppose any effort to kill them. We will never justify the mass murder of our enemies. Rather, we will conclude with Jesus that there is no such thing as a "just war." We will realize that war is never just, that war is not the will of God, that war is never blessed by God, that war is not the method of God, and that war is never supported by the God of peace.

When the word "love" is used in the New Testament, in nearly every instance it is the unusual Greek word *agape*. In his book *Stride toward Freedom*, Reverend Martin Luther King Jr. defines *agape* as "understanding, redeeming good will for all, an overflowing love, the love of God operating in the human heart directed toward both friend and enemy, love in action, love seeking to preserve and create community, a willingness to sacrifice in the interest of mutuality." "When I am commanded to love," Dr. King concludes, "I am commanded to restore community, to resist injustice, and to meet the needs of my brothers and sisters."

"Love for enemies is the key to the solution of the problems of our world," Dr. King once preached. "Jesus is not an impractical idealist; he is the practical realist. Our responsibility as Christians is to discover the meaning of this command and seek passionately to live it out in our daily lives."

Nelson Mandela put it this way: "I have never yet met an enemy whom I did not try to turn into a friend."

Such outlandish love is the hallmark of Christianity. Jesus challenges us to practice God's own all-inclusive, all-embracing, unconditional love for the whole human race, not just because it is the only practical option, but because it is the way God relates to humanity. According to Jesus, God loves God's enemies, and we should try to be like God. He commands us to love our enemies "that you may be sons and daughters of your heavenly God, for God makes the sun rise on the bad and the good, and causes rain to fall on the just and the unjust" (Matthew 5:45). If we love our enemies, we will love as God loves and show the world that we are the sons and daughters of the God of peace.

In the same breath as he commands us to love our enemies, Jesus asks, "If you love only those who love you, what credit is that to you? Do not the tax collectors do the same?" (Matthew 5:46). Luke adds a similar line to the first question: "Even sinners do the same" (Luke 6:32). Jesus compares us to tax collectors. Though they are members of the Jewish community, the tax collectors do the dirty work of the Roman Empire by robbing the impoverished masses of their money and thus collaborating with the Romans in their military domination. They profit off the suffering of the poor. Jesus, however, demands that we not hurt anyone, much less live off the pain of others or support oppression and military domination over others. When Jesus asks his Jewish audience if they want to be like tax collectors, they recoil with shock and horror at the suggestion.

Jesus pushes us to the heights of divine love, the highest ideal, the fullest potential of human behavior. He cannot understand our narrow, selfish love. Why do you not want to love everyone, he asks in amazement. Why are you afraid to love? Do you merely want to model your behavior on selfish people, or worse, on brutal military oppressors? Can you aim higher and dare to live the love of God?

The answer is yes. In fact, such all-inclusive love is what the spiritual life is all about, according to Jesus. Love is social, economic, and political. It knows no boundaries. It is the hardest thing to do, yet the easiest, because it is the most gratifying, the most fulfilling, the most rewarding.

By loving our enemies, we see beyond political and national

boundaries with the vision of God into the heart of every human being. We discover the face of God in everyone. We prepare ourselves for the day when we wake up in the house of God, where we will sit down at the banquet table of peace with every human being who ever lived, including our former enemies. We will be ready because we have spent our lives not oppressing or killing our enemies but loving and protecting them. We will feel right at home.

> And if you greet your brothers only, what is
> unusual about that? Do not the pagans do
> the same?
>
> (MATTHEW 5:47)

I n Jesus' day, people greeted one another with the word *Shalom.* They did not just say, "Hi." In fact, the word "hello" was invented by Alexander Graham Bell as a new expression for his invention, the telephone. But in Jesus' time, people said "Peace be with you."

Jesus' whole life was based on this shalom, the peace of God. He wanted to greet every human being with the message of peace. When he rose from the dead, he twice greeted the disciples, who had betrayed, denied, and abandoned him, saying, "Peace be with you." Today, he expects us to live in peace with every human being on the planet, and so to live in peace with the God of peace. He wants our peace to surpass our private family circles, reaching out to the far corners of the planet. Jesus has "a heart as wide as the world," as the Buddhists say, and he expects the same of us.

Jesus asks us to break beyond our usual day-to-day circle and reach out to everyone. He wants us to love not only our sisters and brothers, parents and children, neighbors and friends, colleagues and associates, but people around the world. He expects that we will reach out with love to the marginalized, the excluded, the poor, the hungry, the homeless, the lonely, the ostracized, the immigrant, the imprisoned, the condemned, the enemy, the sick, the elderly, and the dying. He does not want our love to be the usual "same-ol' same-ol'." Rather, he is looking for an unusual love.

As disciples of Jesus today, we must literally go to all others. We must travel to places we normally would not go—to soup kitchens, homeless shelters, prisons, schools, hospitals, war zones, and inner cities—and befriend anyone who is different from us, who suffers, who is oppressed, who is marginalized. Jesus would have us embrace the whole variety of humanity, just as he does. He wants us to break out of the expected cultural mode and do the unusual.

After asking his question, Jesus invites us to be like God, who greets everyone with the gift of peace. "Be perfect, just as your heavenly God is perfect," he concludes. Luke translates this as, "Be compassionate as God is compassionate." Once again, he roots his ethical behavior in a spirituality of compassion, in a theology that sees God as infinitely compassionate. He believes that we too can be infinitely compassionate, that this divine attribute is not exclusive to God. For Jesus, this compassionate, all-inclusive love is what makes us human, and, in fact, what makes us divine, the sons and daughters of the God of shalom.

Jesus invites us to take seriously our faith in a loving, compassionate God and to demonstrate that faith through an unusual love that surpasses the pagan culture to embrace all those on the margins. His love did just that. As his followers, we are called to imitate his bold, new kind of love.

> And if you do good only to those who do good to you, what credit is that to you? If you lend money to those from whom you expect repayment, what credit is that to you?
>
> (LUKE 6:33–34)

n late 2001, a New York college student was riding home on the subway on a freezing December night when he noticed a homeless man sitting across from him. This poor fellow had no shoes. Earlier that day, the student had been discussing with his friends how to put the Gospel into practice in their own lives, "to give without counting the cost." He looked at his shoes and then at the bare feet of the homeless man. They looked the same size.

"Would you like my shoes?" he asked the homeless man.

"Sure!" the man replied.

With that, the student took off his shoes and socks, gave them to the man, and walked home several blocks in the freezing cold. The homeless man rode on through the night, wearing "new" shoes.

Jesus expects us to resist evil and do good, but not merely to do good to those who do good to us. Rather, he wants us to do good even to those who do evil to us. He expects good deeds toward everyone everywhere, whether or not people do good deeds toward us. He asks us to do good beyond the world's expectations because this is what he does, what God does. He wants us to be as good as God, to be lavish with our goodness, to win over evildoers with our steadfast goodness.

Anyone can do good to those who will be good in return. The challenge, according to Jesus, is to break through our selfish presuppositions, to see every human being as our beloved sister and brother, and to show goodness to them because of who they are, regardless of what they may or may not do. Jesus wants us to do the good because it is right to do the good in and of itself, without any expectation of reward.

Goodness, beyond being its own reward, has positive, practical consequences. Relentless goodness toward those who do evil eventually wears them down and overcomes them. Goodness disarms others and inspires them to do good deeds as well. But we have to take the first step. We cannot wait for evildoers to do good. We must do it first.

Goodness also has spiritual consequences. Selflessness stands out, Jesus implies. It catches even God's attention. It will earn us true credit, where it counts, from God.

Similarly, Jesus expects us to lend money to others but not to those who can repay us. He wants us to give our money to those who cannot repay us. He wants us to do good without any expectation of repayment. He turns capitalism upside down. The goal of Gospel economics is not to save money and get rich but to give our money to those in need, without ever wanting to get it back.

Dorothy Day, founder of the Catholic Worker Movement, was inspired "to make it easier for people to be good." Like St. Francis, she and her coworkers practiced this selfless generosity in deliberate obedience to the Gospel of Jesus. They experimented with Gospel economics in their day-to-day lives. They gave everything they had to the poor who could not repay them. They ran houses of hospitality, soup kitchens, clinics, and services of every kind free of charge, no questions asked. They offered goodness toward everyone, including those who hated them, and they expected nothing in return. They were counted poor in the eyes of the world but rich in the eyes of God.

Jesus envisions entirely different economic, political, and social relationships between us. In his vision, everyone gives away everything they possess to those in need, and no one expects anything in return. Everyone shares everything they have, until everyone everywhere has enough. In his realm, no one hoards anything. Rather, people give away what they have with little concern for themselves. People's primary interest is the needs of others.

Given today's widespread destitution, the upside down economics of the Gospel is desperately needed around the world. Christ expects us to do good to those who do evil to us and win them over with our love. He is waiting for us to give our money and possessions to those in need without expecting any repayment. As we practice his active nonviolence and outrageous generosity, he rejoices and consoles us. If we can emulate his lavish generosity, we may come not only to understand him better but may find ourselves serving him among the needy without even knowing it.

Which of them will love more?

(LUKE 7:42)

For Jesus, love is everything. Love is the meaning of life. Love is the way to live. Love is what it means to be human. Love is the solution to the world's problems. Love is the way to end war and injustice. Love is the way to make friends and disarm enemies. Love is the path to happiness. Love is the guide for the next step. Love is the hope of children. Love is the sigh of creation. Love is the greatest power in the universe. Love is the door to resurrection. Love is the Spirit breathed upon us. Love is the path to peace. Love is the antidote to greed, selfishness, misery, and indifference. Love is the opposite of fear. Love is the reason to keep on keeping on. Love is the soul of prayer. Love is the heart of the spiritual life. Love is the greatest challenge, the highest summit, the deepest depth, the farthest horizon, the noblest aspiration, the humblest truth, the brightest light. Love is the vocation of every human being on the planet. Love is the beginning, the middle, and the end of life. Love is the door to eternal life. Love is the way to God. Love is the name of God. Love is the heart of Christ. Love is the answer. Love is the key. Love is all we need.

When Jesus is invited to dinner at the house of a Pharisee, a "sinful woman" stands behind him weeping, bathing his feet with her tears, wiping them with her hair, kissing them, and anointing them with oil. Knowing how shocked the Pharisee is, Jesus poses a story: "Two people were in debt to a certain creditor. One owed five hundred days' wages and the other fifty. Since they were unable to repay the debt, he forgave it for both. Which of them will love him more?"

"The one whose larger debt was forgiven," the Pharisee answers correctly.

Jesus then points out how this woman has shown great love, far more than the Pharisee. Her many sins have been forgiven, he explains, and so she has shown great love. For Jesus, this is the only thing that matters—how much love we show one another.

God forgives everyone. Jesus wants us to realize that we are already completely forgiven and free to love one another with a great love, with all our hearts, with extravagant gestures.

"Which of them will love more?" This is the question for Jesus and for God. The Gospel calls us to practice unconditional love and connects the act of forgiveness with the possibility, quantity, and quality of our love. If we realize how much God has already forgiven us individually and as a race, if we let go and forgive one another, we will be freer to love one another unconditionally. Forgiveness is an essential ingredient for the journey to divine love. Jesus wants us to forgive one another and to spend our lives practicing unconditional, all-encompassing, all-inclusive, all-embracing, nonjudgmental, nonretaliatory love. He only cares about love, and he waits for us to forgive each other so that we might discover the breadth and length and height and depth of God's love.

"Which of them will love more?" Jesus watches to see if we take up his way of forgiveness and love. Daily meditation will lead us to the shocking truth that God has forgiven all of us for our individual and social sins. Awareness of God's forgiveness empowers us to forgive those who hurt or offend us. As we discover that we are forgiven and start practicing reckless forgiveness, we too will wash one another's feet in acts of kindness and gratitude and practice outrageous acts of great love. We will drop everything to love everyone. We will be filled with God's extravagant love, discover lost joy, be disarmed, and transform ourselves and the world.

SIX

HEALING

Do you want to be well?

(JOHN 5:6)

The great desert father of the fourth century, St. Anthony of Egypt, once said that a time would come when everyone in the world would go mad. Everyone will be sick with violence and killing. Anyone who is not mad and violent, who is nonviolent, will be called crazy. "You are mad," they will be told. "You are sick. You are not like us. You need to be put away or killed." As a result, the world will suffer a plague of violence.

Everyone was sick in one way or another in Jesus' day. Those who were physically ill came to Jesus for healing. However, those who were morally and spiritually sick, such as the self-righteous Pharisees and scribes or the dominating imperial rulers and their soldiers, thought they were perfectly fine and did not need healing. They did not want the healing love that Jesus brought. Rather, they turned on him, denounced him as possessed and sick, and eventually killed him.

One Sabbath day, Jesus came to the pool of Bethesda in downtown Jerusalem, where the sick, the blind, the lame, and the crippled gathered each day. It was generally believed that whenever the water bubbled up (probably from a hidden spring), the first ones into the water would be miraculously healed. So they sat by the water, waiting.

Jesus notices a sick man who has been ill for thirty-eight years. Now, Jesus could have stretched out his hand, touched the man, and healed him, as he did the leper. He could have commanded the illness to leave him, as he did for the centurion's son or the Syro-Phoenician woman's daughter. He could have made a mudpack or spit on the person and rubbed his eyes, as he did with a blind man in the Temple. Instead, Jesus asks a question: "Do you want to be well?"

In our age of hospitals, psychiatrists, alternative medicine, therapy, chiropractors, vitamin supplements, diets, brain surgery, and heart replacements, Jesus' question comes as a shock. The healing he brings is not just physical but also spiritual, moral, emotional, psychological, economic, political, communal, and global. Jesus wants to heal the cause of the world's illness. He wants to heal the whole person and the whole human race.

But Jesus does not impose himself on us. He is the world's greatest psychiatrist. Understanding human nature better than anyone, he diagnoses our sickness and sees the solution, knowing that our healing will require a complete, personal, inner conversion, as well as a global transformation. He also knows that we must want to be made well.

Thus, this question reveals Jesus' doubt: He is not sure we want to be well. We seem quite content with our illness. We do not want a doctor, a messiah, a savior, God.

From Jesus' perspective, each one of us is sick; each one of us is broken. We have all been hurt by violence, hatred, fear, indifference, infidelity, idolatry, greed, selfishness, and war. We are a hurting people, and we go on hurting each other. Worst of all, we believe we are well. We do not know we are sick. We do not think we need healing.

Do we want Jesus to make us well? Jesus is not sure—nor are we. We are oblivious to the fact that we are broken and that we could be made whole, so we do not ask for healing and wholeness. We have grown so used to being sick, so used to the way things are, that we cannot grasp our critical need for divine surgery. We do not want the healing Jesus brings because we are afraid of change, we are afraid to see the holy doctor. Instead, we prefer to take our chances and tell ourselves that we are well, when in fact we are miserable. We fear the freedom and responsibility that healing and wholeness bring. Very simply, we want to remain sick.

If we swallow our pride and ask for the healing that only Jesus can give, Jesus will grant our request.

By the pool of Bethesda, the sick man tells Jesus that he has nobody to put him in the water before it stops bubbling. Jesus looks at him and issues the command: "Rise, take up your mat, and walk."

When Jesus heals us, he calls us out of our slavery to sickness, violence, and death into the new life of wholeness, nonviolence, and resurrection. "Rise up! Take up your mat! Walk! From now on, you are free. You are well. You are made whole. Follow me on the path of wholeness, nonviolence, and life, and join me in making others well."

It is an offer we cannot refuse.

Who touched me?
(LUKE 8:45; MARK 5:30)

There was a woman who had been hemorrhaging for a dozen years. Doctors had been no help; in fact, they had made her condition worse. She had spent all her money on remedies, to no avail. As a result, the woman was declared unclean by society. When Jesus passes by on some important business with a wealthy synagogue official, and the crowd presses in on him, the woman comes up behind him and touches the tassel hanging from his cloak. "If I just touch him," she thinks, "I will be cured."

Instantly, the woman knows that she has been cured. But she does not expect what happens next. Jesus stops in his tracks, turns around, and asks, "Who touched me? Who has touched my clothes?"

"You see how the crowd is pressing upon you," his disciples point out, "yet you ask, 'Who touched me?' Everyone's touching you!" But Jesus feels the power go out from him. "Who touched me?" he asks, looking around.

The woman is caught. She hoped to be healed anonymously, without interrupting Jesus, without causing a scene, without anyone finding out. She knows she is "an unclean woman," ostracized by righteous holy men. If Jesus knows she has touched him, he might yell at her, like every other man, for making him unclean too.

But it's too late. The woman has broken the law and must face the consequences. So she approaches Jesus "in fear and trembling, falls down before him and tells him the whole truth."

What happens next is as astonishing as the miraculous cure. Jesus looks at the woman and, rather than scolding her, he affirms her, loves her, and gives her back her dignity. "Daughter, your faith has saved you. Go in peace and be cured of your affliction."

Jesus feels the power go out of him, but he does not want to be a magician. Rather, he desires a personal relationship with each one of us, with every human being who ever lived. He is not some magic, impersonal god, a healing machine. He is a human being who wants to look us in the eye, love us, and be loved by us. He wants to know us as his daughters and sons. He wants to save each one of us individually, with his own personal touch, so that we might live with him intimately in peace forever.

Jesus practiced what Dorothy Day called gospel personalism. In light of his radical personalism, his question makes sense. In asking "Who touched me?" he wants to know who is close to him, who wants him, who is being healed by him. Over time, Jesus turns away from the crowds and moves closer toward each one of us individually, calling each of us by name, announcing that we are his friends. He is learning the hard lesson that crowds can quickly turn into mobs, and mobs cause riots. Here, in this moment, Jesus sees that the crowd eventually will turn on him and shout out "Crucify him, crucify him!" So, aware of his own impending death, he looks for the touch of faith, hope, and love from us. He looks for our individual response, and he intends to heal and save us, one person at a time.

Jesus' question leads us to ask some of our own: Have I ever touched Jesus? Do I want to touch Jesus with the same determination as the woman with the hemorrhage? Dare I touch Jesus, risk having him find out, and turn toward me in my brokenness and weakness? Do I want Jesus to know that I touched him? Am I willing to enter that intimate relationship with him that he desires with me?

At some point, each one of us has touched Jesus. Mother Teresa says we touch Jesus in the poor and the homeless. Martin Luther King Jr. says we touch Jesus in the struggle for justice and racial equality. Philip Berrigan says we touch Jesus in the pursuit of nuclear disarmament. Dom Helder Camara says we touch Jesus in every act of compassion. Mahatma Gandhi says we touch Jesus in the life of nonviolence. Thomas Merton says we touch Jesus in our contemplative prayer and solitude. Dorothy Day says we touch Jesus when we welcome and house the homeless. Oscar Romero says we touch Jesus when we liberate the oppressed. Henri Nouwen says we touch Jesus in one another whenever we recognize each other as a beloved daughter or son of God.

When we touch Jesus, he turns around and asks us to identify ourselves, tell him our stories, and get to know him. He heals us— but he wants more. He needs our companionship, our presence, our love. He wants to be our brother, our companion, our friend.

The Gospel invites us to tell him, as did the heroic woman, when we touch him, how he is healing us, and who we are. If we dare, we will not be disappointed.

What is your name?

(MARK 5:9; LUKE 8:30)

J esus asks the most basic, the most human, the simplest of questions—the first and most ordinary question we all ask one another: "What is your name?" He wants to know our names, our hearts, our very selves. In the presence of Jesus, the incarnation of innocence, love, and compassion, our hearts are involuntarily exposed. When we meet Jesus and tell him our name, we reveal to him our true self. As we give him our love and our violence, he sees our light and our darkness. He recognizes both the saint and the sinner within. No one can hide in the presence of Jesus. All hearts are revealed.

When Jesus travels to the other side of the Sea of Galilee, into the enemy territory of the Gerasenes, he is immediately confronted by a demoniac who thrashes around the tombs, hurting himself, cursing at passersby, and threatening everyone. He denounces Jesus, who calls upon the demon to leave him. No one had ever approached the sick man, who lived in the cemetery. No one talked to him. Maybe they did not even know his name. But they certainly did not go near him or try to help him. Jesus, on the other hand, starts talking to him the minute he gets out of the boat. Because no one introduces the sick man to Jesus—in fact, probably no one knows his name—he asks this most human of questions: "What is your name?"

Mark and Luke record that the possessed man answers with the politically charged Latin term *legion*. Everyone in those days knew that a legion was a Roman military unit made up of hundreds of brutal Roman soldiers. By calling himself legion, this poor man tells Jesus that he is possessed by the Roman Empire, that he is occupied by a foreign, pagan, military force, that he is oppressed, crushed, being killed by war-makers. The man reveals everything—the cause of his possession, the physical consequences of militarism, his need for Jesus' healing peace.

The rest of this dramatic exorcism account is loaded with military language and imagery. In effect, Mark says that when we give ourselves over to imperial domination, join the Army and the Air Force, and support war and nuclear weapons, we are possessed by death. We go insane and live life as in a cemetery, even though we think we are well, wise, and sophisticated.

When Jesus commands the unclean spirit to leave the man, the demon enters a herd of pigs, who immediately rush over a cliff and kill themselves on the rocks below. The whole town is horrified to see the possessed person now sitting peacefully in his right mind and to witness the destruction of their entire economy. They beg Jesus to leave, and he does. In effect, the people do not want the healing he brings, the peace of mind he offers, the freedom from military occupation he makes possible. They realize that to be healed means they will no longer be subject to imperial violence. They will be free—but they will not be able to prosper from war and weapons anymore.

If we want liberation from Jesus, we too must be willing to pay the price: economic upheaval. We will have to find another form of work. We will no longer be able to support "Roman warriors," get scholarships from the Pentagon, earn huge salaries by making nuclear weapons at Los Alamos, or live comfortably while maintaining the Trident submarine base. Being healed requires that we spend the rest of our lives in work that affirms human life.

When we sit with Jesus' question, we may ask ourselves who we are. How will we answer Jesus when he asks us what our true name is? We need to reflect on the question, so that we do not answer as the culture would have us answer, as the demoniac answered, saying, "My name is America. My name is Republican. My name is U.S. soldier. My name is Wall Street broker. My name is U.S.A." In his presence, with this question, he will lead us to our true self, our true name, and we will find ourselves in our right mind once again.

In the Catholic Christian community, as we come of age, we celebrate the sacrament of confirmation. We stand before the community and declare that we want to follow Jesus for the rest of our lives. As part of the ceremony, we take a new name, usually the name of a saint. We announce that we want to side with the saints who followed Jesus and become like them. We no longer want to be just Americans or New Yorkers or people of a certain territory, language, race, age, or culture. Rather, we want to be people whom Jesus recognizes. We want Jesus to call us by our true name.

But if we want to be healed by Jesus, we must state our true name and tell him who we are. We may find in the process that he renames us, just as he renamed Simon, Peter the Rock. This exchange with Jesus will begin an eternal intimate relationship with him. From now on, he will know us, we will know him, and we will want to be healed by him and live in peace with him forever.

My friend, the Buddhist monk Thich Nhat Hanh, wrote a poem about this question. "Call Me by My True Names" concludes:

> I am the child in Uganda, all skin and bones,
> My legs as thin as bamboo sticks.
> And I am the arms merchant,
> Selling deadly weapons to Uganda.
> I am the twelve-year-old girl
> Refugee on a small boat,
> Who throws herself into the ocean
> After being raped by a sea pirate.
> And I am the pirate
> My heart not yet capable
> Of seeing and loving.
>
> My joy is like Spring, so warm
> It makes flowers bloom all over the Earth.
> My pain is like a river of tears,
> So vast it fills the four oceans.
>
> Please call me by my true names,
> So I can hear all my cries and laughter at once,
> So I can see that my joy and pain are one.

Please call me by my true names,
So I can wake up
And the door of my heart
Could be left open,
The door of compassion.

How long has this been happening to him?

(MARK 9:21)

Jesus, the great healer, does not perform magic acts with a wave of a wand. Rather, Jesus asks diagnostic questions to understand our individual plight, so that he might help us heal and remain healthy.

When a man brings his possessed son to the disciples for healing, and they are unable to heal the boy, the man begs Jesus to intervene (Mark 9:14–29). When the boy is brought forward, he starts, falls to the ground, rolls around, and foams at the mouth. Jesus asks, "How long has this been happening to him?"

The question is simple and direct, but it is also patient and compassionate. Jesus is interested in the boy's life story, the history of his affliction, and the cause of his suffering.

"Since childhood," the father replies, "it has thrown him into the fire and into the water to kill him. But if you can do anything, have compassion on us and help us."

"If you can!" Jesus says. "Everything is possible to one who has faith."

"I do believe," the father responds. "Help my unbelief."

When Jesus declares, "Mute and deaf spirit, I command you: Come out of him and never enter him again," the boy convulses again. Jesus then takes him by the hand and raises him, and slowly he stands up. Later, Jesus tells his disciples that this kind of demon "can only come out through prayer."

Jesus apparently knows all the various kinds of demons that can possess us. He is the only one who is not possessed by the demons of the world, which always try to kill us. Because Jesus is a person of deep contemplative prayer, he is not filled with demons but with God's Holy Spirit. Instead of being controlled by violence, he is filled with God's compassion, peace, and love.

The lesson in this question is straightforward: If we want to heal one another, disarm one another, and save one another from the forces that kill, we need to be people of contemplative nonviolence who give over our inner violence to God. We need to be people of regular daily prayer, people who sit with the God of peace and love. Only through this lifelong discipline of solitude, silence, meditation, and communion with God will we, over time, learn to live and breathe in the Holy Spirit of peace, even while others around us foam at the mouth with the demons of war. Centering ourselves in the God of peace and love, we will be able to call each other to the sanity of nonviolence, even in the midst of a world of nuclear violence. The prayer will heal us and turn us, like Jesus, into healers. Not only will we heal one another of our specific individual ailments, but, through the name of Jesus, we will heal the entire culture.

The question and the love behind the question show the human side of Jesus and invite us to offer that same care for one another. They offer hope that there may be a solution, that we do not have to endure our afflictions by ourselves, that life is not all bad. As we inquire about each other's personal health, problems, trials, and pain, we may be inspired to point out solutions, remedies, and simple human possibilities for healing and transformation.

The human touch of Jesus makes all the difference. The more we can be human with one another, the more we can show concern for one another, the more we care for one another, the more we will know the healing power of compassion. But this kind of loving concern, care, and compassion can only blossom in the heart of humankind if we are first and foremost people who take time each day with God in silent communion. As we are slowly transformed by contemplative prayer, all those around us will be transformed as well. The spirit of compassionate healing will work through us, perhaps without our even knowing it.

Which is easier, to say to the paralytic, "Your
sins are forgiven," or to say, "Rise, pick up
your mat and walk"?

(MARK 2:9; MATTHEW 9:5; LUKE 5:23)

When I was serving as a chaplain at Ground Zero after September 11, several firefighters told me about the legendary Franciscan priest and fire chaplain Mychal Judge, who was killed that terrible morning. Apparently, whenever Judge entered a room full of firemen for a benefit dinner or gathering, he would blurt out, "You are all doing God's will, so all your sins are forgiven." Everyone would applaud.

But word got around, and he was called into the cardinal's office and told never to forgive sins publicly again. He went right on doing it. For Mychal Judge, forgiveness was the hallmark of the Gospel.

When four men lower their paralyzed friend through the ceiling into the house where Jesus is preaching, Jesus is amazed at their faith and announces to the shocked religious authorities that the paralyzed man's sins are forgiven.

"What? Forgiven? Who but God alone can forgive sins? Why do you talk like that?" The authorities are appalled and outraged. Once again, they begin to plot his murder.

Jesus, however, is merely pointing out how much the four friends care for the paralytic. They have created a community of concern for their friend, and they are determined to get their friend to the Holy One, no matter what. They not only forgive the paralytic; they love him and give their lives for his healing. They are a community of faith, hope, nonviolence, and love in action. Jesus sees their forgiving, compassionate love and joins his love with it. "My child, your sins are forgiven," he says, "by your friends and by me too."

Jesus is wildly extravagant with forgiveness; he forgives anyone and everyone. But who of us can stand such forgiveness? I once preached on this famous Gospel episode to a conservative Catholic congregation, consisting primarily of retired military officers. I concluded my comments by saying that we too are called to forgive, to forgive all those who ever hurt us, to forgive all those who hurt the human race. "From now on," I said, "we forgive our parents, our children, our brothers and sisters, our friends, our neighbors, our community members, our church leaders, our countrymen and women, all our fellow human beings. We forgive everyone, even the unforgivable. We forgive Adolf Hitler, Saddam Hussein, Bill Clinton, and George W. Bush. You name them, we forgive them. Then, we can pray the Lord's Prayer and trust in God's forgiveness of us. We will be able to say with integrity, 'Forgive us our trespasses as we forgive those who trespass against us.'"

The congregation was clearly disturbed. "We cannot forgive Saddam," one pious woman said to me. "How dare you mention Bush's name in connection with Hitler or Saddam or Clinton! Only God can forgive those people. You ought to be ashamed of yourself. We don't want to hear your opinion of the Gospel anymore."

That experience taught me that times have not changed much from Jesus' day. We are not as far from the scribes and Pharisees as we might think. We too reject Jesus' message—his love, his forgiveness, his way of nonviolence.

"Which is easier," Jesus asks, "to say to the paralytic, 'Your sins are forgiven,' or to say, 'Rise, pick up your mat and walk'?"

Jesus is telling us that it is, in fact, easier to say, "Rise, pick up your mat and walk." In other words, it is much easier to command the healing of the body than to realize a healing of the spirit.

Forgiveness is perhaps the hardest thing in life, yet it is the one thing that can bring the greatest healing. It is at the core of the spiritual life for Jesus. Over and over, he links forgiveness to prayer. When we pray, he insists in the Gospels, be sure to forgive all those who have hurt you.

Jesus risks his life announcing God's forgiveness. He forgives everyone and calls us to forgive everyone, but then as now, the world cannot tolerate such outlandish forgiveness. The religious authorities charge Jesus with blasphemy and eventually execute him for his outrageous behavior in God's name. Yet, even as he dies, Jesus forgives. He forgives those devout religious leaders who condemned him and those soldiers who killed him—and he forgives us as well.

Forgiveness is connected to healing. Only when we forgive others will we find the inner peace that will lead to our psychological, emotional, spiritual, and physical healing. Jesus even demonstrates that forgiveness and healing together lead to resurrection. "Rise!" Jesus commands the paralytic. "Rise," Jesus commands us. "Rise to the ultimate new life of resurrection. Forgive one another and love one another, and you will be able to heal one another and raise one another to the new life of resurrection."

SEVEN

VISION

Do you see anything?

(MARK 8:23)

As Jesus walked by, he saw humanity blind from birth," we read in John's Gospel (9:1). Most translations record that he saw "a man blind from birth," but the original Greek can be read in the singular or the plural.

Certainly, from all the various statements and healing episodes in the Gospels, Jesus considers every human being to be blind. What's more, the Gospels declare emphatically that Jesus is the only one who knows that we cannot see; he is the only one who can see, and he is the only one with the ultimate vision of God.

Jesus tries to heal our blindness, to help us see, and to give us the vision of God. He gives us sight any way he can, from commanding the blind to see to putting spittle on our eyes and laying hands on us to asking if we can see anything yet. He is the light of the world, and he is determined to lead us out of the dark night of our shared blindness.

Once, while visiting the village of Bethsaida, a crowd brought a blind man to Jesus and begged him to heal the poor man. With deep personal concern, Jesus took the blind man by the hand and led him outside the village, away from the crowd. According to Mark, Jesus puts his spit on the man's eyes, and then lays hands on him.

"Do you see anything?" Jesus asks.

"I see people looking like trees and walking," the man answers. Jesus lays hands on his eyes a second time, and then the man sees clearly.

The healing of this blind man is more than a miraculous tale of a physical cure. It is a parable about the gradual enlightenment of the disciples of Jesus—then and now. All of Jesus' followers are slow to grasp the way and the truth of Jesus. We need time to learn from him. He has to work hard to help us to follow him. Just like the blind man who needs a second blessing from Jesus before he can see clearly, we too need many blessings and graces from Jesus before we can comprehend his path, his vision, and the way before us.

If we imagine Jesus asking us if we "see anything," how would we respond? What do we spend our lives seeing? We look at Dan Rather and the CBS Evening News. We watch Madonna's latest video on MTV. We sit glued to a football game and eat popcorn while watching the latest movie. We glance at the celebrity pictures in People magazine at the doctor's office or the National Enquirer while standing in line at the grocery store. But do we see anything worth seeing? In fact, what do we consider worth seeing? Do we want to see with the eyes of Christ, to see with the vision of God? Dare we look at the world from the perspective of Jesus?

At the beginning of John's Gospel, when Jesus first meets his future disciples and they ask him where he lives, he responds with the biblically charged invitation, "Come and see." Later, when he tells Nathaniel how he sees him sitting under the fig tree, and Nathaniel responds with amazement, Jesus declares, "You will see even greater things than this" (John 1:50).

Jesus wants us to see even greater things. He wants us to have the fullness of his own vision, not to see into the future or to bilocate, but to see with the eyes of love which recognize all others as our brothers and sisters. In the end, he wants us to see him, the Holy Christ, present in every human being. He wants God to reign on earth as God reigns in heaven, which means he wants us to behold "the beatific vision" here and now.

Do we see anything? The Book of Proverbs says, "Without a vision, the people perish." If we do not welcome the healing vision of Jesus, we are doomed to destroy ourselves through our blindness, leading one another in darkness and never toward the light.

We need to recognize our blindness, beg for healing, let Jesus bless us in our contemplative prayer, and welcome the gift of his vision, so that we eventually learn to see him in one another.

We do not want to be blind any longer, or to see poorly, as if people looked like trees, walking. From now on, we want to see enemies as friends, neighbors as brothers and sisters, those labeled as nonhuman as fully human. We want to see all people as God's own beloved children.

You see all these things, do you not?

(MATTHEW 24:2)

The gospel tells us that after walking for several years on a peace pilgrimage to Jerusalem, Jesus weeps when he finally arrives. "If this day you only knew the things that make for peace," he says through his tears, "but now it is hidden from your eyes. For the days are coming upon you when your enemies will raise a palisade against you. They will encircle you and hem you in on all sides. They will smash you to the ground and your children within you, and they will not leave one stone upon another within you because you did not recognize the time of your visitation" (Luke 19:41–44).

Jesus weeps over Jerusalem's complicity with the empire. The people's preference for imperial violence and rejection of his divine nonviolence led to Jerusalem's actual destruction by the Romans in the year 70.

In Matthew's version, the disciples point out the grand buildings of the Temple with awe and wonder. "You see all these things, do you not?" Jesus asks them in reply. "Amen, I say to you, there will not be left here a stone upon another stone that will not be thrown down" (Matthew 24:1–2).

Jesus can see that the violence of his times, including the inevitable failure of revolutionary violence, will lead to Rome's total annihilation of Jerusalem. But Jesus also weeps because in Jerusalem he sees that the whole world rejects his gift of divine nonviolence in preference to human violence. He sees that violence in response to violence only leads to further violence, that war never solves our problems, that revenge and retaliation lead only to destruction, and that unless we adopt the way of creative nonviolence, we are doomed to a global holocaust.

Jesus weeps, but he does not give up. He takes action. Luke records that Jesus proceeds directly into the Temple and turns over the tables of the money changers in an act of nonviolent resistance. "My house shall be a house of prayer," he announces, "but you have made it a den of thieves." For this dramatic civil disobedience, he is arrested, tortured, and executed. He gives his life resisting imperial violence, and he never stops trusting and hoping in the God of peace. When God raises him, he greets his friends with the consoling words "Peace be with you," and then he sends them forth to carry on his mission of nonviolent resistance.

Today we live in a world of even taller buildings, greater power, enormous wealth, and ever more terrifying violence. Surely God cannot stand our arrogance, greed, nuclear weapons, and bombing campaigns. Jesus still asks us, "You see all these things, do you not? If you continue along your path of war and greed, crushing and killing millions of people around the world so that you can maintain global hegemony, you will inevitably be destroyed." Every empire eventually falls. It will happen to the United States too, unless we change our ways, dismantle our weapons, and serve suffering humanity.

Our task is to take up where Jesus left off. As our country wages war on the peoples of the world, we follow the nonviolent Jesus who weeps over war and who acts in the name of peace.

Christian peacemaking begins with grief. We grieve for those who suffer and die from our bombs and wars. We weep for the destruction of our own Jerusalems, for the people of Iraq, Palestine, and Colombia, for the world's poor, for New York City and Washington, D.C., for the world's crucified people. We weep for ourselves. Like Christ, we feel the world's pain. Yet, as our hearts break, we must understand this as the beginning of grace, wisdom, and peace. We cannot love our neighbors and our enemies, as Jesus did, if we do not first enter their pain, as he did. We cannot show compassion without standing in solidarity with those who suffer, especially with those who suffer from our bombs.

As we weep and grieve, we repent of the sin of war and begin the Gospel project of conversion which leads to public, nonviolent action. Like Jesus, we do not stop with grief and tears. Nor do we stand in awe before our government's buildings, weapons, and power. Rather, we act, and keep on acting for peace. We turn over the tables of the culture of war and disrupt the culture of violence. We disturb the culture's false peace and demand true peace with all peoples, and in this we join the struggle of the nonviolent Jesus and witness the peace of the risen Christ.

In these days of despair, we side with Jesus, grieve with him, weep with him, act with him, and learn from him the things that make for peace. We take seriously his commandment to love our enemies, and we live by his last words, to put down the sword.

As we side with Jesus and share his tears, his passion, and his resurrection, we take up his prayerful, public, prophetic, and proactive nonviolence. This means that we take quality time for prayerful non-

violence, repenting of the violence in our hearts, asking God to disarm our hearts, and welcoming God's gift of contemplative peace. We
stand up publicly in his spirit of nonviolence, just as the early Christians did. We practice prophetic nonviolence by breaking the silence
of the church and the complicity of the masses to speak the truth of
peace, that we must stop all war, dismantle our own nuclear weapons,
and pursue nonviolent responses to conflict. As people of prophetic
nonviolence, we repent of our nation's global terrorism, and announce God's reign of peace. Finally, we engage in proactive nonviolence. Our Gospel nonviolence must not be passive or weak. Rather,
if it is to resemble the life of Jesus, it must be active, creative, and
provocative. It risks our own suffering and our participation in his
cross. We vigil, march, fast, agitate, lobby, speak out, organize, cross
lines, and resist war. We weep, we see, we act—and we welcome Jesus'
gift of peace.

Can a blind person guide a blind person? Will not both fall into a pit?

(LUKE 6:39)

One of the many casualties of war is the imagination. In a world
blinded with thirty-five wars, massive starvation, and tens of
thousands of nuclear weapons, people cannot even imagine the possibility of peace—a world without war, poverty, or nuclear weapons.
We can no longer envision such a world because the culture of war
has robbed us of our imagination of peace.

Two hundred years ago, a handful of brave, faith-based people
dared to imagine a world without slavery and dedicated themselves to
building a movement to abolish it. The abolitionists disrupted the
country and changed the world. Now we need to imagine a world
without war, poverty, and nuclear weapons. We need to imagine ourselves building a global movement to abolish this triple axis of evil.

The fact that war, poverty, and nuclear weapons have never been
abolished does not mean that they cannot be abolished. When Nel-

son Mandela became president of South Africa, he unilaterally dismantled their six nuclear weapons in the world's only true act of nuclear disarmament. Someday the United States and every nation with nuclear weapons will dismantle their arsenals, and all nations will pledge never to wage war again—but only if we dare dedicate our lives to this vision of peace, like the first abolitionists.

We live in a time of deep moral and spiritual blindness, a blindness that can lead us over the brink to global self-destruction. We do not know what we are doing, nor can we see the way out of our madness.

Into this world of blind violence comes the nonviolent Jesus, a visionary of peace. This Jesus calls his disciples to be visionaries of nonviolence, people who can envision peace and see the way forward toward a new future without war.

Communities of faith, conscience, and nonviolence may be the only ones that can see into the eyes of our enemies and recognize them as our sisters and brothers; the ones who can insist on the truth of peace, lift up the vision of peace; help others imagine a world without war, poverty, or nuclear weapons; the ones who can lead us away from the brink of destruction toward a new life of cooperation, solidarity, justice, and disarmament.

As disciples of the visionary Jesus, our mission is to uphold that vision of peace and nonviolence, to lead one another away from the pit of destruction, and to point the way forward toward the light of a more peaceful and just world.

Two thousand years ago, Jesus saw the depths of our blindness and self-destructive tendencies. "Can a blind person guide a blind person?" he asked gently. The answer is implied: no. "Will not both fall into a pit?" he asked again. Of course. Neither will see the pit and both will fall into it.

Jesus does not condemn us for our blindness, but he does point out that blindness and calls us to see. He is the light of the world, and he insists that the time of darkness is over. We are meant to see one another, to see the truth, to see God clearly.

Imperial presidents, their generals, and their oil-billionaire leaders cannot lead blind people on the path toward peace, equality, and justice if they themselves are blind. Instead, they will lead all of us over the edge into the pit of global destruction, possibly toward nuclear holocaust. All of us—leaders as well as followers—share the world's blindness, according to Jesus' question. Jesus wants to heal us all, to give us eyes to see, and to lead us forward, not into the pit of death but toward the fullness of life.

If we have eyes to see, we will avoid the pit of death and discover the way to life. The first task, then, is to ask God for the gift of vision.

Do you see this woman?

(LUKE 7:44)

In Jesus' day, women were not considered fully human. Rather, they were the property of men. They were ordered to do as they were told by men and for men. They could be beaten, abused, raped, and murdered, and it did not matter because they were not equal to men. According to the law of Moses, they were considered "unclean." God had ordained it that way.

Men have not changed all that much since Jesus' day. Most of the two billion people who suffer hunger, poverty, homelessness, violence, and warfare are women and their children. We men have yet to stop our violence against women.

Jesus will have none of it. He honors women as "Daughters of Abraham." When he dies on the cross, only his women friends remain faithful to him. All the men abandon him, betray him, deny him, call for his crucifixion, mock him, torture him, and kill him. When he rises from the dead, according to all four Gospels, he appears first to women.

When Jesus dines at the house of Simon, a pompous, self-righteous Pharisee, a woman appears and stands behind Jesus. She weeps at his feet, bathes his feet with her tears, wipes them with her hair, kisses his feet, and anoints them with ointment. The Pharisee, of course, is appalled. He judges the woman as a sinner with a bad reputation and judges Jesus for allowing her to touch him. Yet the Pharisee does not say anything. He wants to appear pious in the presence of the Holy One, but his heart is full of rage and condemnation.

Jesus turns to the woman, Luke records, and then says to Simon, "Do you see this woman?" Jesus is never one to ignore a problem. He does not pretend there is no proverbial white elephant standing on the living room table. He points to it and asks a question. "Do you see this woman?"

The Pharisee is shocked. He wants to ignore the woman, harbor his resentment, and put up a pious front. He desperately wants to answer, "No. What woman? I don't see any woman."

Jesus' question is addressed to all the men of the world. "Do you see women? Do you see them not as objects to abuse but as human beings to honor and cherish? Do you see how you have hurt them? Do you see how you have terrified them, punished them, oppressed them, starved them, raped them, and killed them? Do you see the presence of God in women?"

Jesus also addresses his question to the church. Patriarchy and violence against women have been shameful hallmarks of the male-dominated Christian tradition. Today, Catholic women cannot receive all seven sacraments in the church, only six; they are denied ordination. They are not treated as equals in the Catholic community. When Jesus asks his question, "Do you see this woman?" he is inviting the male-dominated leadership of the church to open all ministries to women, who are, after all, the heart and backbone of the church.

"When I entered your house," Jesus tells Simon the Pharisee, "you did not give me water for my feet, but she has bathed them with her tears and wiped them with her hair. You did not give me a kiss, but she has not ceased kissing my feet since the time I entered. You did not anoint my head with oil, but she anointed my feet with ointment. So I tell you, her many sins have been forgiven; hence, she has shown great love. But the one to whom little is forgiven, loves little." Then Jesus turns to the holy woman (who is never named, even though the male evangelist names the Pharisee). Jesus says, "Your sins are forgiven." The others at table say to themselves, "Who is this who even forgives sins?" But he says to the woman, "Your faith has saved you; go in peace" (Luke 7:36–50).

Jesus wants all men to reject patriarchy, sexism, and violence against women. He wants us to see women as he sees them: as our beloved sisters to be honored and respected, treated with dignity, and given equal rights.

If we men open our eyes to the presence of God in women, we will wash their feet and begin to show great love. On that day, our Lord will say even to us men, "Your faith has saved you; go in peace."

What if you were to see the Son of Humanity ascending to where he was before?
(JOHN 6:62)

Over and over again, Jesus tries to teach us who he is, who God is, what it means to be human, how to live in God's peace, and why we should do what he says. But few can grasp his words. Especially in John's Gospel, the authorities, disciples, and crowds repeatedly criticize Jesus. Nonetheless, he keeps offering new images to help people understand his mission and his life.

At one point, when he explains that he is the bread of life come down from heaven, the disciples say, "This is just too hard. Who can accept it?" (John 6:60). They think he has lost his mind. For Jesus, however, this is just the beginning. "You ain't seen nothin' yet!" he responds. "What if you were to see the Son of Humanity ascending to where he was before?" he asks them. In effect, he says, "You think this is hard, but what if you were to see me rise from the dead, appear behind locked doors, ascend into heaven, and judge the whole human race from my throne at the right hand of God?"

In other words, we have barely begun to comprehend God or understand our reality from God's perspective. We cannot even imagine where we are headed, what eternal life will be like, and whom we will meet there.

What do the disciples do when they eventually see Jesus, the Son of Humanity, ascending to where he was before? The faithful few see Jesus first being "lifted up" on the cross, then rising from the dead, and finally, according to Luke's Gospel (24:50–53), actually ascending into heaven on the clouds. "They did him homage," Luke concludes, "and returned to Jerusalem with great joy and they were continually in the Temple praising God."

The disciples return to the scene of the crime, where Jesus turned over the tables and brought down the house. They go back to praise God, sing hymns, and testify to his glory. Eventually, according to the Acts of the Apostles, they too start disturbing the peace, speaking out against his crucifixion, teaching about his resurrection, and face regular arrest, torture, imprisonment—and eventually their own executions.

What would we have done if we saw such marvels? If we saw Jesus ascend into heaven, if we can contemplate Jesus alive and at home in the paradise of peace, we too would lose our fear, disrupt the world's false peace, and announce the coming of God's reign of peace and justice. We would sing God's praises, turn over the tables of injustice, and face harassment, persecution, arrest, imprisonment, and even death, like Martin Luther King Jr., Ita Ford, Oscar Romero, Jean Donovan, and Mahatma Gandhi.

We too have seen marvelous things. As followers of Jesus, we know where we are headed—toward our own ascensions into heaven.

EIGHT

COMPASSION

Which one of these three, in your opinion,
was neighbor to the robbers' victim?

(LUKE 10:36)

Jesus is compassion personified. The Evangelists write that, "When he saw the crowds, his heart was moved with pity" (Mark 6:34). He feels compassion for suffering people and then takes action. He wants us to do the same.

But who of us dares show such radical compassion? The world insists that only saints like Mother Teresa can demonstrate true compassion. The rest of us tell ourselves that we are not saints, that we cannot become saints, that we are too busy, so we do not have to be that compassionate. Thus, we let ourselves off the hook.

COMPASSION

But Jesus sees it differently. "Be as compassionate as your Father in heaven," he commands us (Luke 6:36).

When Jesus says that we are to love our neighbors as ourselves, a lawyer tries to justify himself and asks, "Who is my neighbor?" In response, Jesus tells the famous parable of the Good Samaritan, how a man traveling on the dangerous road to Jericho was robbed, beaten, and thrown into a ditch. Two religious leaders, a priest and a Levite, passed by the man and kept on walking. But a Samaritan came along "and was moved with compassion at the sight."

Samaritans were the hated enemies of Jews. Jesus ups the ante by using a Samaritan as the model of compassion. It would be like saying that the only compassionate people today are those we hate the most: the people of Iraq, Palestine, and Afghanistan, the Muslims, homeless people, those who are gay or lesbian, death-row inmates, the disabled, children, and women. For Jesus, it is usually the people we ostracize who are the most faithful, the most loving, the most compassionate in God's eyes. The Samaritan cared for the beaten victim, tended to his wounds, took him to a hotel, paid his expenses, and promised to come back and look after him.

Instead of answering the lawyer, Jesus puts forth a question: "Which one of these three, in your opinion, was neighbor to the robbers' victim?"

The lawyer, of course, cannot bring himself to say the name of his enemy, "Samaritan." So he answers, "The one who treated him with mercy."

"Go and do likewise!" Jesus orders. And with that, he commands us to show compassion.

How do we answer his question? Who is our neighbor? We may want to say that our modern-day priests and Levites are holy, righteous, devout people. But are our religious leaders, priests, ministers, nuns, rabbis, bishops, and cardinals "neighbor" to the poor of the world? Do they first and foremost show compassion to those in need? Or are they too busy administering their congregations, managing their bank accounts, directing building campaigns and fund-raising projects, attending cocktail parties, speaking at conferences, and maintaining their power and control over others?

Jesus does not want religious leaders full of pomp and arrogance. Rather, his priority is that we always act neighborly to those in need, that we always be moved with compassion toward the victims of the world. Instead of acting like cold-hearted religious leaders, Jesus wants us to learn from our enemies how to show compassion. The parable of the Good Samaritan is as provocative as it is helpful. The "foreigner"—the despised one—does not care about religious authority and power, only compassion.

Dare we say the names of our enemies, witness their strengths, and learn compassion from them? Dare we follow the example of the compassionate people of Iraq, the oppressed people of Palestine, the poor and marginalized of the world?

Jesus asks for our opinion. He wants us to go and do likewise, to be as compassionate as our enemies. He tells us to be as compassionate as God.

Woman, where are they? Has no one condemned you?

(JOHN 8:10)

When the self-righteous Pharisees and chief priests bring a woman "caught in adultery" into the Temple area where Jesus is teaching the crowds, they want not only to stone her to death, but also to catch Jesus in violation of the Mosaic law so they can kill him too. The man who would have also been caught in adultery, of course, is not brought forth. Men were human beings with their own code of justice. Women deserved to be condemned to death. In the eyes of men, women were not considered human beings.

How does Jesus respond to the angry, murderous authorities? He bends down on the ground, starts drawing in the sand with his finger, and, in the process, disarms them. With patient, mindful nonviolence, Jesus leads them from anger and violence toward truth and clemency. Because he does not cooperate with their righteous indignation and instead bends down to doodle in the sand, Jesus draws the men's attention away from their violence and toward his human, childlike peace. He opens a way for them to hear his new commandment. When he finally has their attention, he straightens up and declares, "Let the one without sin be the first to throw the stone."

This announcement stuns them all, and today it remains one of the most astonishing commandments in all religious literature. Suddenly everyone realizes their own sinfulness. Most important, the brutal religious authorities recognize through Jesus' statement that they too have violated the Mosaic law, which teaches that any person who sees a couple in the act of adultery is also guilty of sin and deserving of condemnation.

In the presence of Jesus, scales fall from our eyes, and we suddenly realize our sinfulness, our guilt, our shame. In the company of the one who is without sin, we see how far we are from true holiness. We lose our moral superiority and self-righteous indignation. We turn away from violence. We are disarmed.

One by one the authorities drop their stones and walk away, beginning with the elders. After a while, the entire Temple is empty. In that moment, Jesus not only condemns the death penalty and saves the woman's life, he summons humanity to recognize its sinfulness, repent of its sins, feel contrite and humble, and turn away from violence toward others.

Imagine the poor, terrified woman, dragged from her home by the righteous religious leaders; imagine her fear as they prepare to stone her to death in the holy sanctuary. After the rabbi Jesus intervenes and the crowds disappear, the woman remains alone in the huge Temple area, standing before Jesus, shaking, relieved, still terrified.

The story could have ended there. Worse, Jesus could have turned on her and denounced her for getting into trouble in the first place. He could have scolded her, or he could have ignored her and walked away.

But Jesus is not like the rest of us. He always responds with compassion and reaches out with a human touch. "Woman, where are they? Has no one condemned you?" His questions are so simple, so obvious. He knows the answers already. Everyone knows the answers. So why does he ask such obvious questions?

I think Jesus wants to restore the woman's dignity. He engages her in simple, loving conversation. He draws her out, gets her talking. He treats her like a human being.

"No one, sir," she answers him.

"Neither do I condemn you. Go and sin no more." Jesus grants clemency to the woman and then lets her go. Not only that, he abolishes the false image of an angry, violent god waiting to condemn us all.

Today, Jesus continues to engage those we condemn. He dialogues with those on death row, with our enemies, with all those we want to kill. He shows them respect, builds up their dignity, and draws them out. He saves them, one person at a time, and then asks them if they have been saved from condemnation.

If we dare side with the condemned, as Jesus does, we will one day realize that Jesus is saving us from our sinfulness. One day he will ask us his simple, obvious question and restore our dignity: "Where are all those who want to kill you? Has no one condemned you, even though you are indeed guilty of sin?" In turn, we will look at the disarming, peaceful Jesus and answer, "No one, sir."

With the eyes of compassion, Jesus will then look upon us and say, "Neither do I condemn you. Go and sin no more."

Why do you make trouble for her?

(MARK 14:6; MATTHEW 26:10)

So many women spend their lives serving, helping, loving, and making peace, and so many men make trouble for them. When I see the faces of poverty in photographs from the Third World and the world's war zones, I see women trying hard to survive, to protect their vulnerable children, and to serve God.

Nowhere is this more striking and haunting than in Iraq, where I visited the hospitals and met countless children dying of relievable diseases because of the unjust U.S. sanctions that killed more than a million Iraqis between 1990 and 2003. The death toll of Iraqi children would be the equivalent of a September 11 attack killing two World Trade towers of children every three weeks for over a decade.

Beside each bed in the Baghdad hospital sat a crying, grieving mother, dressed in black. Each one looked like the grieving Mary, mother of Jesus, holding her son's dead body, as depicted in Michelangelo's *Pietà*.

But the scenes in that hospital are no ancient work of art. This grief is reality for hundreds of thousands of Iraqi women, holding their crucified children. If the women are Mary, and the children are Christ, then we are the crucifiers, the imperial Roman soldiers deliberately, systematically killing Christ, "making trouble" for disenfranchised women in Iraq and elsewhere.

Our feminist Gospel calls men everywhere to stop harassing, hurting, abusing, and killing women and their children. We men need to ask ourselves, "Why are we violent to women? Why do we make trouble for women?" If we look deep within us at the roots of our violence and sexism, we would discover our own brokenness and would turn to God for healing so that we could become nonviolent toward ourselves and all people. As we ponder the life of Jesus, we men can learn from him the way of compassion, nonviolence, and equality and can discover God's compassion toward us.

When Jesus enters Bethany on the outskirts of Jerusalem, shortly before his execution, he dines at the house of a leper (Mark 14:3–9; Matthew 26:6–13; John 12:1–11). A woman comes forward with an alabaster jar of perfumed oil, breaks the jar, and pours the oil on his head. Immediately, of course, the men start protesting: "Why do you waste this expensive perfume?" Mark records. "It could have been sold for more than three hundred days' wages and the money given to the poor." "They are infuriated with her," Mark concludes.

Matthew's version says the men are "indignant" and tells us exactly who these enraged men are: the male disciples.

John's Gospel goes even further. The woman who anoints Jesus, including his feet, is Mary, the sister of Lazarus, whom Jesus raised from the dead. The male disciple who denounces Mary is none other than Judas Iscariot, who will later hand Jesus over to the authorities for execution. Judas condemns the woman, "not because he cared about the poor," John writes, "but because he was a thief and held the money bag and used to steal the contributions" (John 12:6).

"Leave her alone," Jesus says in defense of Mary, and all women. "Why do you make trouble for her? The poor you will always have with you, and whenever you wish you can do good to them, but you will not always have me. She has done what she could. She has anticipated anointing my body for burial" (Mark 14:6–9).

Jesus had been trying to prepare his disciples for his execution and death, but they refuse to listen to him. He knows that the authorities will arrest him, try him, and legally execute him as a criminal and revolutionary. As a victim of the death penalty, his body will not have the benefit of being anointed.

Contrary to the male disciples, this female disciple listens to Jesus and accepts his destiny. She anoints him and encourages him on his journey to the cross. She supports Jesus and does what she can to help him save humanity. She prepares him for his death.

John's Gospel carries the story even further. Jesus is so apparently shocked, stunned, and encouraged by the woman's radical and courageous behavior that he learns from her, and later, during the Passover meal, he bends down and washes his own disciples' feet as an act of preparation for their martyrdoms and deaths. Jesus anoints his disciples and tells us to anoint one another, to help one another face our cross and martyrdom.

How will we men respond to Jesus' question? Do we make trouble for Jesus and then get angry, resent Jesus' defense of women, and, in the end, betray Jesus as Judas did? Or dare we learn from the nonviolent Jesus, not to make trouble for women—or anyone—ever again?

NINE

THE MEANING OF LIFE

What profit is there for one to gain the
whole world and forfeit his life?

(MARK 8:36; LUKE 9:25; MATTHEW 16:26)

One day in fifth-grade social studies class, we read about Martin Luther's Reformation of the church and a Counter-Reformation led by Ignatius Loyola. Ignatius had been a soldier in the Basque country of Spain, where he was severely wounded by a cannonball during battle. He spent nearly a year recovering in bed when, apparently, this question hit him like a second cannonball. His decision to take it seriously led him eventually to walk to the mountain monastery shrine of Montserrat, where he spent the night in prayer, put down his sword, and began a new life of service. Later he founded a radically new religious order of priests: the Society of Jesus, also known as the Jesuits.

Jesus' question was printed right there in black and white in my social studies textbook: "What profit is there for one to gain the whole world and forfeit his life?"

I distinctly remember looking up from my book as we read this out loud in class and turning around to see if my classmates were as shocked as I was. Could this Jesus be serious? Could this question be true? Doesn't it make the most sense?

The question stunned the saint with the funny name, we were told, but I found myself equally bowled over. What good would it be to have a great life, make a fortune, become famous and powerful, only to lose my soul and miss out on eternal life? It would not be worth it, I concluded. The point of life is not to forfeit it, to lose one's soul, and to go to hell. Rather, the point of life is to live it to the fullest here and now and forever in eternity.

Like St. Ignatius, I began to ponder the Gospel of Jesus, and I realized that the fullness of life carries certain guidelines, such as selfless love, boundless compassion, active nonviolence, relentless forgiveness, justice for the poor, and the giving of one's life for suffering humanity, like Jesus on the cross. Eventually I found new meaning to my life and entered the Society of Jesus.

We all make choices about our lives: what we will do, how we will live, what goals we will pursue. In the end, we choose the kind of life we want, even if we are born in suffering and poverty. We can be selfish, resentful, violent, and mean—or we can be loving, kind, nonviolent, and compassionate.

There are countless examples of people who deliberately choose to gain the whole world. In an interview in the early 1980s, Dick Clark asked the young rock star Madonna what her plans were. She replied with a mischievous grin, "To rule the world!"

Jesus cautioned against such dreams. Is it worth gaining the whole world and losing your soul? As we look at the rulers who gained the whole world, from Caesar, Charlemagne, and Napoleon, to Hitler,

Stalin, and Mussolini, to Truman, Nixon, and Reagan, we see they had unlimited power. They were the top of the heap, king of the hill, in charge of everything. But Jesus asks a hard question: What became of their souls? What becomes of us spiritually when we gain imperial, worldly power? The gospel warns of a harsh judgment and urges serious reconsideration when tempted with worldly power and domination.

The day before India's leader Mahatma Gandhi was assassinated, a reporter asked him for advice. "Have nothing to do with power," Gandhi replied. After a lifetime in the public eye as the hero of political liberation, Gandhi learned from Jesus to run in the opposite direction of the world, to renounce the world's power, to seek powerlessness. Try not to win success, reach the top of the heap, or dominate others, Gandhi recommended. Instead, discover the fullness of life at the bottom of the heap. Protect your soul. Stand with the powerless and discover the power of powerlessness, like Jesus on the cross.

The Gospel advocates an upside-down logic, the opposite of every worldly value. For Jesus, the goal is to gain life, to enter the fullness of life here and now and so also to gain eternal life after our physical deaths. Contrary to the rest of us, Jesus always keeps in mind this long-haul perspective of life after death. He urges us to set our sights on God's reign of love in heaven. He wants us to gain heaven, to become saints in God's eyes, in total disregard of the world's traps and temptations.

Gaining the world comes at a terrible ultimate price. When Satan tempts Jesus in the desert and offers him all the kingdoms of the world, there is one big catch: Jesus will have to bow down and worship Satan, and in that act, Jesus will lose his soul. But Jesus chooses to keep his soul and his relationship with God as his number one priority. He rejects the temptation of total global domination and instead clings to his soul, his life, his God. In the process, Jesus suffers the world's violence but reveals God's resurrection.

Jesus is vindicated by God. From his vantage point, he tells us to choose that same difficult path of downward mobility, powerlessness, service, humility, nonviolence, voluntary poverty, and solidarity with the poor. In that way, we may forfeit the world, but we will gain our souls and enter eternal life, like him. We will be materially poor but spiritually rich. Our treasure will be in heaven, and we will spend eternity rejoicing with God and the human race.

What could one give in exchange for his life?

(MARK 8:37)

In "The Ballad of John and Yoko," John Lennon sings of the trials and tribulations that he and his wife suffered from the media after they were married. Their outspoken stand against the Vietnam War led the authorities to harass and persecute them. In the process, they began to dig deeper into the meaning of life. They started tithing ten percent of their income to charity and supporting causes for peace and justice.

"Last night the wife said, 'O boy when you're dead, you don't take nothing with you but your soul,'" Lennon sings to an upbeat Beatles' melody. Suddenly the music stops and he shouts out, "Think!"

Living in New York City, I used to walk by John Lennon's home, where he was shot five times in the back on December 8, 1980. He could not take his wealth, houses, or fame with him, but he must have had a soul to take after struggling for so many years to rediscover his basic humanity, sanity, and peace. Yoko said later that every night before he went to bed, John prayed for the whole human race. His heart had grown wide in love for all people. He had discovered the meaning of life.

Growing up in First World America, many of us dream of making it big. When we are young, we think, "I'm going to be president, a rock star, a movie star, or the quarterback in the Super Bowl. Maybe I'll win an Oscar, the Gold Medal, the Purple Heart, or the Nobel Peace Prize. I'll own a mansion, a private jet, a penthouse apartment, a condo by the beach, a yacht, a fleet of sports cars, reserved seats on Broadway, or front row seats at the Lakers. I'll be the wealthiest person on earth, the most important, the most powerful, the most impressive person in the crowd."

But Jesus warns against such ambitious pride, wealth, power, and domination. If we gain the whole world, he points out, we do so at the price of our soul. When we die, we will lose all we have gained. We cannot take our material wealth with us. If we have focused our energies and attention on gaining material wealth and power, we will miss the opportunity to grow spiritually and attain spiritual wealth.

The Gospel suggests that there is an inverse relationship between the amount of material wealth and personal power we have and the spiritual wealth and personal powerlessness we experience. If we have no spiritual depth to us when we die, the gospel declares, we risk losing our souls. Our selfishness prevents us from loving others, meeting their needs, and growing "rich in the sight of God."

The Gospel tries to prepare us for that sudden day when we stand before the throne of God and face our judgment. In that moment, our lives will suddenly flash before us. As we see how we have spent our days, we may realize that we wasted our short, precious lives in selfish pursuit of money, possessions, power, and honor.

Every spiritual tradition insists that there are spiritual consequences for what we do throughout our lives. What we choose to do with our lives will have positive or negative spiritual consequences, depending on whether we seek positive goals or negative goals.

If we spend our lives in selfish pursuits, we may find ourselves one day standing before God trying to make a deal. "Okay, God," we will say, "I give you my mansion, yacht, bank account, home, job, and weapons, in exchange for eternal life." But it will be too late. Our earthly treasures will not exist in the realm of the spirit. We will discover that our heavenly vault is empty.

"What can you give in exchange for your life?" Jesus asks.

"Think!" the late John Lennon shouts out at us.

Your life is precious, and your soul is all you have. In fact, even your soul, your very being, does not belong to you. Rather, it belongs to God. It is a gift from God and it will return to God. When you die, God will ask for an accounting of your life, your soul. If you wasted your time on material possessions and worldly power, there will be little love within your being to offer God. This will be a bitter realization. You will be spiritually bankrupt with nothing to give in exchange for eternal life.

Jesus summons us to pursue God with all our hearts, souls, minds, and strength, beginning right this moment, while we are still alive and breathing. He says, "Drop all selfish concerns this minute, let go of your life as you know it, and spend the remainder of your days loving and serving everyone, giving your life for God and God's reign of justice and peace. Surrender your life to God. Lose your life—and when you die, God will give it all back to you and more, for an eternity of peace with God and the rest of humanity in paradise."

Jesus exemplifies the selfless life. He had nothing to show for himself—no home, no car, no yacht, no awards, no medals, no honorary doctorates, no bank accounts, no land, no worldly power, no Nobel Prize. Instead, he was tortured and killed and died naked on the cross in total vulnerability.

Yet Jesus lived life with more daring, more passion, more chutzpah, more nonviolence, more compassion, more love, more truth than any person who ever lived. He died full of life—so much life that death could not contain him, and he quickly rose from the dead and lives on for eternity.

Jesus knows that nothing lasts forever, except our loving souls. He teaches us that the one who lets go of her life with total disregard of possessions, pride, privilege, and power, the one who widens her heart to embrace the whole human race in love, even to the point of giving her life for others, has already entered eternal life. That person will not seek to exchange honor, possessions, or power for her life. She will already be fully alive in the presence of Jesus. She will recognize herself in him and find herself at last at home.

> Can any of you by worrying add a single
> moment to your life span? If even the
> smallest things are beyond your control,
> why are you anxious about the rest?
>
> (MATTHEW 6:27; LUKE 12:26)

Life can be filled with worries from hour to hour. We worry about our children, our spouses and parents, our homes and jobs. We worry about breakfast, lunch, and dinner, friends and relations, work and recreation, health and sickness. We add worry upon worry upon worry.

On top of our personal day-to-day worries, there are the big worries of the world: the threat of terrorism, the existence of nuclear weapons, the possibility of nuclear war, the fear of poverty and disaster, the inevitability of illness. The greatest worry of all, of course, is death. We worry about the pain of dying, a sudden death, and what happens when we die. This worry is so overwhelming, in fact, that we deny we are going to die. Some of us live with a deep-down terror about the end of our existence. If we could, we would do whatever it takes to add more time to our lifespan. But because there is nothing we can do to control completely the extent of our lifespan, we worry.

"Can any of you by worrying add a single moment to your life span?" Jesus asks. The obvious answer is no. Not one of us can add a single moment to our life span by worrying.

Jesus proceeds to give us clear advice: "Stop your worrying. It's pointless. It does not help at all. In fact, worrying only aggravates your life. Rather, concentrate on the most important things in life: God, God's reign, love for one another, mercy and compassion. Seek first God and God's reign of justice and mercy, and everything will be provided for you. You will find fulfillment in life and in death."

Jesus' questions and alternatives are simple and to the point, yet we prefer to cling to our lives as if we are in control. We try to control every aspect of our own life and the lives of those around us. Ultimately our preoccupation with control disguises our futile attempt to avoid suffering and death. Years of this behavior will eventually lead us to attempt to control God or to reject God outright. In the end, this intense effort to control our lives, others, death, and God will fail. When we suffer and die, we lose control of our lives. Just as our birth is out of our control, so too is our death. We will eventually die, if not today or tomorrow, then someday, and we will have to surrender our control into the hands of God.

Every major religion suggests that the key to a peaceful life is the letting go of control and worry and living fully aware in the present moment. If we can live in the freedom of the present moment and center ourselves in the peace of God, we will find life turned upside down. We will no longer worry about the past or the future but will be fully alive to the present. And by being fully present to ourselves, others, and God, we will live our lives to the fullest. When we come to the moment of our death, as Thoreau said, we will not have wasted the gift of life but will have lived it to the full.

"So do not worry about tomorrow," Jesus concluded. "Tomorrow will take care of itself. Each day has enough trouble of its own" (Matthew 6:34).

Let go of your worries. Trust in God. Live each moment in peace. Seek God's reign, and all will be well.

Is not life more than food and the body more than clothing?

(MATTHEW 6:25)

In the forming of this question, Jesus sounds like a Buddhist Zen master. But for Christians, Jesus is much more than a wise teacher. He is the incarnation of the God of peace. He knows how mysterious life and the human body are. He sees how confused, misguided, and lost we are, and he knows that we do not know what to do with our lives or our bodies. But instead of chastising us, Jesus asks a question: "What is the meaning of life?" He challenges us to question the meaning of the human body. Is not life more than food, and the body more than clothing?

Everywhere we look in First World America, we see fast-food chains, gourmet restaurants, and grocery stores literally stocked to the ceiling with every food item imaginable. While millions of people around the world are malnourished, and over fifty thousand people, mostly children, die of starvation each day, most North Americans are obsessed with food. In fact, we suffer a new epidemic: obesity.

We are also obsessed with clothes. The fashion industry is booming, as people spend billions on expensive suits, dresses, coats, and shoes. Hundreds of different magazines are published each month featuring glamorous models wearing the latest designs. Our culture has commercialized the body by socializing people into regularly buying new clothes, while thousands of people walk our city streets homeless and in rags, and in some Third World streets, naked and dying.

Jesus has a completely different perspective on food and clothing. He fasts for forty days in the desert and eventually dies naked, nailed to a cross. He recognizes our addiction to food and clothing and invites us to a deeper meaning of life. He wants us to be human, which means he wants us to take care of ourselves by loving and serving others, especially those in need. He wants us to get beyond food and clothing to the question of reality itself.

Life is more than food. The body is more than clothing. For Jesus, life and the body are for loving and serving God and the human family. If we sit with his question, we may find the strength to redirect our time and energy, even to quit our jobs and start serving the poor. We will place less emphasis on exquisite food and fine clothing and reach out with love and service to those in need. Only then will we be given a clue to the meaning of life and the human body. Only then will we discover the God of love within us and in the poor, suffering, and oppressed. Only through humble service and steadfast love will we be able to open the door to happiness and peace and find that life makes sense.

"Seek first God and God's reign of justice," Jesus declares after asking his question, "and all these things will be provided to you as well." His words are more than an invitation or even a commandment: They are a law of nature. If you seek God and God's reign of peace and justice with all your heart, soul, and strength—if you pursue God and God's reign of nonviolence every day for the rest of your life—you will one day meet God and enter God's reign. And besides that, you will have enough to eat and wear. All your needs will be met. Most important, you will be greatly blessed.

Are you not more important than the birds of the sky?

(MATTHEW 6:26)

Watch the sandpipers run from an oncoming wave, the glorious green, yellow, and red quetzal bird of Guatemala move gracefully from tree to tree, or hundreds of Canadian geese flying in formation high overhead. The spectacular beauty, agility, and flight of these magnificent varied creatures is amazing. The lone hawk hovering over the countryside and the seagull gliding over a shoreline cliff do something we can never do: They fly effortlessly through the air. They are miraculous and mysterious creatures, a sign of God's grandeur.

But in our busy lives, we take birds for granted. In fact, we hardly notice them. If we study them, however, we will notice, as Jesus points out, that they always have enough to eat, they always find shelter, they always find companions, they always manage to raise families. Some even fly thousands of miles south each winter to a warmer climate. "Look at the birds in the sky," Jesus says. "They do not sow or reap, they gather nothing into barns, yet your heavenly God feeds them. Are you not more important than the birds of the sky?"

It is evident that the Creator provides abundantly for these little creatures, as Jesus points out. He could further explain that God the Creator takes care of billions of living creatures right this minute—creatures as small as microscopic insects and as grand as whales.

Jesus values birds and all creatures, as did his disciple Saint Francis, finding God in all things—in their simplicity, beauty, agility, and flight. Yet Jesus declares that we are more important than the birds of the sky. God cares for the birds, he teaches, but God has numbered every hair on our head. God beholds our every move. Most of all, God loves each one of us unconditionally, infinitely, madly, lavishly. We belong to God completely.

"So do not worry," Jesus says. "Trust in God. Focus your attention on God and God's reign of peace and God's love. God will take care of you and all the rest, because God takes care of the birds, and you are far more important than the birds."

This simple question may lead us beyond the beauty of the birds to the love of God. As Jesus points out, we may find the grace to realize that the Creator God cares for each one of us. If we can root our lives in this gentle, pervading love, we will find peace. Then, centered in God's love, we will be able to love those around us. We will be able to show compassion toward every human being on the planet, whether or not they treat us with kindness. Indeed, if we can ground ourselves in the all-encompassing love of God, who loves even the smallest of creatures, we will be able to care for and respect every living creature on the planet.

> Is it lawful to do good on the Sabbath rather than to do evil, to save life rather than to destroy it?

(LUKE 6:9; MARK 3:4)

One day, while teaching on the sabbath in the synagogue, Jesus notices a man with a withered hand. No one cares about the poor man, but Jesus stops what he is doing. He cannot continue speaking about good works without practicing what he preaches. He must do something immediately. He calls the man forward to stand up front, where everyone can see him.

The tension in the room grows. Everyone sits on the edge of their seats to see what Jesus will do next. Instead of healing the man right at that moment and breaking the law in the process, however,

Jesus raises the tension another notch by asking one of his most provocative questions: "Is it lawful to do good on the sabbath rather than to do evil, to save life rather than to destroy it?"

There they are, gathered in the holy sanctuary, presumably on their best behavior, and Jesus asks them about doing evil or destroying life. Why does Jesus ask such a pointed question?

The religious authorities care nothing for the poor and suffering. Rather, they are focused solely on the law, the rules, the ritual, their authority, and their control over God and everyone else. They profit from their support of the empire and maintain their economic and political domination with the threat of violence in the name of God, as disturbers of the peace are punished and excommunicated. Anyone who challenges their authority can be legally stoned to death right there in the sanctuary.

Jesus can see that the hearts and minds of the religious authorities are filled with selfishness, hatred, and violence. When he sees people ignoring or profiting from the suffering of others, he never sits back quietly. Rather, he takes a stand and confronts injustice head on, especially when he sees it in the religious community. He risks dividing a community if it means helping someone in need. In this case, he unmasks the violence of the heart and forces the community to deal with the purpose of the law and religion itself. Through his example, Jesus teaches that the spiritual life should lead us first of all to serve those in need.

So when Jesus heals the man, one would think that the religious authorities would rejoice and be grateful to God for this miracle. Instead, they immediately start to plot Jesus' murder, right there in the holy sanctuary.

By posing his question, Jesus forces the Pharisees and scribes to deal with the truth. Today we are faced with the same challenge: Are we to do good and save life or do evil and destroy life? What is the purpose of the law? Which is legal: defending life or destroying life? What is life about anyway?

Had the Pharisees and scribes answered honestly, they would have declared that it is illegal to do good. It is illegal to save life. Their priority was to maintain decorum on the Sabbath, to obey the letter of the Mosaic law, and to punish any lawbreakers.

Then and now, Jesus cannot tolerate hypocrisy and false spirituality. He cannot permit injustice to go unchallenged. He breaks the law, disrupts the religious gathering, and confronts violence, at the risk of his own life. He does a good deed, helps a poor man, and teaches a lesson about the priority of doing good and resisting evil.

Jesus spends his days doing good and saving life, and he is executed for resisting evil and preventing the destruction of life. He is not concerned with laws, customs, rituals, traditions, religious observances, or obligations if they do not do good and save life. Indeed, if these things are evil and destroy life, he resists them actively and publicly, with total disregard for the consequences.

Jesus wants his followers to do good and save life, to resist evil and prevent the destruction of life. He wants his followers to obey God's law of life and nonviolence. He expects us to give our lives, like him, actively, publicly, and nonviolently, confronting evil and whatever legally destroys life, while doing good deeds for those in need and saving the lives of those in danger.

Yet today's laws continue to legalize evil and the destruction of life. War, nuclear weapons, handguns, Trident submarines, air force bombers, missiles, concentration camps, bombing raids, executions, torture, and abortions are perfectly legal. Homelessness, starvation, environmental destruction, and poverty are perfectly legal. The Pentagon's plans to risk the destruction of the planet through nuclear war are perfectly legal. Today, as in Jesus' day, it is legal to do evil and to destroy life. Likewise, as the examples of Dr. King and Mahatma Gandhi show, it is illegal to do good and save life.

But Jesus' question remains. He would have us do good for one another, save life, and resist every form of evil. He would have us practice civil disobedience to systemic injustice and steadfast obedience to God's law of nonviolence, regardless of the consequences to ourselves, because he knows that we have been created to live life to the full in a spirit of goodness and peace.

> Who is greater, the one seated at table or
> the one who serves? Is it not the one seated
> at table?
>
> (LUKE 22:27)

During the Last Supper, Jesus bends down and washes the feet of his disciples. He announces that he is giving them his body and blood as their food and drink to sustain them on the journey of life. He also says that one of them will shortly betray him and the rest of them will quickly abandon him and run away.

How do the disciples respond to these beautiful events and this disturbing news? They immediately start to argue among themselves about which one of them is the greatest! From our perspective today, the whole episode would be hilarious if it were not so tragic.

The disciples appear throughout the Gospels like the Keystone cops. Jesus is surrounded by a group like the Marx Brothers, the Three Stooges, Lucy Ricardo and Ethel Mertz, and Abbot and Costello all rolled into one. At this climactic moment in his life, as he gives them his very body and blood for their food and drink, they start feuding among themselves about how great they are, totally missing the point of what Jesus is doing for them or how great Jesus is.

Yet I feel only love and compassion for the disciples because I see the same worldly ambition and ridiculous pomp among church leaders today. And unfortunately, I find it in myself as well. Instead of focusing on the greatness of Jesus, the selflessness of Jesus, the humility of Jesus, the powerlessness of Jesus, the nonviolence of Jesus, the perfect love of Jesus, I get stuck in my own ego and pride, thinking about how great I am, wanting everyone to know my virtues. Everyone in the church does this. Perhaps it is a simple nervous response to the shocking news that Jesus announces.

But Jesus does not chastise the disciples. According to Luke's account, he simply starts teaching them once again that they must not seek power or domination over others. From now on, they are to be as humble and powerless as he.

"The kings of the Gentiles lord it over others, and those in authority over them are addressed as Benefactors," Jesus says, "but among you it shall not be so. Rather, let the greatest among you be as the youngest, and the leader as the servant. For who is greater, the one seated at table or the one who serves? Is it not the one seated at table? Yet I am among you as the one who serves" (Luke 22:25–27).

Jesus calls us to an entirely new way of living. Instead of drawing attention to ourselves and having people applaud us and wait on us, we are to give ourselves in selfless service to one another, without any desire for attention, reciprocation, or honor. We are to consider ourselves the least, the youngest, the last, the humblest, because in Jesus' worldview the greatest is the smallest. The most powerful is the most powerless. The one in charge is the one least in charge. The highest ambition is to be the lowest servant in the human race.

As Jesus summons us to this upside-down ambition, he embodies it more than anyone else. St. Paul explains that Jesus emptied himself completely when he died on the cross with perfect humility, powerlessness, service, and poverty. He became the last and the least among the whole human race and is therefore raised up as the first and the greatest human being who ever lived.

Jesus explains this divine way of life as he sits with his friends at the Passover meal, after washing their feet and giving them his body and blood. As they argue among themselves, he asks them a simple question: "For who is greater, the one seated at table or the one who serves? Is it not the one seated at table?"

The world insists that the ones who are seated at table and waited on are the greatest human beings. The world honors and exults those great ones—the rulers, the emperors, the rich, the powerful, the presidents and dictators. But in Jesus' realm, those who serve are the greatest. Humble, meek servants, from St. Francis and St. Clare to Dorothy Day and Mother Teresa, are the great ones in his eyes. The Gospel infers that since Jesus is the real lord and master of the disciples, they should serve him, wait on him, wash his feet, and give their lives in defense of him. But Jesus points out to them—and to us—that he has done just the opposite. He has come as their servant, as our servant, as the slave of the whole human race, to give his life in humble service to everyone. Since he the teacher has done this, the Gospel concludes, all disciples and followers must do likewise. We are to be humble servants of one another. We are to be powerless, selfless, loving, nonviolent servants of all, even to the point of giving our lives in service for others, for the whole human race. This is the meaning of life, according to the Gospel. Serve others, and you will be truly great. Be the least of all, and you will be the greatest. Become a martyr for justice and peace for the whole human race, and you will enter into God's reign and resemble the Master himself.

TEN

THE REIGN OF GOD

What is the reign of God like? To what
can I compare it?

(LUKE 13:18, 20)

In the desert of northeastern New Mexico, where I live and serve several poor parishes and missions, we are surrounded not only by poverty but also by stunning mountains and desert vistas as well as countless deer, buffalo, antelopes, horses, and elk. The people who have grown up in both poverty and beauty have an innate, deep spirituality that I cannot grasp. All they seem to do is work outdoors, help one another, and pray.

During my first week in Cimarron, a small desert town, I began a weekly study of the Gospel of Mark with the high school confirmation class. When we read in that opening chapter that Jesus announced that "the reign of God is at hand," I asked the young people, "What is the reign of God?"

These high school juniors and seniors looked at one another as if to say, "What's his problem? Doesn't he know what the reign of God is?"

Finally, one of them spoke up. "The reign of God is life." He looked at the others and they all nodded in agreement. "The reign of God is all around us, here in Cimarron, in our day-to-day life."

I nearly fell out of my chair. In a million years, I do not know if I would ever have thought of such a simple and profound answer. I would expect this kind of answer from the great Buddhist master Thich Nhat Hanh or the Trappist monk Thomas Merton but not from a teenager.

The reign of God is life. The reign of God is peace. The reign of God is love. The reign of God is our community of compassion and kindness. The reign of God is nonviolence. The reign of God is as close as our hand held up to our face. The reign of God is here.

I think Jesus would have liked that young person's answer. The one thing Jesus spoke about more than anything else, the main point in all his teachings, was the reign of God. He did not preach about himself or even about God. Rather, he talked about this mysterious, beautiful image, "the reign of God." Most translations refer to it as the Kingdom of God (or the Kingdom of Heaven), but many people now prefer a less patriarchal, more inclusive phrase. Some call it the realm of God, the empire of God, or the "kin-dom" of God. Martin Luther King Jr. described it as "the Beloved Community."

But what is the reign of God? How do we describe it? What is it like? Where is it? The reign of God is not of this world, Jesus tells Pilate just before Pilate orders his execution (see John 18:36). It is another world. The one main difference between God's reign and the kingdoms and nations of the earth, Jesus explains to Pilate, is that if God's reign were of this world, people would use violence to protect Jesus, their king. But God's reign is nonviolent. In God's reign, there is no violence, no killing, no injustice, no hatred, no bombs, no executions, no nuclear weapons, no war. God's reign is a realm of love, peace, compassion, nonviolence, justice, and goodness.

From the minute he first opens his mouth publicly until his final trial before Pilate, Jesus speaks about the reign of God. After John the Baptist is arrested, according to Mark, Jesus takes up John's message and announces: "This is the time of fulfillment. The reign of God is at hand. Repent and believe in the good news" (1:15). After announcing that God's reign is at hand, Jesus appears to change his strategy. He starts to tell stories, descriptive parables with a specific lesson, about God's reign, stories that help the crowds understand it.

But at some point, Jesus sounds as if he is at a loss to describe God's reign. "What is the reign of God like? To what can I compare it?" He tries a variety of images: a man with a dragnet, a pearl of great price. When he first asks this question in Luke, he describes God's reign as the smallest seed that grows to become a big shrub where birds take shelter. "It is like a mustard seed that a person took and planted in the garden. When it was fully grown, it became a large bush and 'the birds of the sky dwelt in its branches'" (Luke 13:18–19). The image evokes Ezekiel's language of the birds of the sky, representing all the peoples of the earth, coming together in peace and harmony (see Ezekiel 31:6).

But then Jesus does something he rarely does: He repeats his question. For Jesus, this may be *the* most important question. "Again he said, To what shall I compare the reign of God?" On the second try, he uses another image. "It is like yeast that woman took and mixed in with three measures of wheat flour until the whole batch of dough was leavened" (Luke 13:20–21).

The religious authorities, of course, repeatedly challenge all this talk about God's reign. They demand to know when it will come. "The coming of the reign of God cannot be observed," Jesus tells them, even though he is standing there in their midst, doing great signs and wonders, "and no one will announce, 'Look, here it is,' or, 'There it is.' For behold, the reign of God is among you" (Luke 17:20–21).

Shortly afterward, Jesus compares God's reign to the life of children. "The reign of God belongs to children," he says. "Whoever does not accept the reign of God like a child will not enter it" (Luke 18:16–17).

What is the reign of God like? The reign of God is that sacred space where everyone loves everyone else unconditionally, where everyone dwells in peace, where everyone acts in perfect nonviolence, where everyone is happy, where everyone rejoices because they are in the presence of God—most of all, where everyone loves and worships the living God with all their being.

The reign of God is within us, among us, and far away from us, all at the same time. It is right here in front of us, and it is nowhere near us. It is the spiritual experience of inner peace and perfect unconditional love, but it is also an eschatological existence, the heavenly place where God lives, where we shall one day live with God. It is that space of vulnerability, innocence, wonder, peace, and joy that children know. It is the presence of our Lord Jesus. It is life.

More than anything, Jesus wants us to know what God's reign is like, to welcome God's reign, to serve God's reign, and to dwell in God's reign. He teaches us to pray for the coming of God's reign and to "seek first God's reign," because then everything else will be provided for us (see Luke 12:31). He wants us to be members of God's reign.

If we are members of God's reign, then we are no longer members and servants of the nations, kingdoms, reigns, and empires of the earth. Rather, our primary allegiance is to God's reign, not the Roman Empire, Nazi Germany, the Soviet Union, or the United States of America. Jesus wants us to serve the living God who has a specific home and place, not any political party or president or prime minister. Throughout our lives, he wants us to ponder God's reign and get ready to dwell there, because that is where we are headed. From now on, we are citizens first and foremost of God's reign.

> To what shall we compare the reign of God,
> or what parable can we use for it?
>
> (MARK 4:30)

O ne of my favorite movies, *Babette's Feast*, dramatizes Isak Dinesen's fable about a refugee woman who flees the French Revolution to a remote Danish village, where she becomes the cook for two pious, elderly sisters. Once the greatest chef in France, Babette ends up making soup for the shut-ins of a country village.

One day Babette learns that she has won the French lottery, so she asks the sisters if she can cook a special meal for them and their village friends. They agree. Babette then proceeds to spend all her winnings on the greatest feast ever made, using only the best imported French gourmet foods. Boatloads of wine, vegetables, and exotic ingredients arrive for this fabulous feast. The devout Christian villagers, however, fear the worst. They secretly pledge not to enjoy this heathen meal but to eat the food solely out of respect for Babette.

The meal begins, and the diners stoically enjoy one delicacy after another. But over the many courses, old resentments are healed and feuding friends reconcile. Sharing true communion, the villagers taste God's reign.

This modern-day parable demonstrates what God's reign is like. Jesus uses many similar stories to teach his disciples and the crowds about the reign of God. More than anything, he wants us to understand God's reign and to discover it within us and among us. "This is how it is with the reign of God," Jesus explains in Mark's Gospel. "It is as if a man were to scatter seed on the land and would sleep and rise night and day and the seed would sprout and grow, he knows not how. Of its own accord the land yields fruit, first the blade, then the ear, then the full grain in the ear. And when the grain is ripe, he wields the sickle at once, for the harvest has come" (Mark 4:26–29).

The Gospels offer a wide variety of parables to help us understand God's reign. It is like a mustard seed, like a man who gave a great feast but the people refused to come, like a man who had a hundred sheep but lost one, like a woman who had ten coins and lost one, like a man who had two sons and the prodigal one returned, like a rich man with a dishonest steward, like a man who gave his ten servants each a gold coin before going on a long trip, like a man who planted a vineyard and went on a long journey, like a king dividing the sheep and the goats. In each case, Jesus draws us into the story and leads us unwittingly to a revelation of God's reign.

"Knowledge of the mysteries of the reign of God has been granted to you," he tells his disciples, "but to the rest, they are made known through parables so that 'they may look but not see, and hear but not understand' " (Luke 8:10). This hard saying, taken from the prophet Isaiah, challenges our priorities. Do we want to attain knowledge of God's reign, like the disciples, or are we merely people who look but do not see and hear but do not understand? The key is to seek God's reign from now on with the same passion as Jesus and his saints, prophets, and martyrs. We want to welcome it, promote it, dwell in it, proclaim it, and never leave it. This goal is the struggle of our lives. We will never quite attain it in this life, but we seek it within us and announce its coming to the world with all its social, economic, and political implications, such as food and justice for the poor and the abolition of war, the death penalty, and nuclear weapons. We too ponder its mysteries, and as we do, Jesus' parables start to make perfect sense.

> Do you think that I have come to establish
> peace on the earth?
>
> (LUKE 12:51)

I sure hope that Jesus came to establish peace on earth. When he was born, the angels could not contain themselves, and they appeared to shepherds in Bethlehem announcing "Glory to God in the highest and peace on earth!" At the center of his greatest sermon, Jesus declares, "Blessed are the peacemakers." The night before he is executed, he says to his friends at the Passover meal, "Peace I leave you; my peace I give you." After he dies and rises from the dead, his first words, which he repeats over and over again, are simple and to the point: "Peace be with you."

Alas, there seems to be no peace on earth. Today dozens of wars explode around the world. Our country, the world's only superpower, acting like a new global imperial bully, maintains tens of thousands of nuclear weapons, sells weapons to warring nations on every side of

nearly every war, invades and slaughters those nations if it wants to
steal resources from them or claim their strategic position (as in Iraq,
Panama, Honduras, the Philippines), and threatens the world with a
nuclear holocaust if it does not get its way. We have no peace. As Orwell predicted, we even believe that war is peace. We no longer imagine a world without war. In fact, we have come to the assumption that
war is the common, normal, legitimate, legal way to resolve international crises.

More than ever, we need peace on the earth. I hope and pray that
Jesus, the Prince of Peace, Son of the God of peace, came to establish peace. But suddenly, unlike anything we've heard before, Jesus
gives an immediate and specific answer to his own question: No.

"I have come to set the earth on fire," Jesus declares in Luke's
Gospel, "and how I wish it were already blazing! There is a baptism
with which I must be baptized, and how great is my anguish until it is
accomplished! Do you think that I have come to establish peace on
the earth? No, I tell you, but rather division. From now on a household of five will be divided, three against two and two against three;
a father will be divided against his son and a son against his father,
a mother against her daughter and a daughter against her mother, a
mother-in-law against her daughter-in-law and a daughter-in-law
against her mother-in-law" (Luke 12:49–53).

I think that at the beginning of his public ministry Jesus presumed he had come to establish peace on earth. He hoped that everyone would embrace his good news of nonviolence, that the world
would repent of the sin of violence and war, that all nations would
welcome God's reign of peace. But from the minute he started announcing the gospel of peace, people were shocked and appalled. Instead of accepting his message, people rejected his word of peace,
and rejected him as well. The religious authorities, the imperial rulers,
and those who benefit from injustice denounced him and opposed
him. Instead of unity, Jesus' message brought division. No one could
be neutral about Jesus or his message. Either they accepted him or rejected him outright. In a culture of war, the only possible answer to
Jesus' question was crucifixion.

After several months of division, hostility, rejection, and even death threats, Jesus realized that people would not be able to accept his message of love, compassion, nonviolence, and peace. He understood that eventually the ruling authorities who maintained the war-making empire, the culture of violence, and its religious establishment would have to do away with him if their system of violence was to survive the weight of the truth of his word. Jesus realized that he would not be establishing peace on earth, that before humanity could ever abolish war and welcome his reign of peace, there had to be widespread division and confrontation.

"Peace is not just the absence of war but the presence of justice," Martin Luther King Jr. said. When Dr. King brought his campaign of creative nonviolence for civil rights to Birmingham, Alabama, in early 1963, the white, segregationist establishment denounced him for dividing the community and bringing violence to their city. King retorted that he was merely uncovering the latent violence that lay beneath the surface of the divided, racist city. He said graphically that he had to prick the pustule of racism and segregation and drain the pus before healing could begin. It was as if Dr. King, the holy prophet of peace, said, "I have not come to bring peace, but division."

Twenty-five years ago, when I began my public pursuit of peace, I deliberately ignored Jesus' question and difficult answer. Now, after all these years of peace activism, countless speeches, articles, retreats, sermons, and nearly one hundred arrests and long nights behind bars for antinuclear demonstrations, I think I understand Jesus on this question. I would have thought that everyone would be interested in my invitation to peace, that people would want to hear my biblical reflections on violence and war, that people of faith would welcome my spirituality of nonviolence. But I was mistaken. By and large I experienced widespread rejection. People walked away from me, got upset with me, yelled at me, and told me to be quiet, all because I spoke for peace. Over the years, I have received hundreds of hate letters and several death threats, have been discredited across the country by religious communities, religious leaders, the media, and the government, and have been imprisoned because of my words for peace on earth. In other words, I have not brought peace, as I hoped, prayed, and desired with all my heart. Rather, like Jesus, I have brought division.

These days, I take cold comfort in Jesus' difficult, poetic words. I know he wants peace for all of us above all else, that he gave his life that we might enter his reign of peace, and that he wills for us to know the depths of peace here and now at every level—personally, communally, nationally, internationally, and globally. Jesus still offers his resurrection gift of peace.

Some older versions translate Jesus' answer, "I have not come to bring peace, but a sword." Although this statement sounds like an endorsement of violence, the full text invokes the figurative language of St. Paul and the Book of Revelation. The division or sword Jesus brings is the word of God. The word of God is always divisive. One need only recall family or church conversations during the Vietnam War, the Reagan years, or the two Gulf Wars to know how upsetting the political implications of the Gospel are. But this division or sword, the word of God, does not mean we can bomb or murder one another or vaporize people with nuclear weapons. During the first three centuries, this text was used to support Christian opposition to the Roman military and the prohibition of killing in war. Once baptized, people were forbidden to join the army, kill in war, or support the empire. Because of these political implications, they were almost immediately arrested and killed. Their families were horrified. Relatives would leave them, renounce them, and never speak to them again, or they might be implicated and killed. The word of God, the message of Jesus in other words, divided everyone.

"The Word of God is living and active," we read in the letter to the Hebrews, "sharper than any two-edged sword, piercing to the division of soul and spirit, of joints and marrow, and discerning the thoughts and intentions of the heart" (Hebrews 4:12). Jesus wants us to live in peace. But he knows that few will accept his gift of peace and all its implications. This question invites a lifetime of meditation. Perhaps, if more of us surrender ourselves to his word and gift of peace, we will move from division to unity, from violence to nonviolence, from crucifixion to resurrection, from war to peace. Perhaps it will lead us to focus not on our own national agendas and imperial ambitions but on God's reign of nonviolence, and to seek ways to welcome the God of peace here on earth.

ELEVEN

GOD'S GENEROSITY

Why are you anxious about clothes?

(MATTHEW 6:28)

After Francis of Assisi surrendered his life to the Gospel of Jesus, he gave away the clothing manufactured in his father's factory. When his father heard the news, he blew up, assaulted Francis, and dragged him through Assisi to the mayor and the bishop, demanding that they lock him up. But Francis went one step further. In front of the whole town, he stripped off all his clothes, renounced his father, and announced that he only had one Father, in heaven. With that, he set off into the woods in total poverty. But before he did, the bishop took off his majestic cloak and threw it around Francis. Suddenly Francis was wearing the clothes of the Bishop of Assisi!

Francis gave himself completely to God and God's reign, as Jesus commanded. As a consequence, God provided everything Francis needed, until his last breath, just as Jesus promised.

For Jesus, the most important value, the highest good, the greatest cause, is God and God's reign of justice and peace. Jesus teaches us that God provides for everyone, just as any doting parent would. He calls us to study the lilies of the field and the fish in the deep blue sea to learn just how God takes care of the vulnerable. He invites us to place our faith in our caring, generous God. As we trust in God's generosity, do as God commands, we will help transform our world into the haven of peace and justice that God intended and receive from God everything we need.

"Do not worry about your life and what you are to eat, nor about your body and what you are to wear," Jesus teaches in the Sermon on the Mount. "Why are you anxious about clothes? Learn from the way the wild flowers grow. If God so clothes the grass of the field, which grows today and is thrown into the oven tomorrow, will God not much more provide for you, O you of little faith? So do not worry and say, 'What are we to eat?' or 'What are we to drink?' or 'What are we to wear?' All these things the pagans seek. Your heavenly God knows you need them all. But seek first God's reign and God's justice, and all these things will be given you besides" (Matthew 6:28–33).

If we take Jesus' question seriously, we will emulate Francis, stop spending money on new clothes, give away all our extra clothing to the Catholic Worker or the Salvation Army, donate the money we save to Oxfam America or Catholic Relief Services, and discover God's intimate, generous care for us. We will realize our true dependence on God, a greater awareness of God's loving presence, and a profound new perspective on the true needs of the poor. We will allow God to provide for us, while we become people of great faith.

Jesus' question will take us down a new spiritual path in pursuit of justice for the poor, a deepening of faith, and a true reliance on God. It will draw us from selfishness and the illusion of our independence toward selfless concrete action on behalf of the needy, and a practical dependence on God. Ironically, the one who asked this question about anxiety over clothing was stripped of his clothes and nailed naked to a cross, where he died completely vulnerable, helpless, and utterly dependent on God. His total faith and dependence on God led to the most dramatic event in human history: his resurrection. His trust in God bore good fruit and continues to transform the world.

Madison Avenue will never call us to such difficult spiritual heights. Rather, our consumer culture tells us that we are nothing if we do not wear the latest styles. As a result, we are anxious about our image and spend billions of dollars annually on clothing. We waste our time cruising the mall, flipping through thousands of items of clothing, all the while becoming members of a culture of anxiety, far removed from the peace of Christ.

But Jesus calls us back to the highest priorities. He tells us to seek God instead, to expand our hearts, to plumb the depths of faith, love, and peace, to discover the meaning of life. When we let go of our anxiety over fads and fashions, we will be free to learn the wisdom of the present moment, the peace of Christ, the passion for justice, the truth of God's reign. We will see how everything will be provided, and we will discover just how precious we are in the eyes of God.

> Which one of you would hand his son a
> stone when he asks for a loaf of bread, or
> a snake when he asks for a fish?
>
> (MATTHEW 7:9–10)

Throughout the 1990s, the children of Iraq asked for bread and fish, but we denied their request. Instead, we cut off all food and medicine and left them to die with the stones and snakes of the desert. After we systematically destroyed Iraq's infrastructure, including its water purification systems, children started dying. UNICEF and the United Nations estimate that the U.S. sanctions on the suffering people of Iraq killed at least half a million children under the age of five between the first Gulf War and the second. We turned our backs on needy children and let them die without thinking twice about it.

Tens of thousands of children around the world die each day of starvation. They beg for bread and fish, but we ignore their plea and leave them with only stones and snakes. We do not give them what they need, what they want, what they hunger for. In fact, we do not have a foreign policy that aims primarily to serve, feed, and protect our own children here and the world's children abroad. This question should jolt us into realizing that if we would be more like the nonviolent, loving Jesus, who welcomes children with open arms, we would feed, care for, and protect all the world's children from now on.

According to Jesus, God is a doting, loving, generous parent. God is *Abba*, Daddy. God spoils us. God holds us, feeds us, sings to us, makes us laugh, cheers us up, rocks us to sleep. God consoles us, protects us, and gives us everything we need.

Jesus tries to teach us about God's love, care, and generosity. In this case, he points out how we treat our own children. "Which one of you would hand his son a stone when he asks for a loaf of bread, or a snake when he asks for a fish?"

Jesus knows that his disciples are loving fathers and mothers, that they care for their children, that they would give their lives to protect their children. In the Jewish culture of his time, the relationship between a father and a son was particularly sacred. If the son was hungry and asked for a loaf of bread or a fish, the father would not think twice before handing over such basic necessities. A father would never give a stone or a snake to a hungry son.

Even more, Jesus implies, God gives us all we need. God could never hurt us. God cannot be mean or violent to us. God loves us wildly, infinitely, unconditionally, wanting only the best for each one of us. God is crazy about us. God gazes upon us and beams with joy. God brags to the angels about us, and is overjoyed whenever we turn to God.

Tragically, relationships have deteriorated since Jesus' day. Couples divorce; fathers abandon their children; children starve, suffer, and die early and unjust deaths. But the vocation of parenthood remains a holy calling. Parents are summoned to be as generous as God, to shower children with love, to show compassion to children, to practice nonviolence, to feed, care for, and protect children. Parents are summoned to raise their children as God's holy daughters and sons. In fact, parenting may be our greatest calling. We are created to dwell in God's love and pass that divine love on to our children and future generations.

If we expand our view of family and see with the eyes of God that we are all one family—sisters and brothers of everyone on the planet—we will treat every child on earth as our own son and daughter and meet their every need. No child will starve. No child will suffer. No child will be poor. No child will be uneducated, homeless, or abused. Rather, we will be loving, doting parents, not only to our own biological children but to the children of the world. And in being parents to the world, we will become like God: compassionate and loving.

> What father among you would hand his son a snake when he asks for a fish? Or hand him a scorpion when he asks for an egg? If you then, who are wicked, know how to give good gifts to your children, how much more will the Father in heaven give the Holy Spirit to those who ask him?
>
> (LUKE 11:11–13)

Children are the most precious gift we have. The wonder, joy, innocence, truth, and purity of childhood are signs of the divine in our midst. With reverence, awe, and selfless love, we serve our children and give them anything they need—a fish, an egg, whatever is good for them to eat. The only danger of such sanctity, as Thomas Merton once wrote, is that we become so enamored of the holiness among us that we fall down and worship children and even one another.

In an effort to explain God's goodness to us, Jesus points to the goodness shown by a parent toward the child. "What father among you would hand his son a snake when he asks for a fish? Or hand him a scorpion when he asks for an egg? If you then, who are wicked, know how to give good gifts to your children, how much more will the Father in heaven give the Holy Spirit to those who ask him?" You give good things to your children, he observes, and yet you are wicked. Likewise, God who is perfect goodness can give only good things to us.

At our worst, some of us would indeed give snakes and scorpions to our children. We leave the world's starving, sick children to snakes and scorpions. But at our best, we do give good gifts to our children. But God is even better, Jesus explains. God is always generous, gracious, kind, and nonviolent. God gives us whatever we ask for.

However, Jesus' question goes even deeper. He speaks of our "Father in heaven" who "gives the Holy Spirit" to "those who ask him." These three phrases explain not only the nature of God and the mind of Jesus but also, the spiritual life itself.

First of all, God is our Father in heaven. Unfortunately, we have grown bored and complacent about this title after reciting the Lord's Prayer so many times. This understanding of God has lost its power, its shock, its subversive intimacy. For millennia, God was portrayed as mean, violent, and warlike. God was someone to fear, avoid, hide and run away from. God was angry, wrathful, vengeful. God created us so he could throw us into an everlasting hellfire.

But Jesus throws out these false images of God. He invites us, rather, to recognize and feel God's parental love. He invites us to experience God as a doting parent who calls us "my beloved." He teaches that God rejoices at our birth, celebrates our life, holds us in loving arms, protects us, feeds us, cares for us, weeps with us, and does whatever is necessary to help us. If the Gospel's patriarchal language is a stumbling block, the image of God as a loving mother may help us understand Jesus' revelation about God.

Next, Jesus instructs that God gives us the Holy Spirit. He is talking about bread and fish, but then he starts talking about the

Holy Spirit. For Jesus, the Holy Spirit is as necessary, even more essential, than food and water. The Gospel invites us to ponder what our loving, divine Parent would want to give us. From God's perspective, what is the best gift God could give us? For Jesus, the answer is obvious: The best gift God can give each one of us is God!

God wants us, as God's beloved children, to be filled with God's very own spirit. To be God's beloved sons and daughters means we live in God's spirit of love and act and speak to one another just like our loving, divine parent. We resemble God, and become like God, beings of infinite love, peace, and compassion.

What does it mean to live in the spirit of God? St. Paul writes simply that we know if we are living in the spirit of God if we can see the fruits, the signs, of the Holy Spirit in our lives. He names these fruits of the spirit: love, joy, peace, patience, kindness, generosity, faithfulness, gentleness, and self-control (see Galatians 5:22–23). If we have these characteristics, these graces, these attitudes in our day-to-day lives, we are living in the Holy Spirit. Because we are fallen creatures, sinful, violent people, we have not yet attained the perfection of the spirit, and so the Gospel invites us to beg for the spirit.

This is the clincher at the end of Jesus' question. Just as a hungry child must ask the parent for bread and fish, so too we must ask our beloved God for the Holy Spirit. We have to let God know our needs, just as children let their parents know their needs. We all need the Holy Spirit of God. But God is so modest, so determined to respect us with the great gift of free will, and has been so continually rejected, that God knows if we do not want God's spirit. God gives us the freedom to live as we choose. That is why we need to beg God to fill us with God's spirit that we may live the best way for ourselves and all.

We need God's spirit to be our true selves, to survive in this world, to grow into mature sons and daughters of God. Because we are spiritual beings with souls, we need God's spirit to live just like the roots of a tree need water to grow and flourish. In order to find our true vocation, to become the people we were created to be, we need to call out day and night for God to give us God's own spirit.

We have to spend our short time on earth preparing to return to our heavenly home with our beloved Father/Mother God, where we will live in the fullness of the Holy Spirit. The shocking, surprising good news within Jesus' question is that all we have to do is ask for this gift and we shall receive it.

How many loaves do you have?

(MATTHEW 15:34; MARK 6:38, 8:5)

Once, after the disciples returned from their mission to proclaim God's reign, Jesus invited them to come away to a deserted place for a few days of rest. When they arrived at that place, they discovered that a large crowd had followed them.

The Gospels say that Jesus looked upon the people, all alone out there in that deserted place, and felt compassion for them. "His heart was moved with pity for them," Mark writes, "because they were like sheep without a shepherd" (6:34). So he started to teach them again.

After another long day, the disciples finally approach Jesus and say, "This is a deserted place and it is already very late. Dismiss them so that they can go to the surrounding farms and villages and buy themselves something to eat."

"Give them some food yourselves," Jesus replies.

"How are we supposed to feed all these people?" the disciples object. "Are we to buy two hundred days' wages worth of food and give it to them to eat?" (We are told that there were five thousand men present, "not counting women and children." Women and children did not count in those days, so they were not counted. But if we count them, we know there were probably twenty thousand women, because women are always more interested in the spiritual life. If all those women followed Jesus into the desert, they could not have left their children home. They would have brought their children with them, so there were probably another ten thousand children!)

"How many loaves do you have?" Jesus asks. "Go and see."

When the disciples return and report that there are "five loaves and two fish," Jesus tells them to get the people to sit down in groups of hundreds and fifties. Then, "taking the five loaves and the two fish and looking up to heaven, he said the blessing, broke the loaves, and gave them to his disciples to set before the people; he also divided the two fish among them all."

"They all ate and were satisfied," Mark reports.

Jesus inspired everyone to share what they had with one another. That is the miracle! Why else are we told that he sat them down in groups? Jesus formed small, manageable, human communities among the crowd, where everyone could get to know one another and relate humanly to one another. They had been listening to Jesus teach them about love, service, and sharing. Now, at the end of their retreat, when they were tired and hungry, he was instructing the people to create groups among themselves. They would have looked up and watched him sitting on the hilltop, lifting up the bread and fish, and sharing it with his friends. So they would have done likewise, imitating the Holy One.

But where did all this food come from? To begin with, the women would never have gone out into the desert without bringing food along for their children. So when these women saw Jesus take the bread and fish and bless it, they immediately would have taken out their small portions of food, broken the pieces, and shared the food with the members of their group. And they would have been happy to do so, because Jesus would have inspired them through his teachings to love the people around them and to give what they have to one another.

Mark records the same event two chapters later, only this time Jesus feeds "four thousand men" on the other side of the lake, in enemy, pagan territory. In that setting, Jesus asks the same question: "How many loaves do you have?" The Gospels make it clear that Jesus fed everyone on all sides, that he called everyone on all sides to share what they had with one another, that he was reconciling people everywhere. Besides the Crucifixion story and the turning over of the tables in the Temple, the miracle of the loaves and the fish is the only episode recorded in all four Gospels.

Taken alone, this question opens up an array of insights and concerns. Today we live in a world of hunger, where up to fifty thousand people, mostly women and children, die of starvation every day. Over eight hundred million people are malnourished at all times, while over two billion people live in total destitution without clean water, electricity, health care, or a balanced diet. The First World, with its corporate billionaires and Wall Street ethic, teaches us not to share our resources with one another. Rather, we are to make as much money as we can, hoard as much food and as many possessions as we can, and get ahead of others at any and all cost.

The Gospel, on the other hand, proposes an upside-down economics. In fact, Jesus' economics go against the entire direction of the world. He asks us: "How many loaves do we have in our breadboxes, our refrigerators, our grocery stores, and our local communities and nations, at a time when people around the world are starving to death? Go and see," he commands us.

Jesus wants us to form small, manageable, human communities, where we can relate to one another and share what we have with one another so that no one is hungry anywhere ever again. Following Gospel economics, everyone on the planet is supposed to have adequate food, drink, housing, health care, education, employment, and peace.

If we dare risk sharing the little we have with those in need around us, the Gospel insists, we will be doing the work of Jesus, and miracles will happen. In fact, there will be tons of food left over. Instead of resisting the commandment to feed the hungry, as the disciples initially do, we can share our loaves and fish with one another, live out the economics of God's reign, and rejoice in the miracles around the world.

If God so clothes the grass in the field that grows today and is thrown into the oven tomorrow, will God not much more provide for you, O you of little faith?

(MATTHEW 6:30; LUKE 12:28)

In the Sermon on the Mount, Jesus urges us not to worry about food, drink, or clothing. He refers to nature to make his point. He connects God's care of the earth with God's even greater care for us. "If God so clothes the grass in the field that grows today and is thrown into the oven tomorrow, will God not much more provide for you, O you of little faith?" he asks, according to Matthew and Luke.

Jesus, you could say, practices Buddhist mindfulness. He looks deeply at nature. He notices the details of creation. This contemplative practice helps him understand not only the way of God but what it means to be human. He sees the birds of the earth, the lilies of the field, and the grass that grows wildly. He concludes that the beauty of the created world reveals a God who cares. God cares for the birds, the flowers, the animals, and the sky. God "clothes" the grass of the field, which we burn without thinking twice about it.

If God takes such care of the grass, "clothing" it and allowing it to flourish, Jesus asks, what is God's attitude toward us? Jesus concludes that God has even greater care for us. He knows that we are the beloved of God, that we are worth far more than grass, that God takes great personal interest in us and cares for us individually and collectively as a devoted, doting parent. He insists that the God who provides for the natural world also provides for us. And so, he concludes, we have nothing to worry about. Our every need will be met, he teaches. All we have to do is believe in God and trust God—and everything will be provided for us.

Yes, God loves creation, Jesus points out, but God loves each one of us even more. Therefore, have faith, he says. Trust God. Let God provide for you. The one great commandment he issues in this context is helpful and to the point. "Seek first the reign of God and God's justice" (Matthew 6:33). That is the task before us.

The key to such trust comes in the phrase at the end: "O you of little faith." Our lack of faith is the problem. If we truly believed in God, if we knew God's existence, if we understood God's loving care, we would trust God to provide for us. But deep down within us lurk dark corners of doubt, where we do not believe in God, where we fear that we are really alone. So we worry and conclude that we must provide for ourselves because no one else cares for us. We worry about everything because we think there is no God, no meaning to life, no one to provide for us.

In the end, the Gospel insists, faith makes all the difference. We need to grow in faith. The question then is: How do we grow in faith? Daily prayer is a first step, along with Bible study, communal worship, friendship, solidarity with the poor, and good deeds for justice and peace. In a sense, we have to act as if we believe and live as if we believe, and over time we will discover that we do in fact believe in God because we have experienced God's loving care firsthand.

As we grow in faith, we become more like Jesus, like contemplatives and mystics who trust the providential care of God, who seek first God's reign and God's justice, and who dare to give our lives for others in the struggle for justice and peace, as Jesus did on the cross. Like Jesus, we will know that our lives are in the loving hands of God.

> Will not God secure the rights of God's chosen ones who call out to God day and night? Will God be slow to answer them?
>
> (LUKE 18:7)

If we are weary, burned out, cynical, despairing, or lacking faith, we may respond, at first glance, in the affirmative. "Yes, God is slow to answer. Yes, God is slow to respond to those who call out day and night. Look around the world. Everywhere we see the rights of the poor, the rights of children, the rights of the Third and Fourth World peoples trampled with no sign of God's help. Indeed, God is very slow to answer those who call out day and night," we lament with heavy and discouraged hearts.

In a world of structured, institutionalized injustice, where the rich and the powerful flourish and the poor and the oppressed get ignored, beaten, starved, bombed, and killed, there is little evidence of God's quick assistance, of God's justice, of God's active concern.

Where do we see God quickly answering the plea for justice and human rights for the poor and oppressed?

These questions, like all the others, cannot be answered immediately. Rather, they require time and meditation. They invite prayerful consideration, studious observation, and actual experimentation.

The text of this question appears only in Luke's Gospel, at the conclusion of the parable of the judge and the widow, in which Jesus tells "about the necessity for them to pray always without becoming weary" (18:1). The widow goes to the judge and demands a decision in her favor against her adversary. The unjust judge does not care about her and has no intention of rendering a verdict of justice for her. Eventually, however, the judge concludes, "While it is true that I neither fear God nor respect any human being, because this widow keeps bothering me, I shall deliver a just decision for her lest she finally come and strike me!" Jesus then goes on to instruct: "Pay attention to what the dishonest judge says. Will not God then secure the rights of God's chosen ones who call out to God day and night? Will God be slow to answer them?"

The parable and the questions teach us about the nature of God. God is honest, just, and attentive to the cries of the poor and the oppressed. According to Jesus, God will always bring justice for the widows, the poor, and the oppressed peoples who cry out for justice. "I tell you, God will see to it that justice is done for them speedily!" Jesus announces.

Following the teaching of the Gospel, God will take action for justice and peace if we but issue our plea day and night. This is the lesson of the Gospel. God will respond to those who beg for justice and human rights. God will grant our requests. Whether or not we see it, whether or not God's action makes the evening news, whether or not we see the clouds open in a spectacular revelation of divine light, God is acting for justice on behalf of those who call out for justice. God is a God of justice!

Jesus promises that God will hear the prayers of those who ask for justice, human rights, and peace and will meet our demands. But

Jesus goes even further. He pledges that God will answer our prayers for justice and peace *quickly!*

The question then becomes: Who of us calls out to God night and day to secure justice and human rights for the poor of the earth? Who cares much for the poor, for justice, for human rights? Do we really pray night and day for the coming of God's reign of justice and peace here and now, with all its social, economic, and political implications?

Perhaps occasionally we get on our knees and ask God for global justice and peace, but we soon give up. The Gospel, however, challenges us not to give up. Jesus wants us to cry out night and day to God for justice, peace, and human rights for all the poor, and to trust that God will hear our prayers and answer. So while we should pray for our relatives, our health, our friends and neighbors, and our work, the Gospel summons us to pray for justice, peace, and human rights for all the poor and the oppressed of the planet.

In response to the Gospel, let us start a new practice of praying at various intervals during the day and into the night for the specific needs of the world's poor and the oppressed. Let us pray: "God of justice, bring justice to those who suffer injustice. Liberate the oppressed. Feed the starving. House the homeless. Heal the sick. Educate all children to read, write, and live in peace. Give medicine and health care to those who have none, especially to those with HIV, AIDS, and cancer. End every war on the planet. Dismantle every nuclear weapon. Abolish every gun, bomb, land mine, death row, and weapon of mass destruction.

"God of justice, bring justice to the Palestinians, the Sudanese, the Iraqis, the Sri Lankans. Dissolve all the drug dealing, death squads, violent revolutionary gangs, military units, U.S. bombing raids, and the U.S. military occupation of Colombia. Bring healing, justice, and peace to all the people of Latin America. Bring healing, justice, and peace to all the people of Africa. Bring healing, justice, and peace to all the people of Asia. Bring healing, justice, and peace to all the people of Australia and the Southern Pacific.

Bring healing, justice, and peace to the poor in North America and Europe.

"Give us your reign of justice and peace, right now, today, this very minute!"

According to Jesus, if we take up this prayer crusade and storm heaven night and day for the rest of our lives, in one long demand for the great gifts of justice, human rights, and peace, God will answer our prayer, give us justice and peace, transform the world, abolish injustice and war, and change every heart so that the human race will learn to live in peace and nonviolence.

> Ten were cleansed, were they not? Where are the other nine? Has none but this foreigner returned to give thanks to God?
>
> (LUKE 17:17–18)

The only prayer Jesus ever utters in the Gospel of John occurs in chapter 11, just a few days before his death, when he stands in front of the tomb of Lazarus and prays, "Thank you, God, for hearing me." His prayer is a prayer of thanksgiving, for Jesus is a person of gratitude.

On one occasion in Luke's Gospel, ten lepers call out to Jesus saying, "Jesus, Master, have pity on us." Jesus sends them home, and on the way they are healed. One of them, a Samaritan, one of the hated enemies of the Jewish people, immediately returns to thank Jesus.

"Ten were cleansed, were they not?" Jesus asks. "Where are the other nine? Has none but this foreigner returned to give thanks to God?" Jesus cannot comprehend why all did not return to give thanks.

Today Jesus continues to wonder, in disappointment and amazement, why we do not express our gratitude to him for all he is doing for us. "Haven't all of you been healed?" he must ask. "Why haven't you all returned to give thanks to God? Why have only your hated enemies, the people you have bombed and killed for decades, the people of Iraq and Palestine, Nicaragua and Guatemala, El Salvador and Vietnam, given thanks?"

When we are kind and generous yet receive only ingratitude in return, we are hurt and resentful. We may even walk away saying, "I'll never do anything nice for those people again!"

But that's not God. Rather, God always helps us, heals us, and guides us. God has done so much for us and continues to do good things for us, right up to this moment. God creates us, loves us, and gives us family and friends. God gives us this beautiful creation: the gift of life, the gift of each breath, the gift of each day, the gift of animals and clouds and rain and snow and sun and moon. God gives us the Eucharist. God gives us Jesus, the gift of peace. We have much to be grateful for.

Despite our ingratitude, indifference, and lack of love, God continues to love us, help us, heal us, and guide us, all the while waiting for us to say thank you. That is the first and last prayer for the rest of our lives.

Gratitude is one of the key ingredients in the spiritual life. If we are angry, we can move toward gratitude and name whatever it is we are grateful for. If we are sick, we can move toward gratitude for the people who help us through life. If we have been hurt, we can move toward gratitude and name all the kind, loving things God has done for us. If we are stuck in despair or boredom or gossip or fear or depression or frustration or sadness or poverty or loneliness or resentment, we can move toward gratitude and count our blessings and discover the peace and joy of Jesus.

Whatever we have been through, we give thanks to God.

Whatever we go through, we give thanks to God.

Whatever we suffer, we give thanks to God.

Whatever we endure, we give thanks to God.

Whatever the future brings, we give thanks to God.

We pray, "Beloved God, thank you for all the blessings you give us: for the gift of life, the gift of creation, the gift of one another, the gift of families and friends, the gift of our community. Thank you for loving us and healing us and helping us and giving us your peace and calling us to love and serve you by loving and serving one another. Thank you. Thank you. Thank you forever! Amen."

Like the mystics, we pray, "For all that has been, thank you. For all that is to come, yes."

TWELVE

FAITH

Where is your faith?

(LUKE 8:25)

When I was imprisoned for eight months with Philip Berrigan in the mid-1990s for demonstrating against nuclear weapons, Philip and I began a detailed, daily study of Mark's Gospel. Since we were not allowed outside during our entire time in jail, we had plenty of time to ponder each verse.

We soon realized that Jesus' greatest concern was the question of faith. Although that might seem perfectly obvious to anyone, neither of us had spent much time grappling with the meaning of faith and its opposite, faithlessness.

Jesus clearly wants his disciples to believe in God and in him. According to the Gospel, everything eventually comes down to faith. Just before he is killed, Jesus tells his disciples that their faith should be so strong they can move mountains. He instructs them to pray always, forgive one another, and live in trust. He demonstrates the depths of faith throughout his arrest and execution, when he never gives up on his beloved God.

Philip and I concluded that all the world's problems come down to the question of faith. If we Christians would plumb the depths of faith, as Jesus did on the cross, we would likewise give our lives resisting evil and transforming the world. We Christians would no longer support war, pay for war, work for the military, wage war, seek wealth, or hold dominating power over others. Rather, our deep faith in Jesus would lead us to follow him on the way of the cross in active nonviolent resistance to systemic injustice. Our lives would be turned upside down. We would side with the poor, resist the forces of imperial violence, and practice creative Gospel nonviolence. We would love one another and love our enemies and, in the process, discover the faith that moves mountains. The whole world would see our faith and give greater glory to God.

But alas, we no longer possess the faith that moves mountains. We claim to believe in God and in Jesus, but our daily lives show not an astonishing faith but a dismal lack of faith. In particular, the problem is not with so-called "unbelievers." Rather, the global horrors of war, injustice, and idolatry find their cause in so-called "believers" who should know better but go right on with the culture of war, practicing faithless idolatry and offering lip service to Jesus.

Later, while studying the collected works of Mahatma Gandhi for a book I was editing, I discovered that Gandhi also concluded that the world's problems stem from a lack of faith in God, especially among those who publicly claim to hold such faith. Politics, hunger, violence, war, the proliferation of armaments, and nuclear weapons are matters of life and death, spiritual matters, Gandhi declared. Our violence and greed betray our pledge of faith and demonstrate that we really place our trust in weapons, governments, money, and power, not in the way of Gospel nonviolence, voluntary poverty, and powerlessness.

Jesus speaks about faith more than any other topic. In this instance, after telling his disciples to cross to the other side of the Sea of Galilee, he gets in the boat and promptly falls asleep. When a ferocious squall breaks out, nearly capsizing the boat, the terrified disciples wake him, shouting, "We are perishing!" He immediately calms the storm, then turns to the disciples and asks the pointed question: "Where is your faith?"

We certainly can understand the terror of the disciples. A squall would frighten any of us. But the Gospel always carries many layers of meaning. In this case, the storm symbolizes much more than the challenges of nature. The key to understanding this episode is that the disciples are traveling to the other side of the lake. But what is on the other side? The hated enemy! Jesus has been teaching about love of enemies, and now he orders his disciples to join him in practicing what he preaches. He tells them to travel across the lake into enemy territory. Loving one's enemies and reconciling with those we hate are not problems for Jesus. Rather, they are the quintessential works of faith.

So Jesus is calm and sleeps through the journey. He is not afraid to love his enemies, to reconcile with those hated by his culture. The disciples, on the other hand, are terrified at the prospect of encountering their adversaries. They do not want to love their enemies. After all, this is unheard of! Nothing like it had ever been tried. They fear that they will be immediately killed. The storm symbolizes the terror involved when we love our enemies nonviolently and reconcile with those we hate.

The same fear takes over today if we dare contemplate loving the enemies of our country. During the 2003 U.S. invasion of Iraq, Christian peace activists like my dear friends Jim Douglass and Kathy Kelly traveled to Iraq to stand with our enemies and demonstrate Gospel nonviolence. They were willing to give their lives for our enemies. By flying across the world to Jordan and driving through the desert into Baghdad, they journeyed to the other side like Jesus and the disciples. Such a controversial life-and-death journey can be understood only as a matter of faith. The only way to walk into a war zone and stand with one's enemies while the bombs are falling is with faith in the living God of peace. My friends demonstrated shining faith. They put their faith into practice.

"Where is your faith?" Jesus' question can be taken two ways. He may be asking simply if we have any faith. "Do you believe in me?" he asks. "I thought you believed in me, but do you?" Every day we have to choose to believe in God and in Jesus. We answer, "Jesus, our faith is in you. We believe in you; help our unbelief. Help us to believe even more. Give us the faith that can move the mountains of war and systemic injustice. Let us be your faithful people."

We may also hear Jesus asking: "Where have you placed your faith? Do you believe in me, or do you believe in something else? Is your faith placed not in me but in America, the president, money, the Pentagon, your nuclear arsenal, your weapons of mass destruction, your armies, your Trident submarines, your F-16 fighter bombers and destroyers?"

We need to examine what a deep, profound faith would mean concretely for our lives. If we really believe in God, we will no longer trust in the idols and weapons of the world. Rather, we will trust in God. We will no longer seek to make money to sustain us but will trust in God to sustain us. We will no longer try to do our will but God's will. We will no longer be obedient to the nations of the world but to God. We will have problems with the world and struggle through life, but we will come to know the living God and discover the depths of faith.

Do you believe in the Son of Humanity?

(JOHN 9:35)

After Jesus heals a blind man in the Temple, the religious authorities attack the healed man and excommunicate him for defending Jesus. When Jesus hears the news, he does something he never did before: He goes back in search of the healed man. Jesus finds him outside the Temple precinct. The Gospel hints that Jesus too has been excommunicated. Jesus asks the man, "Do you believe in the Son of Humanity?"

"Who is he, sir, that I may believe in him?" the man replies.

"You have seen him," Jesus says, "and the one speaking with you is he."

"I do believe, Lord," the man answers, and with that, he falls down at Jesus' feet and worships him. It is one of the most remarkable scenes of the Gospel.

At first thought, we may presume that Jesus goes to console, thank, or congratulate the man after suffering the attack of the religious leaders. But Jesus has a much more pressing mission. He wants to know if the man has any faith and, particularly, if he has faith in the Son of Humanity?

Who is this Son of Humanity? The Son of Humanity is a mysterious phrase that Jesus uses more than any other title to describe himself. He takes it from the Book of Daniel, chapter 7, where Daniel describes a wild dream he had. After he saw a series of nightmarish visions about terrible beasts who rule the world, Daniel wrote that he saw:

> One like a son of humanity coming,
> On the clouds of heaven;
> When he reached the Ancient One
> And was presented before him,
> He received dominion, glory and kingship;
> Nations and peoples of every language serve him.
> His dominion is an everlasting dominion
> That shall not be taken away,
> His kingship shall not be destroyed. (Daniel 7:13–14)

This powerful vision of the Son of Humanity describes "the Anointed One of God," the Christ who saves humanity and rules heaven and earth alongside the Creator. In apocalyptic literature, the Son of Humanity is a nonviolent king. Eventually all beings will obey and worship him. Jesus takes this title for himself because he knows himself as the Christ of God.

For the first and only time in all four Gospels, someone who has been healed by Jesus proceeds to stand up publicly and defend Jesus against his attackers. None of the disciples ever do this. Instead they all abandon Jesus under pressure. But this man actually speaks out for Jesus, suffers for Jesus, is verbally abused and kicked out of the religious establishment. Jesus, concluding that he has finally found one person who truly believes in him, is willing to give his life for him.

When Jesus asks the formerly blind man, "Do you believe in the Son of Humanity?" the man does not hesitate to respond. He says yes, calls Jesus "Lord," and falls down and worships him. He enacts the proper attitude before the Christ, the Son of Humanity. It is the first time in John's account when someone actually worships Jesus.

Today, Jesus continues to heal us and give us sight, but do we stand up for Jesus, speak out for Jesus, defend Jesus, obey his teachings on strict nonviolence, and suffer the consequences of our obedience? If we do, Jesus will seek us out, like he does the blind man in John's Gospel, and put the question to us: Do you believe in the Son of Humanity, the one who comes on the clouds of glory, who holds eternal dominion over the nations of the world, and whose reign will never be destroyed?

From now on, we say yes and accept the political consequences of our faith in Christ and his reign of peace. We are no longer citizens of this world and our nation. Rather, we are servants and citizens of his eternal reign in heaven. Like Daniel, we no longer obey the idolatrous war-making presidents, rulers, and generals of the world. Rather, we worship the nonviolent Christ and welcome his dominion. Like the once blind man who came to see Christ with his own eyes, we claim our proper place in the universe, at the feet of Jesus, adoring and worshipping the Son of Humanity.

Do you believe that I can do this?

(MATTHEW 9:28)

Jesus comes to give us vision to see reality, to see one another as brothers and sisters, and to see him present in our midst as the Son of Humanity, the Christ of God. But this healing gift of vision requires participation on our part. The one necessary ingredient that we need in order to receive his gift of healing vision is faith.

Matthew's Gospel tells of two blind men who "followed Jesus, crying out, 'Son of David, have pity on us!' " When Jesus enters a house, they approach him, so Jesus puts the question to them, "Do you believe that I can do this? Do you have faith in me? Do you believe that I can grant you vision?"

"Yes, Lord," they reply. "We do believe in you." Through the eyes of faith, they affirm Jesus not only as "the Son of David," a very high honor in those days, but now as their Lord, as God.

With that, Jesus touches their eyes, and says, "Let it be done for you according to your faith." They immediately receive the gift of vision and look upon the Christ. Jesus gives them vision to see because they believe in him.

If we come before Jesus as we are—blind, deaf, dumb, paralyzed, sick, and hurt, with all our needs and brokenness—Jesus will first inquire about our faith. He will ask us if we believe in him. The question may come in different forms, but in the end he wants our faith. Faith moves his compassionate heart to reach out, touch us, and heal us.

"Do you believe that I can do this?" he asks us.

Deep down, there is some dark place within each of us that does not believe in Jesus. We have grown tired, cynical, bitter, lazy, hopeless, hateful, and ideological. We have lost our faith. We do not believe that Jesus can grant us vision, heal our brokenness, disarm our hearts, or transform the world. Does he know we do not believe in him? Does he want our faith to act within us and in the world? Does he want us to cooperate with his healing, saving touch? Ultimately, do we refuse to believe?

Deep down, a large part of us does, in fact, believe in Jesus. Standing before the Christ, we hear his question. Knowing our own brokenness, we fall to our knees and respond like the two blind men: "Yes, Lord, we believe in you. We believe you can give us vision, heal us, disarm our hearts, and transform the world. We believe you can change our lives for the better, help us to live in peace and love, and reconcile our relationships with one another. We believe you can abolish war, weapons, the death penalty, poverty, starvation, AIDS, cancer, and nuclear weapons. We believe you can grant us the fullness of life here and now on earth and, one day, entrance into your reign of peace and nonviolence. With you, Lord, all things are possible. We believe; help our unbelief!"

With that declaration, Jesus will smile and say to us, "Let it be done for you according to your faith."

Faith makes all the difference. Believing is seeing. All we have to do is say yes.

O you of little faith, why did you doubt?

(MATTHEW 14:31)

Matthew records that Jesus "made the disciples get into the boat and precede him to the other side" of the Sea of Galilee, while he dismissed the crowds. Then, Jesus goes up on the mountain by himself to pray. The boat is tossed about by the waves and the wind. Then, in the middle of the night, Jesus comes toward them—walking on the water!

The disciples are completely terrified and cry out in fear. "Take courage, it is I!" Jesus says. "Do not be afraid."

"Lord, if it is you," Peter yells back at the ghost, "command me to come to you on the water."

"Come," Jesus answers.

Peter steps out of the boat into the rocky waves of the Sea of Galilee and starts walking on the water toward Jesus! But once he sees the strong wind, he becomes frightened again and starts to drown. "Lord save me!" Peter cries out.

Immediately Jesus stretches out his hand and catches him. "O you of little faith, why did you doubt?" he asks Peter.

The scene is so dramatic and surreal that it is hard for us who have little faith to comprehend the question. Peter's actions seem reasonable. He tries to be with Jesus, to walk on the water, to obey Jesus, but the wind, the waves, and the fear take over.

The images of crossing the Sea of Galilee refer to Jesus' commandment that we love our enemies. He wants his disciples to cross "to the other side" and reconcile with their hated enemies. In this instance, he forces the disciples to get into the boat and go ahead without him. He wants them to go places where they would rather not go, to seek out those "on the other side," to trust in God and reach out with love, regardless of the consequences. But such a journey can be made only with great faith.

For Jesus, crossing to the other side is as easy as walking. He walks on water to the other side, into enemy territory. For the disciples, crossing the sea is totally terrifying. It is like facing a squall, a wind storm, and their deepest fears. It means confronting the real possibility of death.

Jesus reassures the disciples and commands them not to be afraid. Peter responds by engaging Jesus, who calls him out onto the water. Apparently Peter can walk on the water as long as his eyes are focused on Jesus. If he stays centered on Jesus, he can do anything, including walk on water. But the minute he takes his eyes off Jesus, he notices the wind and the waves and starts sinking. He cries out for Jesus to save him, and Jesus quickly grabs his hand.

I do not hear a trace of anger or frustration in Jesus with this question. I always think of Jesus smiling and encouraging his friend Peter as he pulls him up and they get into the boat. I figure Jesus is pleased that Peter at least tried.

When we hear the question asked of us, we know that it can apply to many areas of our lives, from dramatic near-death moments, to our own attempts to reconcile with our adversaries and love our enemies, to the everyday struggles of life. In each case, Jesus sees our weak faith and wants to know why we doubt. He expects us to trust him completely, to keep on walking forward toward him, to fix our eyes on him, oblivious to the waves beneath us, the wind against us, and the fear within us.

The Gospel invites us to cast aside our doubts and fears, to walk the waters of peace and nonviolence, and to trust in God. Faith in Jesus will lead us across the waters of life to the other side, to the new land where he has great plans for us. In the process, our little faith will grow, and we will learn to worship Jesus like the disciples did.

Do you not yet have faith?

(MARK 4:40)

Life is a journey in faith. If we dare stand against the systems of violence, war, and nuclear weapons, as Jesus taught, we need deep faith in the God of peace and justice. If we dare venture toward the other side to love our enemies, as Jesus taught, we need deep faith in the God of love and reconciliation to survive opposition and persecution. If we dare to stand with the poor and the ostracized, as Jesus taught, we need deep faith to see Christ in their eyes and not be discouraged by the world's indifference and hostility. If we dare meet suffering in a spirit of peace and befriend death with openness and tranquility, as Jesus taught, we need deep faith to surrender our very being into the arms of our compassionate God, the God of life and resurrection.

Living in the desert among the poorest people in the nation is an experiment in faith. When I moved from the Upper West Side of New York City into the remote desert of northeastern New Mexico to serve several churches and missions, the outgoing pastor sat me down and said, "You are going to need a lot of faith to live and work in this isolated place. Nothing happens. No one comes here. Nothing can be done to change things. Life is a matter of day-to-day survival and trusting in God. Out here, the people have nothing, except faith." I am learning from these desert people the meaning and possibilities of faith. They have no money, no distractions, and few idols. All they have is the natural beauty around them, each other, and God.

Over the years, I have presumed that my faith would grow. But to my chagrin, I discover not deeper wells of faith but deeper abysses of faith. But I do not let this revelation discourage me, because I see the same dynamic right in the Gospel. At the end of John's Gospel, Jesus finally invites Peter to the life of faith and discipleship. You would expect that by now Peter would be the greatest, most faithful disciple of all; after all, he has been through a lot with Jesus, but Peter's life of faith is just beginning.

Life does not necessarily bring greater faith. Rather, for most of us, life brings greater challenges, and with them, doubt, fear, and despair. Each day we are invited once again to trust in God. We may think we have mastered faith, but like Peter we are always abecedarians. Just when we think we have reached the heights of faith, some new crisis arrives and the process begins anew. If we are to be faithful, we have to choose to believe in God and act in faith every single day of our lives. Day by day, again and again, in those moments of doubt, Jesus turns to us and asks, "Do you not yet have faith?"

In Mark's account of the crossing of the Sea of Galilee, a violent squall breaks out, the disciples become terrified, and the boat starts to sink. Meanwhile, Jesus sleeps soundly through the whole episode. Finally, the disciples wake him up and cry out, "Do you not care that we are perishing?"

Mark records that Jesus "rebuked the wind and said to the sea, 'Quiet! Be still!' The wind ceased and there was great calm." Then Jesus asks, " 'Why are you terrified? Do you not yet have faith?' They were filled with great awe and said to one another, 'Who then is this whom even wind and sea obey?' "

Jesus cannot believe our lack of faith. What more does he have to do for us, he wonders. He has taught us, healed us, and demonstrated the daily practice of faith by his own steadfast example. He suffered and died for us, gave us his body and blood, rose for us and sent us his spirit. Yet, he knows that many of us do not believe in him, do not care about him, or at best struggle to believe in him. "If they do not believe the words of Moses, then they will not believe even if someone should rise from the dead," he once said. Jesus has done everything humanly possible for us, but we continue to resist him, doubt him, and refuse to believe in him.

But what is even more disturbing is that, in many cases, those who parade around as the most faithful are in fact the least faithful. As Jesus experienced in his explosive encounters with the Pharisees, scribes, and the Sadducees, public religious observation does not necessarily flow from a heart of faith. We may engage in religious ritual for all the wrong reasons: for power, honor, ego, control, even wealth. Sometimes the pillars of the church turn out to be the meanest people in the community. When push comes to shove, they place their faith not in God but in themselves, their idols, the nation, and their own violence. It was the faithful—the Pharisees and the Sadducees— who plotted against and killed Jesus. The same dynamic happens in our own religious congregations today. Doubt, despair, violence, betrayal, denial, abandonment, and apostasy come from within the community of faith.

And yet, within the weakness of community, we also find enormous strength. Even though community holds the temptation to power and faithlessness, we need one another to uphold our faith. We cannot live the life of faith alone. We need the community of faith to bolster our own faith, keep us on the journey, and push us ahead toward greater acts of fidelity.

Compassion, forgiveness, and nonviolence are always signs of faith. When people refuse to resort to violence no matter what and trust in God for their security and protection, they have entered the life of faith. If people care for the poor, do not accumulate wealth, forgive those who have hurt them, and remain open to all people, regardless of race, creed, gender, orientation, age, or nationality, they have embarked on the journey of faith. When they do it together, they bring the Gospel to life in our own times.

In the end, faith requires the complete surrender of our hearts and lives to God. We have to let go of control, ideology, and possessions and place ourselves in God's hands. As we give ourselves to God in faith, we learn who we are, who God is, how dependent we are upon God, and how close God is to us. As we walk with our faith community, we discover what it means to be brothers and sisters, children of our beloved God. As we approach death, we can let go and open up even more to God in a spirit of love, gratitude, fearlessness, and trust, knowing that God not only exists, but loves us, cares for us, and waits to welcome us home for all eternity.

Why are you terrified?

(MARK 4:40; MATTHEW 8:26)

Thomas Merton wrote that fear lies behind all our personal problems and every crisis in the world. He said that fear is the root of war. Henri Nouwen said that fear is the opposite of love. Because we are afraid, we put our defenses up, strike out at one another, and fail to love.

But why are we so afraid? Because we come into the world full of fear. Someone strikes us, and we cry out in fear. Our parents let go of us for a moment, and we are terrified. We are raised in fear, live in fear—and die terrified.

We fear everything. We fear life, one another, people who are different, the government, our enemies, God. We fear heights, spiders, snakes, and wild animals. We fear illness, poverty, unemployment, hunger, homelessness, and imprisonment. We fear fire, plane crashes, earthquakes, hurricanes, and tornadoes. Most of all, we fear death.

We're so like the disciples; they were always afraid. They feared what Jesus said, what he did, and what he thought. They were scared when Jesus was transfigured and God spoke from the clouds; when the storm rocked their boat; when Jesus walked on water, healed the sick, and raised the dead; when Jesus challenged the authorities and spoke of the cross. Perhaps they were most afraid that night in the Garden of Gethsemane, when Jesus was arrested by the Roman soldiers. They feared that they too might be arrested and executed as agitators and revolutionaries.

"Be not afraid," Jesus says over and over again. He did not live in fear and did not want his followers to live in fear. Rather, he lived life to the full, with perfect love toward everyone. He was fearless, and he spoke the truth with total disregard for what others thought about him. He believed in God and in himself, no matter what others said. He resisted injustice and faced martyrdom on the cross, overcoming the ultimate fear of death.

When Jesus and his disciples are crossing the Sea of Galilee in a boat, a violent squall comes up and waves break over the boat, filling it up. Jesus is sound asleep on a cushion in the stern, but the disciples are terrified. They wake him up and say, "Teacher, do you not care that we are perishing?" In Matthew's version, Jesus asks, "Why are you terrified?" Then he calms the wind and the sea. In Mark's version, he calms the wind and sea, then asks, "Why are you terrified?"

Jesus does not understand why his friends are terrified when he is there to protect them. Likewise, he cannot grasp why we are so afraid today, although we claim to believe in him. If we believe in God, if we trust Jesus, then we have nothing to fear. Jesus will protect us against anything and everything. Even our very survival is guaranteed: When we die, we shall rise and live in paradise with him.

"Do not be afraid," Jesus says as his parting words at the Last Supper. And if we are his followers, we will hear these words and rely on them when we face whatever terrifies us. Jesus has given us these words so that we can renounce our fears and live in peace with ourselves, with God, and with one another.

Why are we afraid? This question is ripe for our daily meditation. As we listen to Jesus ask us about our fears, as we contemplate his crucifixion and resurrection, as we experience the peace of his presence, our fears melt away. Our hearts expand, our faith grows, and we find ourselves able to love everyone.

When the Son of Humanity comes, will he find faith on earth?

(LUKE 18:8)

Jesus tells a parable about prayer, the urgent needs of the poor, and God's swift action for justice. But he seems to stop in midthought and wonder out loud about our lack of faith. Yes, God will bring justice quickly to those who ask for it, but the real question may be, Will anyone believe in the Son of Humanity in the future?

In every encounter, Jesus looks for faith. But over and over, his expectations are dashed. He begins to wonder if anyone believes him, if anyone will ever believe him, if anyone will believe in him thousands of years down the road, when he one day returns.

"When the Son of Humanity comes, will he find faith on earth?" Today this question must still rest heavy on Jesus' heart. Humanity has achieved so much over the past few centuries. We have learned to fly, sent people to the moon, cured plagues, halted epidemics, replaced hearts, cloned sheep, and prolonged human life. Yet we haven't ended hunger, obliterated poverty, overcome racism, stopped sexism, served children, honored the elderly, employed every adult, protected animals, saved the environment, abolished nuclear weapons, or learned to resolve conflicts nonviolently.

At a deeper level, we have not been able to plumb the contemplative depths of spirituality and faith in our Creator, the Son of Humanity, or the Holy Spirit. Although the majority of North Americans claim to believe in God, our culture reflects a lack of faith in God. All we need do is look around us to see the ultimate confidence we place in money, power, ego, fame, possessions, war, nuclear weapons—in everything but God.

If we care about Jesus, then our job is to believe in him and go deeper into faith in every area of our lives. That means we have to act as if God exists, as if our lives depend on God, as if we do not worship false gods, as if we no longer obey the authorities of this world, as if we mean what we say, as if we practice the teachings of Jesus, as if we are as nonviolent and loving as he is, as if we know that God will protect us. And acting like that means we give away our lives selflessly to serve and protect the poorest people of the planet.

We have to practice the faith that does justice, the faith that makes peace, the faith that loves enemies, the faith that resists evil, and the faith that bears good fruit for God and future generations. In the end, our goal is to serve Jesus, and he desires our faith. He needs us to support him and believe him. He has promised to return, and he wonders if there will be any faith when he does.

Our bold faith now contributes to that great day of peace in the future when the nonviolent Son of Humanity returns to earth. As we sow seeds of faith and remain faithful to Jesus every day of our lives, we do our small part to hearten and support the one we believe in.

> But if you do not believe the writings of Moses, how will you believe my words?
>
> (JOHN 5:47)

We've all heard of the Ten Commandments. Most of us can name a few of them: Thou shalt not kill. Thou shalt not steal. Thou shalt not commit adultery. After that, though, most of us get a bit fuzzy.

When Moses came down the mountain with those holy tablets, he set the basic guidelines for human behavior and divine obedience. He was the great prophet of the Jewish people. Moses was God's instrument to liberate the Jews from slavery in Egypt, God's instrument to offer God's law for God's people, God's instrument for the Passover memorial meal and its subsequent fulfillment in the Eucharist, God's instrument to lead the chosen people into the promised land, and God's instrument to pave the way for the Messiah. Moses is one of the greatest figures not just in Jewish history but in human history. He is the beloved, obedient servant of God. He is the one person in the Hebrew Scriptures whom God converses with face-to-face.

The Jewish culture of first-century Palestine idolized Moses, his Commandments, and his law. In fact, the Pharisees, scribes, and Sadducees prided themselves on keeping every letter of the Mosaic law. Unfortunately their passion for the law eventually turned into violent law enforcement, outright brutality, and murder. They grew to claim the law as their own, and those who did not obey their law were harassed, ostracized, and excommunicated. The religious authorities might even execute people right there in the holy sanctuary in front of the Torah itself. The spirit behind the law did not matter, only strict adherence to the letter of the law. These religious death squads killed many people for breaking the Mosaic law. Their violence, of course, led them to violate the whole purpose of the law.

When Jesus appears, he calls everyone to live in the Spirit of the law, to practice mercy, seek justice, and worship the living God with love and peace toward one another. He denounces those religious leaders and legal experts for misinterpreting the law to suit their own ambitions, for disobeying God, and for not really believing what Moses said. "You do not believe in the God of Moses," he declares pointedly. And even when he tries to explain the meaning of the law and the life of Moses, the authorities refuse to listen. Rather, they forbid him to teach and reject him completely. From day one, they launch one long steady attack upon him. Deep down, they must have known that if Jesus was right, everything they had done was not only wrong but unjust, unlawful, and ungodly.

"I do not accept human praise," Jesus tells the religious authorities. "Moreover, I know that you do not have the love of God in you. I came in the name of my Father, but you do not accept me; yet if another comes in his own name, you will accept him. Do not think that I will accuse you before the Father; the one who will accuse you is Moses, in whom you have placed your hope. For if you had believed Moses, you would have believed me, because he wrote about me. But if you do not believe the writings of Moses, how will you believe my words?" (John 5:41–43, 45–46).

The Pharisees, scribes, and Sadducees, of course, are insulted and infuriated. They increase their attacks, threaten to kill him, plot against him, and on several occasions pick up rocks to stone him to death. Finally they succeed in having him publicly executed.

Jesus told the religious authorities of his day that since they did not believe the teachings of Moses, whom they claimed to honor, they would never believe in him, whom they regularly dishonored. If we follow the logic of his question through to our own times, we can ask ourselves: Do we believe the teachings of the holy ones we claim

to honor, from Moses and the prophets, to the apostles and evangelists, to the martyrs and the saints? Do we heed the words and example of our own modern-day saints, the great figures of our era such as
Mother Teresa, Pope John XXIII, Martin Luther King Jr., Mahatma
Gandhi, Dorothy Day, Archbishop Romero, Ita Ford, and the Dalai
Lama? If we do not follow the stunning example of such luminous
holy ones, do we not delude ourselves by thinking we actually believe
the words of Jesus? If we honor the words of Jesus with our lips but
refuse to practice them in our hearts, how different are we from the
scribes and the Pharisees?

Most of us put these saints on a high pedestal but ignore their
teachings and examples, and go about doing as we please. We dismiss
them and prefer instead to listen to our culture's celebrities, media
stars, power brokers, scandal makers, generals, and imperial leaders.
But if we continue to ignore the teachings of the saints, we may end
up like the self-righteous, pious Pharisees, who missed the whole
point of the spiritual life and colluded with the empire in the great
sins of war and systemic injustice. If we are not careful, the saints of
our time will one day stand before us and judge us.

If we want to believe in Jesus, we need to take seriously the life of
Moses, as well as the prophets, apostles, evangelists, martyrs, and
saints. We need to follow their example, become saints and prophets,
and believe the words of Jesus with all our hearts. This task must become our number one priority and will require all our energy, but in
the end we will receive the same reward Moses and the saints received.
We will be blessed.

Why this commotion and weeping?

(MARK 5:39)

Jesus wants us to live in perfect peace, perfect love, perfect trust, perfect joy, and perfect faith. He cannot grasp why we are content with
anything less. He does not understand why we cling to doubt, fear,
despair, sadness, depression, vengeance, resentment, hostility, and

war. "Be perfect as your heavenly God is perfect," he commands us. "Do not let your hearts be troubled. Have faith in God. Have faith also in me. Peace I leave with you. My peace I give you. Do not let your hearts be troubled or afraid."

In the face of violence, rejection, and death, Jesus stays calm. He remains at peace, centered in the presence of his beloved God. He does not get flustered or disturbed, except when our lack of faith leaves us believing in the false gods of death and the idols of violence.

Once, while on his way to heal the daughter of Jairus, an official with the Capernaum synagogue, Jesus is interrupted by a sick woman with a hemorrhage (see Mark 5:21–43). The woman sneaks up behind him, touches his garment, and is healed. When Jesus stops to find out who touched him, and the woman comes forward and confesses, Jesus says to her, "Daughter, your faith has saved you. Go in peace and be healed of your affliction." Just then, people arrive saying that Jairus's daughter has died. "Disregarding the message that was reported," Mark records, "Jesus said to the synagogue official, 'Do not be afraid; just have faith.' " He then takes Peter, James, and John with him to the official's house, where he finds a loud commotion with "people weeping and wailing loudly."

"Why this commotion and weeping?" Jesus asks. "The child is not dead but asleep." They ridicule him, so he puts them out, leads the parents and disciples inside, takes the girl by the hand, and tells her to rise. The young girl is healed and gets up immediately.

Jesus has no possessions, money, home, car, bank account, worldly power, weapons, or material wealth. Yet he has a limitless faith in God. There is no trace of doubt in him. In the face of the worst crisis, he never fails to believe that everything is possible with God. He believes in himself and in God. He knows that he can move mountains, walk on water, heal the lame, give sight to the blind, make the mute speak, save lives, and raise the dead—and he wants his followers to have that same enormous faith and trust in God. "You will do greater things than I," he says to them.

Our commotion, weeping, and wailing in the face of catastrophe and death reveal for Jesus our lack of faith. If we have faith in God, we would not carry on, Jesus declares. Rather, we would believe in God, trust in the resurrection, and ask Jesus to raise our loved ones to eternal life. We might even rejoice in the death of a loved one, knowing that God can do anything, that their death may bring greater glory to God, that our loved one has entered paradise, that God has welcomed them into God's house of love and joy. When Trappist monks hear that one of their brothers has died, they do not weep, wail, or make a commotion. They immediately say, "Alleluia!" They know that their brother has gone to a better place: home to our beloved God. They shout for joy!

For Jesus, death is not the worst disaster. Rather, death is a simple transition, like the daily experience of closing our eyes and falling asleep. Resurrection is like awakening from a deep sleep into the new life of eternity in God's house of peace. What concerns Jesus is what he calls "the second death," that final judgment that could send us to a desolate eternity without the God of love.

Jesus wants us to "find peace in him" (John 16:33). His question invites us to reflect on what upsets us in our daily lives and in the disasters of the world. He wants us to look at how we handle the suffering and death of others and how we prepare for our own suffering and death. He does not want us to make a commotion about anything nor to weep even in the face of death. Rather, he wants us to live in the serenity of his spirit, and to possess his complete joy. He desires that we go deep into the life of faith and trust in the power of the Resurrection.

From now on, no more commotion. No more weeping. No more wailing. We are people of resurrection, life, peace, love, and joy. Alleluia!

Why does this generation seek a sign?

(MARK 8:12)

When Jesus asks this question, he is not responding to a demand from his friends, the disciples. They were not asking for a sign. They had seen him heal the sick, walk on water, calm a storm, give sight to the blind, feed thousands of people, raise the dead, and change into dazzling, white light. Instead, they were trying to keep up with him, to follow him to martyrdom. They were probably too scared to ask him for further evidence that he was the Messiah.

Rather, the religious authorities wanted a sign. "The Pharisees came forward and began to argue with Jesus," Mark records, "seeking from him a sign from heaven to test him." They argue with him, test him, attack him, denounce him. They seek to prove him wrong, to defeat him, and, if necessary, to do away with him. And how does Jesus respond to this ugly confrontation? Jesus "sighed from the depth of his spirit."

To sigh from the depth of one's spirit is to be deeply moved and profoundly sad. In this account, Mark offers an intimate glimpse into the heart and feelings of Jesus as a person. Jesus is discouraged by these holier-than-thou religious men. One might expect them to welcome Jesus' miraculous gifts and teachings, but, instead, they confront and challenge him. They never welcome him, never thank him, never love him. They are not open to God or the truth. They can only respond with violence and hostility. When Jesus sighs from the depth of his spirit, he realizes that they will never accept him, that organized religion will always reject him, and that his dreams will be dashed and nailed to a cross.

"Why does this generation seek a sign?" Jesus asks. "Amen, I say to you, no sign will be given to this generation." Then he leaves them, Mark writes. He gets into a boat and goes off to the other shore (see Mark 8:11–13). In other versions, Jesus announces that the only sign they will be given is "the sign of Jonah." Just as the prophet Jonah was released from the belly of the whale after three days, so, too, Jesus will rise from the dead after three days in the tomb.

Today we still seek signs because we do not believe in God. Because we are scared. Because we have been hurt by everyone we have ever met and cannot comprehend a loving, gentle God. Because we think we need proof and evidence before jumping to the outlandish conclusion that a benevolent Supreme Being exists. Because we do not

FAITH

want to change; we are comfortable with the way things are, however bad they may be. Because we want to remain in control, in charge, in power. If there really is a God, then we are no longer in control.

Yet we do not need to seek a sign. We have already been given thousands upon thousands of signs of God's existence and the veracity of Jesus. Because Jesus' extraordinary life, teachings, and example as told in the Gospels remain the most amazing story in all literature and human history. Because no one could have invented such stories and teachings. Because Jesus gave us the Eucharist, the simple but astonishing communal meal that leads us not only to reconcile with love for one another but for God. Because we have the extraordinary lives of countless saints, martyrs, prophets, and apostles, and thus we have the truth of love, justice, and compassion. Because we have the power of active, creative nonviolence, as demonstrated by Mahatma Gandhi in the Indian revolution, in the Civil Rights movement, and in the revolution in the Philippines. Because we have the daily miracles in our own lives—the birth of a child, the love of a spouse, the ability to see, the gift of the next breath, the joy of being alive. Because we have the wonders of creation that bring us to the edge of awe. Because we have the remarkable people of our own generation, such as Mother Teresa, Thich Nhat Hanh, Nelson Mandela, Dorothy Day, Daniel and Philip Berrigan, Dom Helder Camara, Jean Donovan, Ita Ford, Thomas Merton, the Dalai Lama, and Martin Luther King Jr.

What more do we need? Why do we think we need a sign about God or about Jesus or about what we are called to do? Have we not been given more than enough?

Before baptizing a forty-year-old man named Sam Minor at the Easter Vigil Mass in my parish in Cimarron, New Mexico, I asked him, "Why do you want to become a Christian?" Sam replied, "Growing up out here in the desert, seeing the spectacular beauty of the mountains, the big sky, and the animals, I never doubted the existence of God. I do not understand how anyone could ever doubt God's existence. I was always headed toward Jesus and the love of God, because I am surrounded every minute by concrete evidence of the existence of a loving, generous God. I'm just formalizing what I have long believed and known."

Indeed we have what we need to live a life of faith, hope, and love. We are surrounded by the beauty of creation. We hear the stories of those who have gone before us. We experience the wonder of children and those we love. We understand that one day we will die, and our spirit will travel to an even better place. As we take time to pray, we feel loved and blessed. We know we are on a journey toward our beloved God and God's realm of peace, so we go forward filled with hope. We spend our days doing the noble work that Jesus left us— loving one another, serving those in need, seeking justice, practicing nonviolence, resisting evil, abolishing war and injustice, and envisioning the coming of God's reign of peace here on earth.

No, we do not need more signs. We do not need to harass Jesus. We do not need him to sigh from the depth of his spirit. From now on, we want to make Jesus happy, to console him, to cause him to rejoice. We will do the things he desires. We will love him, serve him, thank him. Most of all, we will believe in him.

> Then to what shall I compare the people
> of this generation? What are they like?
>
> (LUKE 7:31; MATTHEW 11:16)

No one was greater than John the Baptist, Jesus declared on several occasions. He must have loved John. He clearly learned from John. After John's arrest, Jesus picked up where John left off: calling people to repent and welcome God's reign. As he later reflected on John's life and death, and the rejection they both faced from the Pharisees and other religious officials, Jesus sought an image to help people see what they were doing, what they were choosing, and how they were rejecting the prophets in their midst.

"To what shall I compare the people of this generation?" he asked. "What are they like? They are like children who sit in the marketplace and call to one another, 'We played the flute for you, but you did not dance. We sang a dirge, but you did not weep.' For John the Baptist came neither eating food nor drinking wine, and you said, 'He is possessed by a demon.' The Son of Humanity came eating and drinking and you said, 'Look, he is a glutton and a drunkard, a friend of tax collectors and sinners.' But wisdom is vindicated by all her children."

Jesus put a mirror up to the people who were rejecting him so they could see themselves as they were. He was trying to help them see themselves and what they were doing to him. The religious leaders did not like what they saw, of course; they did not like to hear him say this, and they proceeded to do away with him.

What is Jesus saying about us? To what does he compare us? How does he describe the people of our generation?

Here at the beginning of the third millennium, we North Americans are creative, successful, and efficient. Yet, in comparison to people elsewhere and throughout history, we are the most violent, warlike, selfish, destructive people of all time. While we develop the capacity and intent to destroy the entire planet, and hoard the world's resources, billions suffer in misery and hunger. While we turn away from our neighbors and try to get ahead, we pollute the earth and the sky so much that we threaten to destroy the environment itself. We even send radioactive materials into outer space and risk destroying space itself.

To what does Jesus compare us? We are like spoiled children who have everything they could ever need but who demand more, throw temper tantrums, beat up other kids, and rage out of control. Such angry, violent, selfish children do not feel loved, do not love, and do not know how to love. They grow up to dominate, oppress, injure, and kill themselves and others. They become leaders of corporate wealth, imperial politics, and unjust wealth. They have everything but the grace of God. So they have no peace.

Many would dismiss this harsh judgment, but Jesus' words were harsher, which is why the Pharisees killed him. Like the people of Jesus' day, we too need to look into a mirror of truth and see ourselves as we are: a warlike, imperial people. We believe we are faithful and devout, but our wars, our weapons, our greed, and our indifference say otherwise. We do not understand what we do to others.

Jesus wanted his people to change, and he wants us to change too. He knows that self-reflection can help us grow into the people God wants us to be. For Jesus, it is never too late to change. He desires that we become the greatest generation the world has yet known: a people of pure love, devout service, creative nonviolence, social justice, and true peace.

> How can you believe, when you accept
> praise from one another and do not seek
> the praise that comes from the only God?
>
> (JOHN 5:44)

I do not accept human praise," Jesus announces (John 5:41).

We, on the other hand, spend our lives seeking human praise. We want praise from everyone: our parents, our brothers and sisters, our teachers and classmates, our friends, our neighbors, our local community, our church, our nation, our world. We want praise, honor, and recognition. We want an Emmy, a Tony, the Oscar, the Pulitzer, the National Book Award, the Congressional Medal of Honor, the Purple Heart, the Nobel Peace Prize. Or we want all of the above.

Jesus wins none of those awards, never aspires for recognition, and decidedly never seeks human praise. Rather, he despises praise and honor because he knows that it is not from God. He only wants whatever God wants for him.

For Jesus, the only recognition worth pursuing is from God. He wants to be held in high esteem not by humanity but by God. He understands better than anyone that human honor and recognition pass away, but the respect, honor, and recognition of God are everlasting. It is the only thing worth pursuing, the only recognition we should seek.

But we do not seek the praise of God. Although we might claim to care for God, perhaps believe in God, and even think about God, we really have our eyes set on others. We ask ourselves: Do they like me? Do they approve of me? Do they think I am as great as I know I am? Does the world honor me? Do others realize just how great I am? When will I get the attention I deserve? When will the world praise and honor me?

For Jesus, such pursuits are a sheer waste of time. If we seek the approval of others and not the praise of God, we will not receive the praise of God. In fact, we will not even believe in God.

The Pharisees did precisely this. They talked a good deal about God, but mainly they sought the honor, praise, and attention of humans. If people did not show them respect, honor, and praise, if people did not recognize them as holy and righteous, those people might face punishment and excommunication. The Pharisees got the praise of others through their showy outfits, their commanding presence, and their violent threats. They sought the praise of others and gladly accepted it. They relished the applause.

Throughout history, we see this phenomenon from Caesar and the emperors to the feudal lords and kings and queens, to presidents and prime ministers and generals and military leaders. Everyone seeks human praise, accepts it, and feels justified, even as they kill, oppress, and dominate human beings.

"How can you believe, when you accept praise from one another and do not seek the praise that comes from the only God?" Jesus asks.

His question goes even deeper, however. Not only does he not want us to seek praise from one another, he does not want us to accept praise. Rather, he wants us to seek the praise that comes from "the only God" (a rare and unusual description of God).

But how do we not accept the praise of others and seek the praise of God? This question gets to the heart of the spiritual life. Not only are we to become humble and not accept the praise of others, Jesus wants us to spend our lives seeking God's attention and praise.

What is the praise of God? Jesus is the only one who ever receives praise from God, when God calls him "my beloved." We do not know what the praise of God would be like for us, but Jesus wants us to seek it. We can also seek the praise of Jesus himself. But his life, suffering, death, and resurrection are so astonishing, his nonviolent love is so great, that we would have to go as deeply as possible into sanctity to even approach consideration. But he wants us to do precisely that.

If God praises us, if Jesus praises us, then we have received an honor far greater than any award.

> Did I not tell you that if you believe you will
> see the glory of God?
>
> (JOHN 11:40)

The purpose of our life is God's glory," Archbishop Oscar Romero once said. "However lowly a life is, that is what makes it great." We have been created to see the glory of God, to bring glory to God, to become the glory of God. St. Ignatius Loyola sent the early Jesuits to bring even greater glory to God. God's glory is our vocation, our mission, our destiny.

If we believe in God, according to Jesus, we will see the glory of God. These days, however, we have become so jaded between the special effects of *The Matrix* and *The Lord of the Rings* and horrific nonstop news coverage of the U.S. bombings of Baghdad that the glory of God may not interest us or even impress us. We cannot imagine it and no longer desire it. Because spectacular sunsets and natural vistas no longer move us or sustain our attention, neither will the glory of God, we tell ourselves. Because God's glory will not make the front page of the *New York Times*, will not be televised or heralded by the Pentagon, and because the White House seeks its own glory, we become blind to the glory of God.

God's glory will not feature military triumph, imperial power, "shock and awe" bombing raids, or nuclear firestorms. Rather, it will be humble, pure, and peaceful—a disarming presence, a bright light, an inviting, loving glow. It will come quietly, nonviolently, gracefully. In fact, it exists here, now, today, whenever we heal the sick, help the

needy, encourage the discouraged, feed the hungry, house the homeless, liberate the imprisoned, comfort the afflicted, free the addicted,
disarm the violent, give sight to the blind, enable the lame to walk,
grant hearing to the deaf, overthrow injustice, dismantle nuclear
weapons, beat swords into plowshares, and raise the dead. Heaven rejoices at such cosmic events. These are the signs of God's presence in
the world. They are the glory of God, and they bring even greater
glory to God's glory.

In one of the most astonishing episodes in scripture, when Jesus
approaches the tomb of his dead friend Lazarus, Martha and Mary
complain because Jesus is late. They urge him to pray to God and reluctantly, grudgingly admit that they still believe in him. Jesus then
approaches the tomb and issues a bold, outrageous order: "Take away
the stone."

"Why should we take away the stone?" the people ask among
themselves. What can be done? Why make a scene? So on behalf of
everyone present, Martha, the dead man's sister, objects. "Lord, by
now there will be a stench; he has been dead for four days." Speaking
the popular opinion of the masses, Martha resists the commandment
of Jesus. "No, Lord, we cannot take away the stone," she says. "We
will not do that. There is nothing that can be done. Lazarus is dead
and now he is a stinking, smelling mess. You are too late. Please don't
make a scene. Please don't bother us anymore. Please leave us alone
now. Just say a prayer. You are the Holy One, yes, but nothing can be
done in the face of death. Death gets the last word. Death is the most
powerful force there is. Please don't try to confront death. It's a waste
of time. Besides, you'll embarrass us."

In her attempts to prevent resurrection, Martha does everything
she can to stop Jesus. She cannot handle such hope. She has faith, yes,
but up to a point. What can be done in the face of power? What can
be done to stop the power of death? What can be done to change the
world, end war and poverty, and abolish nuclear weapons? Nothing!

"Did I not tell you that if you believe you will see the glory of
God?" Jesus asks.

Eventually, but reluctantly, the crowd does as he commands: They roll away the stone. With that, Jesus offers a prayer of gratitude, commands the dead man to come out, and tells the crowd to unbind him and let him go free. For this miraculous act of resurrection, the authorities set about to kill Jesus, and Lazarus as well. And when they succeed, Jesus raises himself from the dead, reveals the resurrection again, shows everyone the glory of God, and promises to welcome all his followers into the new life of resurrection.

"To believe is to consent to a creative command that raises us from the dead," Thomas Merton writes in one of his journals. If we believe in Jesus, the Gospel solemnly assures us, we will see the glory of God. We will experience it, taste it, enter it. This is our future.

As followers of Jesus, we can meditate and ask ourselves: When have we seen the glory of God? As we look back over our lives, we will notice the presence of God, see the hand of God at work in us, and recognize God's glory in our midst. The scales will fall from our eyes and we will begin to see the world from an entirely different perspective. The smallest act of love will become, for us, a cosmic revelation. The simplest act of peacemaking in the face of war and nuclear weapons will take on universal implications. The calm presence of peace within us will open up new avenues of God's loving, transforming care. Daily acts of nonviolent resistance to systemic injustice will become new opportunities for God's greater glory. Each step on the road to truth and peace will bear enormous fruit for the God of truth and peace.

Once we start believing, the glory of God starts appearing everywhere. It becomes our daily reality. From now on, God's glory is the milieu of our lives.

Do you not believe that I am in the Father
and the Father is in me?

(JOHN 14:10)

Faith consists in accepting God without asking God to account for things according to our standard," Archbishop Oscar Romero said. "Faith consists in reacting before God as Mary did: I don't understand it, Lord, but let it be done in me according to your word."

John's Gospel explains that throughout his public life Jesus tried to teach us about God, whom he called Father, and about how close he was to his Father. Finally he announced, "The Father and I are one." The Judeans were so appalled by these words that they picked up rocks to stone him to death on the spot (see John 10:30–31).

"If I do not perform my Father's works, do not believe me," Jesus told them, "but if I perform them, even if you do not believe me, believe the works, so that you may realize and understand that the Father is in me and I am in the Father." They tried to arrest him, but he slipped away.

As he gathered with his friends at the Last Supper, Jesus again tried to explain his relationship to God. But his friends were as doubtful as the Judeans. "No one comes to the Father except through me," he told them. "If you know me, then you will also know my Father. From now on you do know him and have seen him" (John 14:6–7). If you see me, in other words, you have seen God.

"Master, show us the Father," Philip said, "and that will be enough."

"Do you not believe that I am in the Father and the Father is in me? The words that I speak to you I do not speak on my own. The Father who dwells in me is doing his works. Believe me, that I am in the Father and the Father is in me, or else believe because of the works themselves" (John 14:10–11). Jesus tried to convince the disciples, just as he tried to convince the religious authorities. In the end, however, they all abandoned him. No one believed him.

How different are we from those doubting disciples? Do we believe that Jesus is in God and God is in Jesus?

We might answer, "Well of course we believe that Jesus is in God and God is in Jesus." But if we dare make that statement, then should not our lives be radically altered? Should not our lives dramatically reflect this bold declaration of faith in Jesus of Nazareth? If we believe that Jesus is in God and that God is in Jesus, then we must renounce our selfish lives, adhere to his teachings, do what he says, and believe in his works.

If God is in Jesus, then everything Jesus says is right. The Creator of the Universe speaks through this troublemaking carpenter. Because Jesus has the words of eternal life, we know the will of God for each one of us. From now on, we love one another and love our enemies. We sell our possessions, give our money to the poor, put away our swords, reject the world's violence, beat our swords into plowshares, dismantle our nuclear weapons, resist the institutions of injustice, abolish war, and take up the cross.

Like Jesus, we too practice steadfast, loving nonviolence, regardless of the consequences. We too willingly give our lives for others, even if that means facing persecution, harassment, imprisonment, and martyrdom. The martyr we follow is God incarnate. Our lives have been transformed, and we are headed toward resurrection.

Do you believe now?

(JOHN 16:31)

W hat people don't realize is how much religion costs," novelist Flannery O'Connor writes: "They think faith is a big electric blanket, when of course it is the cross. It is much harder to believe than not to believe."

At the end of the Last Supper, according to John's account, the disciples say to Jesus, "Now you are talking plainly and not in any figure of speech. Now we realize that you know everything and that you do not need to have anyone question you. Because of this, we believe that you came from God."

"Do you believe now?" Jesus asks them. "Behold the hour is coming and has arrived when each of you will be scattered to his own home and you will leave me alone" (John 16:31–32).

The minute we make any big claims and bold pronouncements of faith, Jesus immediately asks in response, "Do you believe now?" He knows our weaknesses, our doubts, our fears. He knows that as soon as the next crisis comes, we will turn away from him, doubt him, and reject God once again.

"Do you believe now?" The question stands before us at this present moment. This is the great desire of Jesus, that we believe in him with all our hearts and souls.

Do we believe in Jesus right now? Yes and no. Yes we believe. But no, there is a part of us that still does not believe. We have doubts— but we want to believe! We desire to grow in faith and follow Jesus. We pray to believe, we act in faith, and we try to live in the presence of God without a trace of doubt.

The question gently invites us to believe once again, and to keep on believing, even in the face of personal crisis, doubt, loss, and global catastrophe. "If you feel you can't believe," Flannery O'Connor concludes, "you must at least do this: Keep an open mind. Keep it open toward faith, keep wanting it, keep asking for it, and leave the rest to God."

I would add, keep returning to inner peace, seeking the peace of God, sitting in the peace of God, opening your heart to God. Simply be with God. Be with Jesus. Love God, listen to Jesus, breathe in God's Holy Spirit. In the process, you will become people of faith and learn to trust God more and more. You will be able to follow Jesus, do the things he did, and look forward to meeting him face-to-face one great day.

"I have told you this so that you might have peace in me," Jesus says after asking this question (see John 16:32–33). He does not reject us or chastise us. Rather, Jesus wants us to believe in him and find peace in him. That's all we have to do.

THIRTEEN

TRUTH

> If I am telling the truth, why do you not
> believe me?
>
> (JOHN 8:46)

Perhaps more than any other public figure of the last century, Mahatma Gandhi spoke most frequently about truth as the goal of life. Like few others, he endeavored to live in the truth. "I am devoted to none but truth," he writes, "and I owe no discipline to anybody but truth. I am but a seeker after truth. I claim to be making a ceaseless effort to find it. To find truth completely is to realize oneself and one's destiny, to become perfect."

Gandhi subtitled his autobiography "The Story of My Experiments with Truth." He even coined a new word, *satyagraha*, meaning "truth force," to describe "the relentless search for truth through steadfast active nonviolence" that lay at the root of his campaigns for justice, peace, and freedom. Gandhi's pursuit of truth led him to practice creative nonviolence as the only means toward positive social and political change. His search for truth pushed him to seek justice and independence. He engaged in civil disobedience, was arrested repeatedly, spent over six years in prison, and in the end was assassinated by his opponents, who could not grasp the truth. Gandhi's life became a shining revelation of truth.

But who cares about truth? When Jesus stood before the ruling authorities to be sentenced to death for opposing imperial injustice, he spoke about the importance of truth, "For this I was born and for this I came into the world, to testify to the truth. Everyone who belongs to the truth listens to my voice" (John 18:37).

"What is truth?" Pilate asked. He had never heard of truth and had no interest in it. We are not that different. Truth is not our number one pursuit. We do not stake our lives on the truth. Instead, we seek power, domination, oil, money, control, military might, political rule, and fame—anything but truth.

Jesus was constantly attacked by the ruling authorities of his day because he insisted on the truth. The Pharisees, scribes, and Sadducees denounced him, dismissed him, and threatened him because they hated the truth. But Jesus did not write them off. Rather, he tried to persuade them, to reason with them, to lead them to the truth of God. But ultimately they did not care about God or life or love or him; their only concerns were power, prestige, and domination. So they attacked and attacked until at last they succeeded in doing away with him.

"If I am telling the truth, why do you not believe me?" Jesus asks at one point. He is so pure and simple that he seems completely amazed at our resistance to the truth. He proceeds to answer his own question: "Whoever belongs to God hears the words of God; for this reason you do not listen, because you do not belong to God" (John 8:47).

"If I am telling the truth," Jesus asks us, "why do you not believe me?" He presumes we are interested in the truth, that we want to know the truth, that the truth is important to us. If we want to grow in faith and believe in Jesus, perhaps we need to adopt the strategy of Mahatma Gandhi and embark on a fearless pursuit of the truth. We can experiment with the truth in our own personal lives and publicly in the world. The more we chase after the truth, the more our faith will grow.

As we commit ourselves to the truth, we will reject whatever is untrue and spend our days "doing the truth." As the gospel declares, we will learn to listen to Jesus, hear the words of God, and discover that we belong to God. Finally, we will believe in Jesus.

Is it lawful to cure on the Sabbath or not?

(LUKE 14:3)

Jesus wants to know if we care about the truth. He wants us to seek the truth. He knows that if we pursue truth, we will do God's will, love one another, and come to realize who he is.

While dining at the house of a Pharisee, according to the Gospel of Luke, Jesus sees a man suffering from a disease called "dropsy," so he puts this question "to the scholars of the law and Pharisees." "Is it lawful to cure on the Sabbath or not?" They are silent, so Jesus heals the man and sends him on his way. Then he puts another question to them: "Who among you, if your son or ox falls into a cistern, would not immediately pull him out on the Sabbath day?" Luke writes simply that the Pharisees are unable to answer his question.

In a similar story in Matthew's Gospel, Jesus heals a man with a withered hand on the Sabbath, violating the Sabbath law that forbids work, so the authorities ask him, "Is it lawful to cure on the Sabbath?" (Matthew 12:10–13) In response Jesus asks them, "Which one of you who has a sheep that falls into a pit on the Sabbath will not take hold of it and lift it out? How much more valuable a person is than a sheep. So it is lawful to do good on the Sabbath." With that,

Jesus says to the man, "Stretch out your hand," and the man is healed. In both accounts, the religious authorities denounce him for breaking their law and set about to kill him. His eventual murder is perfectly legal, following their law to the letter and missing entirely the whole point of the spiritual life.

Jesus views everything from God's perspective: from the truth. He observes God's law and knows the truth—that we are created to love and serve one another, that love is the fulfillment of any human law.

"Is it lawful to cure on the Sabbath or not?" Jesus asks. He pushes us to question the meaning of life, the law, and God's will. What is the purpose of the Sabbath, and, for that matter, of any religious custom, tradition, ritual, or law? What does God want us to do? Are we supposed to obey the law or God, who is above even the law? Does God want us to follow the letter of the law or the spirit of the law, which seeks life for everyone?

At one point in the Sermon on the Mount, Jesus explains that the law of Moses was given to help us live in peace. He then goes on to fulfill the law through his teachings of nonviolent love and embodying the law of God. God's law requires our ultimate obedience, his life testifies. He wants us to do God's will, live in God's reign of love, and adhere to God's gift of life for everyone.

But we have lost track of that higher purpose. Over the centuries, we have set up rules and regulations to benefit those in charge, and violators are penalized and punished. We have reached a time when we inflict death on those who do not obey our laws, including the Mosaic law, doing exactly the opposite of what the law originally intended. This perversion of the law and the spiritual life has brought us to the insanity of the law, which legalizes injustice, executions, racism, sexism, war, and weapons of mass destruction. Even in the last century, apartheid was legal. Concentration camps were legal. The vaporizing of Hiroshima and Nagasaki was legal. And the killing continues: The death penalty is legal. Obliteration bombing is legal. The destruction of the environment is legal. The maintenance of thirty thousand nuclear weapons is perfectly legal. And those who object to these laws get severely punished through imprisonment or execution. Sadly the global system of domination is now so total that we all feel helpless and powerless.

Jesus saw where history was headed. He understood imperial domination and the complicity of the religious authorities, and he would have none of it. Rather, he obeyed the law of God and was faithful to God, in total disregard of the legal consequences. He was determined to help, heal, and love others, regardless of what the authorities said. When necessary, he broke civil and religious laws to obey God's higher law. He took whatever nonviolent action was necessary to heal someone in need. Is it lawful to cure on the Sabbath? Of course it is, Jesus announces. We should always cure one another. That is our task in life.

Jesus' question can lead us to probe our own religious traditions, rituals, and liturgies, as well as our civil laws, in the face of global violence and systemic injustice. What would Jesus have us do in such times? Would he tell us to obey the authorities, including religious authority, or would he insist that we speak the truth, resist evil, defend the poor, and take nonviolent action in the service of suffering humanity? Which is obligatory in the eyes of God: doing our duty, obeying civil laws, supporting the lesser evil, and being silent in the face of global injustice—or disturbing the peace, opposing evil, breaking unjust laws, and agitating for a new world without war, weapons, and injustice? What is the purpose of religion, ritual, and tradition? To help us love and serve one another so that life may be full and peaceful for all, or to keep us under control, to maintain the unjust status quo, and to preserve the authority of the imperial establishment?

Jesus always resists the powerful, the rulers, the religious authorities, and the imperial status quo. His life is a series of public, illegal actions on behalf of the poor and disenfranchised. His life is a steady stream of civil disobedience and divine obedience. He is a one-person crime wave. That is why the authorities legally execute him as a revolutionary, a troublemaker, a terrorist.

After his resurrection and ascension, Jesus' friends become filled with his spirit and start speaking out and breaking the law as he did. The Acts of the Apostles chronicles this rhythm from public nonviolent action to arrest and imprisonment, to release and further illegal activity. Eventually, the apostles too are executed as revolutionaries. They refuse to obey the authorities and will not worship the emperor. Rather, they defend the poor and speak the truth. They practice civil disobedience as a way of life and become completely obedient to the God of justice and peace. Peter explains this early on, when he tells the authorities, "We must obey God rather than men" (Acts 5:29).

Jesus' question can lead us, as it did Thoreau, Gandhi, Martin Luther King Jr., and Dorothy Day, to resist injustice and war, cross the line, break unjust laws that legalize systemic violence, and obey God's higher law of truth and justice, regardless of the legal consequences for ourselves. Like Jesus, the early apostles, and the great peacemakers of our time, we too must set about the task of curing each other and curing society as a whole of the madness of violence. We need to allow ourselves to be arrested, imprisoned, even executed. Like Jesus and his friends, we too will follow the spirit of the law in bringing life to others.

> Tell me, was John's baptism of heavenly or
> of human origins?
>
> (LUKE 20:4; MARK 11:30)

Jesus was forever questioning his opponents, who were always struck dumb by his questions. Eventually they tried the same tactic and started questioning him. The Synoptic Gospels conclude with the religious authorities pummeling Jesus with difficult questions in order to trap him. Luke and Mark write that the chief priests, scribes, Pharisees, and elders begin by asking Jesus, "By what authority are you doing these things? Who gave you this authority to do them?"

"I shall ask you a question," Jesus replies. He never lets them off the hook. He is always the real authority, the one with the authority to ask questions. "Tell me, was John's baptism of heavenly or of human origins?" "Answer me," he adds in Mark's version, "and I will tell you by what authority I do these things."

Before they respond, the authorities assess the odds. "If we say, 'Of heavenly origin,' then he will ask, 'Why did you not believe him?' If we say, 'Of human origin,' then all the people will stone us," they conclude, "for they are convinced that John was a prophet." So they tell Jesus that they do not know.

"Neither shall I tell you by what authority I do these things," Jesus replies.

Jesus' question demonstrates not only his method of dealing with the authorities but also his devotion to John the Baptist and his steadfast focus on God. In this case Jesus does not denounce the religious leaders for trying to find out "by what authority" he acts. Indeed Jesus is willing to explain the authority behind his actions. But he does not trust their motivation. He knows that they want to trick him and do away with him. He questions them so that they will see the truth, embrace the truth, and admit the truth publicly. "You shall know the truth," he tells them at one point, "and the truth shall set you free."

Jesus is clearly devoted to John the Baptist. Jesus picks up where John left off, proclaiming God's reign and denouncing injustice. At one point, Jesus announces that John was the greatest man born of woman. His question here forces the authorities to confront the political reality of the recently beheaded John the Baptist and his baptism. Was John's baptism from God or not? If it was from God, then John was right: We are to repent of systemic sin, renounce our complicity with injustice, declare John a holy prophet and martyr, and do as John did. Deep in their hearts, the religious leaders know that John was right and that his baptism was holy. But they cannot confess the truth without also admitting that their lives are a lie, that they need to repent, change their entire spiritual orientation, and become disciples of Jesus.

But even more than showing his concern over John and his baptism, Jesus points us once again back to God. Religious leaders ask him what authority he has, and Jesus asks them about God. Even today his question leads us to God: Where is God? What is God doing? What is from God and what is not from God? These are the ultimate concerns of Jesus. He seeks only God and God's will. He looks for the finger of God acting in the world. He keeps his eye focused on the presence of God. So he asks about John's baptism in connection with God. Is it of God or not? Was John's action of God or not? Are our actions of God or not?

Unlike the religious authorities of his time, we can answer Jesus clearly: "Yes, Jesus, the baptism of John the Baptist was of heavenly origin. It was of God." We can then begin again to live out our own baptismal promises, to deepen our faith in God, to repent of sin, and to enter God's reign of justice and peace. Like Jesus, we can look for the presence of God acting in the world today, discern what is of God and what is not of God, and always choose that which is of heavenly origin.

Show me a denarius; whose image and name does it bear?

(LUKE 20:24; MARK 12:16; MATTHEW 22:20)

The religious authorities recruit King Herod's associates, the Herodians, to entrap Jesus. Together they confront him with a catch-22 question: "Is it lawful to pay the census tax to Caesar or not? Should we pay or should we not pay?"

If Jesus tells them to pay their taxes, he will not only lose the support of the people but he will be siding with idolatry and allegiance to Caesar, who claimed to be God. If Jesus tells them not to pay taxes, he will be in violation of the law, will be branded a revolutionary, and will be subject to capital punishment.

"Recognizing their craftiness," Luke writes, Jesus says, "Show me a denarius," asking for a Roman coin. After they give him one, he asks, "Whose image and name does it bear?"

"Caesar's," they reply.

"Then give to Caesar what belongs to Caesar," he says, "and to

God what belongs to God" (Mark 12:17). Mark reports that they were "utterly amazed." Luke writes that they "fell silent" (Luke 20:25).

All three synoptic Gospels record this loaded exchange. Any first-century Jewish reader would know that faithful Jews were not allowed to carry Roman coins. Those coins portrayed a picture of Caesar. Because Caesar claimed to be God, carrying a Roman coin violated the Ten Commandments. It was idolatrous.

Jesus did not carry any Roman coins. He did not practice idolatry. So why did he ask the religious authorities for a coin? Because when they showed him a Roman coin, their hypocrisy and idolatry were exposed. When he asked them whose image and name were on the coin, he forced them to name Caesar, the false god, and to recognize their complicity with this systemic idolatry. Everyone in the crowd saw their violation of the Mosaic law. That act would have been enough to humiliate the religious authorities. It should have led to their repentance. But it probably only infuriated them.

Ultimately it was Jesus' answer to the religious authorities' question that blew them all away. No doubt they were sure that there was no way out of their question, but Jesus transformed the question into one of his greatest statements and revelations.

For two thousand years we have presumed that Jesus supported the payment of taxes. "Give to Caesar what is Caesar's," we recall him saying, and leave it at that. Even the church has used the first part of Jesus' answer to urge the faithful everywhere to be obedient citizens, to pay taxes, and to do what our rulers tell us. Sadly, we have lost the truth and power of Jesus' statement.

In the 1950s, Dorothy Day used this exchange to reflect on our relationship with the U.S. government and its military might. She opened up the explosive, shocking, revolutionary truth of Jesus' words. "Once you give to God what belongs to God," Dorothy Day explained, "there's nothing left for Caesar! Everything belongs to God! We are not allowed to give anything to Caesar, back then or now."

Jesus' declaration is more than a poetic play on words. It is a biblical commandment with profound social, economic, and political implications. He introduces God into the equation, knowing that everything belongs to God, including our lives, our bodies, Caesar, the whole world. He wants us to surrender everything to God, to give to God what belongs to God. That means we give one hundred percent of our allegiance to God, not to Caesar or the United States or the flag or the Pentagon. God gets all our devotion, attention, energy, and resources.

Jesus' question is as politically explosive today as it was back then. He asks us: Whose image and name is on your currency? What is more important to you, God or money? What belongs to God and what belongs to the United States? Whom do you worship, God or your modern-day Caesars? If we were to ask Jesus about paying taxes to the United States government, he might request a dollar bill, since he would not have any money on his person. Seeing the picture of George Washington, he might well say, "Give to George what belongs to George, and to God what belongs to God." He would expect us to reflect on his words, conclude that everything belongs to God, and give God our entire allegiance.

Would Jesus want us to pay taxes? I do not think so. He had no money and expected his followers to have no money. Dorothy Day took this Gospel personally, advocated voluntary poverty, and possessed hardly any money throughout her life. She took seriously Jesus' words to the rich young man: "Go, sell everything you possess, give the money to the poor, and come, follow me." She connected Jesus' attitude toward money with his stand toward the empire and its requirements. She never paid taxes; rather, she supported those groups that opposed payment of taxes to the United States government, arguing that over fifty percent of every U.S. tax dollar goes to support war and nuclear weapons. The payment of taxes today, she concluded, is just as idolatrous as it was in Jesus' day.

Philip Berrigan went even further. He said that our whole lives must be in resistance to the American culture of war and weapons. He taught that we should not financially support this unjust oppressive system with its tens of thousands of nuclear weapons, and that we

should risk our lives in peaceful civil disobedience and suffer imprisonment for our opposition to this nuclear idolatry. Philip Berrigan
spent over a decade of his life in U.S. jails and prisons for protesting
against war and nuclear weapons. He staked his life on this question of
Jesus and paid a terrible price for it. He tried to give God everything
and give our modern-day Caesar nothing. Like Dorothy Day, he became a shining example of gospel fidelity and discipleship.

Jesus will not let us have it both ways. We cannot serve both God
and money, he says. Seeing the words printed on our currency, "In
God we trust," he would most certainly question our sincerity. He
would point out the many ways we do not trust in God but trust instead in weapons and other idols.

Give everything to God, Jesus commands us. Give nothing to
Caesar, the president, the Pentagon, or the IRS. From now on, we are
servants of God, citizens of the reign of God. We no longer practice
idolatry.

FOURTEEN

UNDERSTANDING

Why do you not understand what I am
saying?

(JOHN 8:46)

T he religious authorities who quarrel with Jesus never understand
what he is saying. Although Jesus speaks to them simply and
clearly, tries to reason with them, invites them to faith, truth, and
love, they refuse to believe him. Once he says to them, "If you cannot
believe me because of what I say, at least believe because of these
mighty miracles." But they feel threatened and do not want to give up
their power. They think they know everything. Who is he to try to explain anything to them?

"We are sons of Abraham and children of God," they say to him angrily. But Jesus responds, "If God were your father, you would love me, for I came from God. I did not come on my own. God sent me. Why do you not understand what I am saying?"

Jesus is a person of deep reflection, self-understanding, and wisdom. He embodies the truth. He must have thought about the religious authorities a great deal, for he proceeds to answer his own question, much to their dismay. "Because you cannot bear to hear my word," he says. "You belong to your father, the devil, and you willingly carry out your father's desires. He was a murderer from the beginning and does not stand in truth, because there is no truth in him. When he tells a lie, he speaks in character, because he is a liar and the father of lies. But because I speak the truth, you do not believe me" (John 8:42–45).

In the end, the religious authorities reject everything Jesus says and does. They refuse to believe in him or accept his truth or face the change they need to undergo. Instead of welcoming his wisdom, they kill him. But as we know, you cannot kill the truth. As William Cullen Bryant writes, "Truth crushed to earth will rise again."

The things Jesus said are direct and to the point: "Love one another. Love your enemies. Forgive one another. Seek justice and God's reign of justice. Be merciful. Be compassionate. Do unto others as you would have them do unto you. Do not be afraid. Trust me."

In New Mexico, along a major highway not far from the Los Alamos Nuclear Weapons Laboratory, a peace group has put up a large billboard that reads, "Which part of 'Thou Shalt Not Kill' do you not understand?"

Why do we not understand what Jesus is saying? Perhaps we don't want to listen. Perhaps we don't pay attention. Perhaps we have lost interest. Perhaps we're too busy. Perhaps we get his voice mixed up with all the other competing voices. Perhaps we don't like the sound of what he is saying. Perhaps we are like the self-righteous Pharisees: We feel threatened; we think we understand everything; we resent God's intrusion; we don't want to change; we're afraid; we're selfish; we're set in our ways; we've lost interest in the truth; we've grown comfortable with the culture of lies and illusion.

To live the spiritual life, according to the Gospel, is to live in the truth. Jesus wants us to be people of understanding. The life of discipleship to the word of God, the things Jesus is saying, requires a commitment to the truth. This commitment, as Catholic Worker Ammon Hennacy once said, needs love, courage, and wisdom. "Love without courage and wisdom is sentimentality, as with the ordinary church member. Courage without love and wisdom is foolhardiness, as with the ordinary soldier. Wisdom without love and courage is cowardice, as with the ordinary intellectual. Therefore one with love, courage, and wisdom is one in a million, who moves the world, as with Jesus, Buddha, and Gandhi."

The Gospel calls us to be people of understanding, who listen to the truth, seek to understand Jesus, accept his words, and put them into practice with the same love, courage, and wisdom that he demonstrated.

Instead of balking at Jesus, we are learning to respond as the disciples eventually responded. We listen to his question, and one day we will find ourselves saying back to him, "Thank you, Jesus, for what you are saying to us. Help us to understand what you are saying. Help us to welcome your truth. Give us the love, courage, and wisdom to accept everything you have to say to us, that we might live in the light of your truth and be your faithful disciples always."

> Do you not yet understand or comprehend?
> Are your hearts hardened? Do you have
> eyes and not see, ears and not hear?
> Do you still not understand?
>
> (MARK 8:17–19, 21)

Mark's Gospel records that Jesus grows frustrated with his disciples because of their inability to understand what he is talking about. At one point, while crossing the Sea of Galilee, he tries to warn them about the Pharisees and King Herod. "Watch out, guard against the leaven of the Pharisees and the leaven of Herod," he says. "Beware them both," he says in effect. "They are both out to get us!"

But the disciples have no idea what Jesus is talking about. Instead, they think he is upset because they forgot to bring enough bread for the journey. According to the original Greek, they had but one loaf. Their misunderstanding, coming after the recent miracle of the loaves, leads Jesus to ask a series of explosive questions.

"Why do you discuss that you have no loaves?" he asks them. "Do you not yet understand or comprehend? Are your hearts hardened? Do you have eyes and not see, ears and not hear? And do you not remember, when I broke the five loaves for the five thousand, how many wicker baskets full of fragments you picked up? When I broke the seven loaves for the four thousand, how many full baskets of fragments did you pick up? Do you still not understand?" (Mark 8:14–21)

Jesus calls his disciples to an entirely new kind of life, but they are more concerned about dinner. He warns them against the evil work of religious and political authorities who oppose God's reign of love and peace, but they think he is talking about shopping for food. He asks them incredulously if they have understood anything he ever said, but they must have looked down and remained silent. Jesus is completely exasperated.

Today this series of questions pricks our consciences and exposes our own lack of comprehension about the teachings of Christ. Everything the Gospels teach calls forth an entirely new way of life, a whole new attitude, a willingness to give our lives for one another, to take up the cross, confront systemic injustice, and welcome God's reign of nonviolence in the world. We, on the other hand, like the Keystone cops disciples, are more interested in dinner. Jesus must be exasperated with us as well.

For the evangelists, the eyes, ears, mouth, heart, feet, and hands are symbols of discipleship to Christ. We see Christ in one another with our eyes, unless we are blind. We hear the word of God with our ears, unless we are deaf. We proclaim the good news of the Gospel with our mouths, unless we are dumb. We love one another with our hearts, unless our hearts are hard as stone. We walk in the footsteps of Christ, unless we are lame. We reach out and serve Christ in one another, unless our hands are withered. Whenever Christ heals the blind, deaf, mute, lame, and those with withered hands, he frees people to become his disciples and to follow him on the way of the cross into God's reign of love and peace.

St. Paul goes beyond the evangelists and writes boldly that we are called to lose our minds and put on the mind of Christ. We are to think like Christ, understand everything like Christ, and comprehend the mysteries of God like Christ. Indeed, he says, we have to let our bodies die so that we no longer live, but Christ lives in us. This is the goal of the Christian life, to become Christ!

"Do you not yet understand or comprehend?" Jesus asks us today. "Are your hearts hardened? Do you have eyes and not see, ears and not hear? Do you still not understand?" As we sit with these questions, we confess to Jesus that, in fact, we do not understand or comprehend, that our hearts are hardened, that we do not see or hear him, that after all we have lived, learned, and witnessed, we still do not understand him or his Gospel. This honest confession of our weakness and need for him is the first step toward healing. We have to ask Jesus for these gifts. We cannot achieve them on our own.

As we sit with his questions, we recognize our brokenness, our vulnerability, our need. We learn to come before God, not claiming to know the answers, but in need of God's grace. Each time we come before God in a spirit of humility and openness, God heals us and transforms us into the Christ-figures we are called to become.

> You are the teacher of Israel and you do not understand this?
>
> (JOHN 3:10)

When one of the leading Pharisees, Nicodemus, "a ruler of the Jews," comes to Jesus in the middle of the night, Jesus tells him that he must be born from above. "No one can enter the reign of

God without being born of water and spirit. What is born of flesh is flesh and what is born of spirit is spirit. Do not be amazed that I told you, 'You must be born from above.' The wind blows where it will and you can hear the sound it makes, but you do not know where it comes from or where it goes; so it is with everyone who is born of the spirit."

"How can this happen?" Nicodemus asks Jesus.

"You are the teacher of Israel and you do not understand this?" Jesus says to him.

Nicodemus never grasps the essential nature of the spiritual life that Jesus teaches. But Nicodemus is not the only one. None of the Pharisees, scribes, chief priests, Sadducees, or elders understood the teachings of Jesus. They were experts in the Mosaic law and the Scriptures. They fasted twice a week, prayed publicly, and wore religious garb to ensure their status as teachers of Israel, yet, as far as Jesus was concerned, they missed the whole point. They knew little of love, mercy, justice, or peace. And in the end, these teachers of Israel ordered his execution.

Jesus' question indicts anyone who claims to be a teacher of Israel, the community of faith. He challenges every priest, minister, rabbi, iman, theologian, preacher, bishop, or cardinal. It was a source of amazement to Jesus, and to thinking people today, that experts in religion so often miss the basic truth of the spiritual life. While theologians and religious leaders can quote chapter and verse of canon law or the latest catechism, few understand the all-inclusive, compassionate, unconditional, nonviolent love of the spiritual life. For example, it is not uncommon to see religious authorities spouting off against abortion, claiming to be pro-life, yet calling for the bombing of Iraqi children, blessing nuclear weapons, justifying warfare, supporting executions, and excluding those who do not meet their self-righteous standard. Few teachers of faith reflect an understanding of the Gospel's consistent ethic of life. Few insist on the sanctity of all life, condemn war and nuclear weapons, or embrace the wisdom of nonviolence. Like the Pharisees of long ago, most religious leaders, teachers, theologians, and especially priests like me find themselves caught up with rules, regulations, laws, power, authority, fund-raising, and control. We do not practice the wild, unconditional love of the Gospel. We do not love our enemies. We do not stand with the poor, carry the cross of resistance to injustice, or risk persecution for the prophetic truth of justice.

Nicodemus lives in each of us, sneaking out to meet Jesus at midnight, questioning his teachings, asking "How can this be?" Each of us is called into the daylight to be a teacher of the Gospel by living the Gospel, proclaiming the Gospel, and witnessing to the Gospel. As we question Jesus about the spiritual life, he asks, "You are the teacher of Israel and you do not understand this?" As we ponder his life, we need to let go of those rules, regulations, laws, and power, and learn to plumb the depths of love, as Jesus taught. Then we will be born from above into the life of the spirit.

> If I tell you about earthly things and you do not believe, how will you believe if I tell you about heavenly things?
>
> (JOHN 3:12)

The question has the air of Zen Buddhism, plain, direct, down to earth, so simple as to be unanswerable. If we do not believe what Jesus says about earthly things, how will we ever believe what he says about heavenly things?

What does Jesus say about earthly things? He speaks in specific terms: the lilies of the field, a mustard seed, a grain of wheat, the harvest, the clouds, the wind, a mountain, a fig tree, the birds. He gives concrete instructions about human life and social behavior, pronouncing all foods good, urging the faithful not to obsess about the cleanliness laws, advising couples to stay married, and upholding the work of carpenters, shepherds, and fishermen.

But while commenting on nature and society, Jesus gives specific guidelines for life. He commands us to love one another, show compassion, feed the hungry, create justice for the poor, forgive one another, put away the sword, love our enemies, and make peace with one another. "Do unto others as you would have them do unto you," he said famously in the Sermon on the Mount.

The ethical standard of Jesus is rejected by most people as impractical, idealistic, and impossible. His circle of friends adopted it only after his death and resurrection, and after a few centuries even the Christian community rejects his ethical norms. Christendom sides with the empire on questions of authority, law, violence, and war. Christians refuse to love their enemies, and the church supports armies to wage war and kill heathens in the name of Jesus.

Jesus wants to tell us about heavenly things—about God, the Holy Spirit, God's reign of justice and peace, the law and the prophets, the Scriptures, and God's will versus human ways. But we continue to reject his teachings because we cannot accept what he is saying; we cannot handle it.

As we meditate on this question, the spirit of Jesus will help us first to accept his social teachings. We will be able to love, forgive, and serve one another more and more. We will even dare to reject the sword and love our enemies, regardless of what our country says. Once we begin to delve into his social teachings and discover his wisdom and truth, we will better understand his teachings about heavenly things, we will learn the truths of the spiritual life, and we will move closer to the living God.

Are even you likewise without understanding?

(MARK 7:18)

Jesus expects the religious authorities to be clueless about the spiritual life, but he is astounded by the repeated lack of understanding of his disciples. At one point, the Pharisees and scribes blast Jesus because his disciples do not follow the law and carefully wash their hands before they eat. "Why do your disciples not follow the tradition of the elders but instead eat a meal with unclean hands?" they ask him (Mark 7:1–23).

"Well did Isaiah prophesy about you hypocrites," Jesus says, quoting the prophet. "This people honors me with their lips, but their hearts are far from me. In vain do they worship me, teaching as doctrines human precepts."

"You disregard God's commandment but cling to human tradition," he charges the Pharisees several times. "How well you have set aside the commandment of God in order to uphold your tradition. You nullify the word of God in favor of your tradition that you have handed on. And you do many such things." Finally, turning to the crowd, he says, "Hear me, all of you, and understand. Nothing that enters one from outside can defile that person; but the things that come out from within are what defile."

By now we expect such confrontations between Jesus and the ruling class. He is committed to the truth and demands understanding from us. The religious authorities are committed only to power and domination. They resist truth and refuse to understand the spiritual life. But Mark notes that this friction sets off sparks with Jesus' disciples as well. "When he got home away from the crowd, his disciples questioned him," the Evangelist writes.

The disciples never really understand Jesus. They are portrayed as unable to comprehend his teachings, but they show us ourselves as well. We would do no better. The disciples' mistakes teach us not to question Jesus but to ponder his questions.

"Are even you likewise without understanding?" he asks them. "Do you not realize that everything that goes into a person from outside cannot defile, since it enters not the heart but the stomach and passes out into the latrine?" "Thus he declared all foods clean," Mark adds in parentheses. "But what comes out of a person, that is what defiles. From within people, from their hearts, come evil thoughts, unchastity, theft, murder, adultery, greed, malice, deceit, licentiousness, envy, blasphemy, arrogance, folly. All these evils come from within and they defile."

In this instance, Jesus teaches us that the key to the spiritual life is not the law, the food we eat, the rules and regulations we follow, the traditions we keep, or the fear of punishment. Rather, the key to the spiritual life lies in the heart. For Jesus, the heart symbolizes the inner life, the divine spark within us, the spirit of God within every human being. He wants us to disarm our hearts, wash our hearts, purify our hearts, transform our hearts. Jesus invites us to understand that the work of the spiritual life goes on within us and flows out from there.

We know this, and yet we do not understand. "Are even you likewise without understanding?" Jesus asks us with a mixture of surprise and disappointment.

Learning from the disciples, we confess our lack of understanding, beg Jesus to explain it once again to us, and focus on the heart of the matter. We need to obey God's commandments, and, as Isaiah writes, turn our hearts to God and fashion them after the heart of Jesus. That's all that counts.

Do you understand all these things?
(MATTHEW 13:51)

The anonymous medieval author of *The Cloud of Unknowing* writes that it is impossible to understand God. Instead we should enter the cloud, dwell in God's love, and rest in God's peace. Such wisdom sums up the spiritual life. We seek spiritual understanding and enlightenment and at the same time let go of the desire to grasp all knowledge and understanding. We plumb the depths of love, compassion, and peace, and in the process enter into the incomprehensibility of God. Living in this "cloud of unknowing," we go deeper into the Mystery, and our lives bear the good fruit of peace and love.

According to this spiritual classic, God does not want us to fully understand God. But at the same time, God wants us to love God with all our hearts, souls, minds, and strength. God allows us to love God fully, to enter into the fullness of God's love, and to know God as love through our experience of unconditional, suffering, nonviolent love.

Throughout his life Jesus tries to explain this spiritual life of active love and repeatedly asks others if they understand him. Rarely does anyone understand, however, especially the disciples. But in Matthew's Gospel, Jesus "rejoices" that God has hidden this knowledge from "the wise and learned" and given it to "mere children."

Jesus tells the crowd the parable of the weeds, in which he compares the reign of God to a man who sows good seed in a field. During the night, an enemy comes and sows weeds. The owner decides to wait until the harvest to pull up the weeds, when he will separate the weeds from the wheat and burn the weeds. Later, at home, the disciples ask Jesus to explain this parable to them. He says that at the end of the world the angels will separate those who did good from those who did evil. "Then the righteous will shine like the sun in the reign of their Father," he explains (Matthew 13:43). He then proceeds to tell them other parables: that the reign of God is like treasure buried in a field, like a merchant who finds a pearl of great price, and like a dragnet thrown into the sea that collects every kind of fish.

"Do you understand all these things?" Jesus then asks them.

"Yes," they answer, and for the first time, Jesus seems satisfied.

Later in John's Gospel, during his prayer at the Last Supper on the night before he is killed, Jesus prays to God the Father for his disciples. "They have kept your word," he says. "They know that everything you gave me is from you, because the words you gave to me I have given to them, and they accepted them and truly understood that I came from you and they have believed that you sent me. I pray for them" (John 17:6–9). The Gospels reveal that in the end Jesus trusts that his disciples understand him. The implication for us is that we too can understand the teachings and life of Christ.

So when Jesus asks us, "Do you understand all these things?" how will we answer him? If we do not understand him, we can confess our lack of understanding and ask him to explain everything again. If we think we understand his teachings about God's reign, life and death, the just and the unjust, the need to drop everything in pursuit of God, and love and compassion, then we can tell him so and ask him to continue teaching us whatever he wants us to know.

The key to our answer lies in our day-to-day behavior. If we understand the teachings of Jesus about God, God's reign, and God's justice, then our lives will reflect his teachings. We will radiate the love of Christ and share that wisdom with one another.

Why do you not know how to interpret the present time?

(LUKE 12:56)

W hen you see a cloud rising in the west," Jesus tells the crowds, "you say immediately that it is going to rain, and so it does, and when you notice that the wind is blowing from the south, you say that it is going to be hot, and so it is. You hypocrites! You know how to interpret the appearance of the earth and the sky. Why do you not know how to interpret the present time?" (Luke 12:54–56). Mark's version states plainly, "You know how to interpret the appearance of the sky, but you cannot interpret the signs of the times" (Mark 10:36).

Jesus wants us to interpret the present time. But what does it mean to interpret the present time? To "interpret" means to explain the meaning of something, to make something understandable, to translate. The "present time" refers to this moment, the years of this current generation. The Greeks had two words for time: *chronos*, meaning chronological time, and *kairos*, meaning the present, urgent moment, God's time, the time beyond time, the *eschaton*. Jesus wants to know why people cannot discern the *kairos* moment, the eschatological time when God stands in their midst.

Why could the people of Jesus' day not explain, understand, and translate the *kairos* moment of the Christ? They could read the weather. They could help their animals. They could interpret the Scriptures. But they could not explain the historic, urgent moment they lived in, because they did not believe in Jesus. They could not grasp that he was the Christ of God. They did not understand who stood in their midst, and so they refused to accept his way of love and nonviolence. As Jesus approached Jerusalem and his martyrdom, according to Luke, he broke down and wept because "they did not recognize the *kairos* of their visitation."

Are we any different today? Do we understand the times we live in today?

Why is it that we cannot interpret the present time, the *kairos* moment at the beginning of the third millennium? Because we are like that first generation of Christians: We have little faith in Christ. We do not obey the commandments of God. We do not risk the suffering love of the cross, confront injustice as Jesus did, practice the creative nonviolence of the gospel, or believe in resurrection. We do not listen to the holy prophets God sends to us—people like Dr. King, Dorothy Day, Daniel and Philip Berrigan, Oscar Romero, Aung San Suu Kyi, Rigoberta Menchu, Steve Biko, Arundhati Roy, Thich Nhat Hanh, Desmond Tutu, Ita Ford, Jean Donovan, or Helder Camara.

Instead we walk passively through life, allowing systemic injustice and war to continue in our names, with our money, and through our silent consent. We do not grasp the magnitude of our present moment, in this post-Hiroshima, post-Christian, post–September 11 age, when the world hangs on the brink of destruction, when our leaders pursue billions for oil moguls while ignoring the suffering of billions of poor people around the world, when we run headlong toward environmental catastrophe. It is a moment of terrible darkness, the hour before the great flood.

We do not interpret these times, these events, these signs. Instead we look the other way. We change the channel. We shrug our shoulders.

If we did interpret our *kairos* moment, we would change our lives, join the struggle for justice, disarm our weapons, feed the starving masses, and give our own lives, like Jesus, to save the planet. It is not too late to open our eyes, to learn how to interpret our *kairos*, and to take up the gospel mission of global, nonviolent transformation.

Why do you not judge for yourselves what is right?

(LUKE 12:57)

W hy do you not judge for yourselves what is right?" Jesus asked the crowds. "If you are to go with your opponent before a magistrate, make an effort to settle the matter on the way; otherwise your opponent will turn you over to the judge, and the judge hand you over to the constable, and the constable throw you into prison" (Luke 12:57–58).

Jesus does not want people to rely on the ruling authorities, magistrates, judges, constables, lawyers, religious leaders, kings, or emperors. Rather, he wants everyone to live in the spirit of love and practice truth, nonviolence, compassion, and mercy. He urges everyone to put away their differences, settle with their opponents, and reconcile with one another. He knows that our failures, mistakes, violence, injustice, lawsuits, and battles will inevitably lead to painful consequences, and he tries to help us avoid this pain because it is simply not worth it.

Jesus told the crowds that they had to learn for themselves to judge right from wrong. Today his teachings sound like kindergarten lessons, but true spiritual wisdom is so simple that children grasp it better than adults. Love one another, Jesus said over and over again, and when you fail to love, forgive and reconcile with one another. Although his teachings are often mistaken as idealistic, they are the most practical. He does not want people to end up in court or in prison. He wants everyone to live in peace and freedom and know the fullness of life and love.

But we have forgotten how to judge between right and wrong. In fact, we have so mixed up right and wrong that right is often treated as wrong, and wrong is often considered right. For example, we execute people to show that people who kill people should not kill people. We do what is wrong supposedly to instruct people about what is right. We bomb innocent civilians and consider it right, even honorable, in order to stop what is wrong. We build nuclear weapons and hail this work as patriotic instead of just plain evil. As George Orwell prophesied, war is peace, peace is war, injustice is justice, and justice is injustice.

On the interpersonal level, we threaten one another with lawsuits, take each other to court, evict one another, divorce one another, try to get our fair share of the estate, and demand our money back. But Jesus urges us to avoid the courts and the authorities, to settle our differences with our opponents, and to live in the spirit of forgiveness and reconciliation, with God alone as our judge and authority. He wants us to judge what is right and to live according to what is right, whether in regard to day-to-day problems or national and global questions.

Why do we not judge for ourselves what is right? Why do we prefer to listen to what the president and the media tell us to do? Why do we fail to form our own opinions, much less use the Gospel as a lens with which to view reality and judge between right and wrong? Why are we proud, angry, resentful, and hurt, refusing to reconcile with anyone, least of all our opponents? Why are we so concerned for number one? Why do we take our chances to get ahead of others, and even risk courtroom drama and imprisonment in pursuit of money, pride, and ambition? Because judging what is right, choosing what is right, doing what is right, and reconciling with others so that we stand in the right before God is no longer our priority. We are concerned with making money, gaining power, acquiring fame, achieving success, and winning honors. We do not judge what is right, settle with opponents, and try to serve others. Instead we give away our power to do what is right and just.

In our society, where wrong is often considered right, we need a community of truth to help us know what is right and do what is right. Our local church community can encourage us to judge what is right, choose what is right, do what is right, and live right before the God of truth. As we learn to do this more and more, our faith will deepen, and we will trust God more and more. We will settle with our opponents, reconcile with everyone, and even begin to love our enemies.

Are you not misled because you do not
know the Scriptures or the power of God?

(MARK 12:24)

T eacher," the Sadducees asked Jesus, "Moses wrote for us, 'If
someone's brother dies, leaving a wife but no child, his brother
must take the wife and raise up descendants for his brother.' Now
there were seven brothers. The first married a woman and died, leaving no descendants. So the second married her and died, leaving no
descendants, and the third likewise. And the seven left no descendants. Last of all the woman also died. At the resurrection, whose
wife will she be? For all seven had been married to her."

"Are you not misled because you do not know the Scriptures or
the power of God?" Jesus asked them. "When they rise from the
dead, they neither marry nor are given in marriage, but they are like
the angels in heaven. You are greatly misled" (Mark 13:18–27).

The Sadducees, along with the Pharisees and scribes, considered
themselves the greatest living experts on the Scriptures and God, and
they thought Jesus was a charlatan, if not a dangerous revolutionary.
When they put this trick question to Jesus, they began by egotistically asserting that Moses wrote for them. Their question shows that
not only did they not believe in resurrection (since they mock it),
they did not care about the Scriptures or God, only about their own
power and domination. They wanted to expose Jesus as a fraud and
maintain their control over the Judaic world.

Today a new generation of bigoted, self-righteous Sadducees,
Pharisees, and scribes is trying to gain control over the Christian
world. But each one of us is prey to religious hypocrisy. With his
question, Jesus tells us all that our problems stem from our failure to
understand the Scriptures and the power of God.

As a people, we North Americans are biblically illiterate. We do
not read the Scriptures; we do not understand the Scriptures; we do
not live in the spirit of the Scriptures. We do not adhere to the commandments of God, take the word of God to heart, or keep the word

of God, as Jesus commands. Few people take the sacred Scriptures seriously and live according to them.

If we understood the Scriptures, we would know that Jesus fulfills the law and the prophets, that he practices creative nonviolence, that he insists we love one another and our enemies, and that he requires renunciation of violence and resistance to injustice, even to the point of our own imprisonment and martyrdom. Daily, we would read, study, and pray over the Scriptures, especially the Gospels, to learn more about Jesus, to understand what he is like, to discover what he wants of us, and to practice his commandments of love and compassion.

Some of us, on the other hand, take the Scriptures literally and miss the entire point of the spiritual life. We concentrate on false, violent images of God that contradict the love commands of Jesus, leading us to defend war, imperial power, and religious intolerance. We ignore the Sermon on the Mount and preach fire and damnation. We reject the cross of nonviolence and condemn those we do not like. "Not everyone who says, 'Lord, Lord,' will enter the reign of God," Jesus said. We may call upon Jesus but end up acting exactly opposite of the way he wishes. Our misreading of the Scriptures and our false images of God mislead us to do evil deeds without knowing it.

We have also misunderstood the nature and power of God. Deep down, the world is in total rebellion against God, resisting God, denying God, killing God over and over again. We think God is impotent and powerless—or that God does not even exist. The world holds up false images of God as either helpless or a cold, brutal tyrant who cannot wait to throw us into hell. Jesus portrays God as active, loving, nonviolent, forgiving, and compassionate, as Thomas Merton wrote, "Mercy within Mercy within Mercy." Because we have not grasped the power of God as unconditional love, active nonviolence, limitless mercy, and boundless peace, we need to contemplate the God of love and peace.

Understanding the Scriptures and the power of God is critically important for Jesus. When he rose from the dead, one of his first acts was to explain the Scriptures to the disciples on the road to Emmaus and to point out the power of God in the nature of the Messiah as suffering servant, the meaning of the cross, and the promise of resurrection. As he spoke, their minds were opened and their hearts were burning.

The great peacemakers of the last century also tried to explain the scriptures and the power of God. Mahatma Gandhi and Dr. King insisted that nonviolence is the key to understanding the spiritual life, religion, the Scriptures, and God. They proposed that we contemplate God through the hermeneutic, or perspective, of nonviolence. As we read the Scriptures, especially the Gospels, from this lens of active nonviolence, the Scriptures explode, and suddenly we discover a testament of creative, divine nonviolence, a dramatic, powerful way to live and act in the world. We realize that God is a God of nonviolence, whose power is far greater than the power of the world, including all nuclear weapons combined. God is the most powerful force in the world, but God's power is far different from the world's power. It is an overwhelming power of nonviolent, merciful love that can transform anything. This hermeneutic of nonviolence transforms the way we live and see the world and helps us to understand the Scriptures, the nature and power of God, the meaning of life and death, the mystery of resurrection, and theology in general. Everything begins to make perfect sense.

Gandhi and King taught that once we reject every form of violence and open up to the possibility of divine nonviolence, we will not keep our hands off the Scriptures. We will study the Scriptures daily and contemplate God hourly, and we will no longer be misled. Rather, we will find ourselves like Jesus, entering the struggle for justice and peace and giving our lives in love for suffering humanity.

Does this shock you?

(JOHN 6:61)

If we are honest with ourselves, everything Jesus says and does is shocking. He wants us to repent, deny ourselves, sell our possessions, forgive everyone who ever hurt us, put away the sword, love our enemies, be as compassionate as God, take up the cross, resist injustice, and lay down our lives for others. Does this shock us? If we take him seriously and meditate on these core commandments, we are not only shocked, we are appalled and terrified.

The specific words in this instance that were shocking pertained to the Eucharist. "Amen, amen, I say to you, unless you eat the flesh of the Son of Humanity and drink his blood, you do not have life within you. Whoever eats my flesh and drinks my blood has eternal life, and I will raise them on the last day. For my flesh is true food, and my blood is true drink. Whoever eats my flesh and drinks my blood remains in me and I in them. Just as the living God sent me and I have life because of God, so also the one who feeds on me will have life because of me. This is the bread that came down from heaven. Unlike your ancestors who ate and still died, whoever eats this bread will live forever" (John 6:52–62).

"This saying is hard," his disciples responded. "Who can accept it?"

"Does this shock you?" Jesus asked them. As he tried to explain himself and the other great things to come, the Evangelist writes that "many of his disciples returned to their former way of life and no longer accompanied him" (John 6:66). They simply could not accept his teachings any longer.

John's Gospel does not record the words of the Eucharist at the Last Supper, but exchanges like this one make it clear that the early community centered itself on the bread and the cup, the body and blood of Christ. Today Christians continue that tradition by gathering regularly to celebrate Christ through this eucharistic meal. We break bread and pass the cup, we read the book, we pray in the name, we breathe in the spirit, and we pledge to live and act as he did. In particular, we feed off Jesus. We become immersed in Jesus. He is our food and drink, the air we breathe, the center of our lives. As St. Paul writes, we actually become Christ. We are his body.

Does this shock us? Probably not any longer. We North Americans have grown complacent. Little fazes us. The body and blood of Jesus? That is no longer shocking.

It is good to celebrate the Eucharist, and to live off the body and blood of Jesus, but we need to be careful that the eucharistic life does not become routine and lose its power and meaning. If the Eucharist does not in some sense shock us into new life and awareness, then we may be missing the force of its original impact, the power of the words of Jesus that challenged the original community so strongly. In many ways, we need to be shocked.

Ultimately our role as disciples is to accept the teachings of our master. Even if we do not understand what he says, and we find his words shocking, we accept them, humbly agree with them, do what he says, and live according to his teachings. Then we will find our way one day into greater understanding. Over time our faith will deepen, peace will blossom within us, and we will become the saints and mystics Christ is looking for. We will fall down at his feet, worship him, and welcome whatever he has to say to us.

FIFTEEN

OBEDIENCE

Why do you call me "Lord, Lord," but not
do what I command?

(LUKE 6:46)

At the culmination of Luke's Sermon on the Plain, after blessing
the poor, the mournful, the hungry, and the hated; after cursing
the rich, the full, the laughing, and the popular; and after commanding us to love our enemies and be as compassionate as God, Jesus
asks, "Why do you call me 'Lord, Lord,' but not do what I command?"

"I will show you what someone is like who comes to me, listens
to my words and acts on them," he continues. "That one is like a person building a house, who dug deeply and laid the foundation on

rock; when the flood came, the river burst against that house but could not shake it because it had been well built. But the one who listens and does not act is like a person who built a house on the ground without a foundation. When the river burst against it, it collapsed at once and was completely destroyed" (Luke 6:46–49).

In Matthew's Sermon on the Mount, Jesus does not ask the question but gives a sober declaration: "Not everyone who says to me 'Lord, Lord' will enter the reign of heaven, but only the one who does the will of my Father in heaven. Many will say to me on that day, 'Lord, Lord, did we not prophesy in your name? Did we not drive out demons in your name? Did we not do mighty deeds in your name?' Then, I will declare to them solemnly, 'I never knew you. Depart from me, you evildoers' " (Matthew 7:21–23).

These crucial texts tell us that Jesus does not care for lip service. Rather, he expects actual obedience to his commandments. He does not egotistically look for us to call him "Lord, Lord." Rather, he wants us to do what he commands. This is his chief concern. He expects us to love our enemies, be as compassionate as God, forgive one another, and follow him on the path of active nonviolence into the world. He wants us to live life to the full and not be destroyed by the flood that will inevitably hit each one of us. And Jesus knows that the only way we can survive life's crises and disasters is to put his words into practice, not just call out to him. We have to do it ourselves. For Jesus, active nonviolence and compassionate love are not only requirements of the spiritual life: They are the only practical way to make it through life.

But who obeys Jesus? Millions of us call him Lord, but few of us love our enemies, show compassion to the weak, or forgive those who hurt us. Jesus marvels at our lip service and daily disobedience and warns us to heed his words. He does not want to say to us, "Depart from me, you evildoers." He does not want us to do evil but to do good.

Why do we call him "Lord, Lord," but not do what he commands? Sure, we like Jesus; we call him Lord and Savior. But most of us fundamentally do not agree with his political and social teachings, so we simply disregard them. We presume, instead, that it does not matter. We think he will not notice. We assume we know better than he does about how to live in our concrete world of the twenty-first century. In fact, we are so brainwashed by the culture that we cannot go against our nation. We must offer our allegiance first to the flag "and to the republic for which it stands." We can never love our enemies, such as the Iraqi people, or show compassion to Muslims and people who are different. That would be un-American. We do as we are told and try to protect our way of life, our interests, our investments, our imperial ambitions. We go along with everyone else. We wave the flag, put up our yellow ribbons, support the troops, sing patriotic songs, ignore the plight of the poor, turn away from the cries of our bombing victims, try to make more money, honor the rich and the famous, and remain silent in the face of war and nuclear weapons—all the while calling out "Lord, Lord!"

If we are not careful, the day will come when we will appear before Jesus only to discover, much to our shock and bitter disappointment, that we do not know him and he does not know us. On that day, he will say, "I never knew you. Depart from me."

Jesus wants us to take his words to heart and put them into practice. He is concerned about what we do with our lives. He has given us concrete instructions about how to live, how to love, how to serve, how to make peace, and how to forgive. This Gospel work is the most important task in life. If we fulfill his commandments, he will know us and we will come to know him—and he will rejoice because of our good deeds.

Why do you break the commandment of
God for the sake of your tradition?

(MATTHEW 15:3)

Why do we break the commandment of God for the sake of our tradition? Because tradition means everything. Tradition is our life, our culture, our world, our god. Tradition is a paramount force in our lives. We do what we do because it has always been done that way. We hold our religious services, perform our rituals, honor the honorable, and maintain our culture—warts and all and worse—because that's the way it's always been. Those who bring change are troublemakers. Our traditions, the culture tells us, must be kept at all costs.

Centuries of fidelity to tradition have elevated our traditions so that now we presume they have been handed down from on high. For many, tradition has become more important than love, life, the needs of the poor, or the peace of humanity. We spend our lives upholding and idolizing our traditions, while the world goes to hell with its wars and neglect of the poor. Yet tradition can be a strong obstacle to life and the God of life. It can prevent us from pursuing God's reign of justice and peace.

The culture of war insists that we keep its traditions running smoothly. This is our highest calling, we are programmed to believe. We observe our secular feast days, honor the culture's symbols, do as we are told, and cheer on our all-American traditions. On Memorial Day and the Fourth of July, we raise the flag, shoot our rifles, and praise our soldiers for killing in the name of God and country. We keep the tradition alive but disregard the commandments of God, such as those bedrock, bottom-line pronouncements: "Thou shalt not kill, thou shalt not steal, put away your sword, beat your swords into plowshares and love your enemies." Placing America and its traditions on the same pedestal as God, if not higher, we eventually forget what God commands. And before we know it, we forget God too. God becomes a sweet, sentimental fantasy or a vengeful idol who fuels our traditions and their aspirations to dominate the world.

This is precisely what the Pharisees did. They placed their traditions, laws, rules, and authority over and above God. They idolized their traditions and in the process broke God's commandments. Jesus' constant attempts to point out this fatal flaw only insulted and infuriated them. Eventually they killed him in the name of their tradition and then carried on with business as usual, with blood on their hands.

If we take Jesus seriously and put his biblical commandments foremost in our lives, sooner or later we will have to break with tradition and follow God's law wherever it leads us. We will resist our nation's wars, protest its nuclear weapons, refuse to join the military, demand that our troops come home, vote for politicians who stand with the world's poor, call for nuclear disarmament, create religious communities rooted in nonviolence, resist the ongoing oppression of the poor, and seek God's reign of justice and peace with all our strength.

As Keepers of the Word we will find ourselves in trouble with the Keepers of the Tradition. People will ask, "Who do you think you are? What gives you the right to break with our traditions? How dare you rock the boat and disrupt the culture!" We will be harassed and persecuted as un-American, unpatriotic, leftist, communist agitators and social misfits. But we will remember God's commandments, and we will notice how others have long forgotten God's commandments. We will even feel compassion for the Keepers of Tradition, because we realize that they do not know what they are doing.

Obedience to God's commandments is the top priority of Jesus and the spiritual life. As we contemplate his commandments of nonviolent love and act according to them, we will find ourselves in opposition to the culture's disobedience. But even as we go against the grain and become marginalized, we will discover a new spiritual freedom in our love for God and God's law. Even if everyone else adheres to tradition in disobedience to God's law, we will obey God's commandments. We may suffer for our stand. We may be wildly misunderstood as being "political," especially by church leaders. But ultimately but we will be found faithful before the God of the commandments, and we will rejoice.

It is never too late to obey God's law. We can begin anew every day to obey God's commandments of love. If more of us turn back to those difficult but beautiful Gospel commandments, not only will our hearts and lives be disarmed and healed, but over time our culture will be transformed from a culture of war into a culture of peace, from a culture of violence into a culture of nonviolence, from a culture of death into a culture of life.

What were you arguing about on the way?

(MARK 9:33)

This question appears in two variations, one right after the other. After Jesus' transfiguration, he comes down the mountain with Peter, James, and John to find a large crowd watching the remaining disciples arguing with the scribes. "What are you arguing about with them?" Jesus asks the disciples (Mark 9:16). A father had asked the disciples to heal his possessed boy but they are unable to drive out the demon, and an argument breaks out. After Jesus heals the boy, he and his disciples leave and begin a private walking journey through Galilee, where he tells them over and over again, "The Son of Humanity is to be handed over to the authorities and they will torture and kill him, and three days after his death, he will rise" (Mark 9:31).

When they arrive at the house in Capernaum, Mark writes that Jesus immediately asks the disciples, "What were you arguing about on the way?" The phrase "on the way" is a first-century term used to describe the journey of Christian discipleship. The disciples grow silent and bow their heads. It turns out they had been arguing among themselves, "on the way," about which one of them is the greatest. Jesus had just explained to them that he is about to confront the forces of injustice in Jerusalem and will be arrested, tried, tortured, and executed, and they ignore his announcement and start arguing about themselves and how great they are! Jesus is about to die, and they focus on only themselves. He is warning them about the horrific nightmare that lies ahead "on the way," and they debate their egotistic ambitions. It would be funny if it were not so tragic.

Jesus could explode, reprimand them, or kick them out. But he does nothing of the sort. Instead he simply proceeds to describe what true greatness looks like. "If anyone wishes to be first, they shall be the last of all and the servant of all," he tells them (Mark 9:35). It is an upside-down vision of the world, a great challenge, and the most noble calling, to spend one's life in service of the entire human race. More than any other human being in history, Jesus fulfills this definition of greatness. He is the greatest of all, and the disciples, at this point, remain clueless.

Today, Jesus still expects his followers to obey his commandments of love and compassion. He calls us to love one another and our enemies. He leads us "on the way" to the cross, to share in the Paschal mystery of suffering, love, death, and resurrection. But how do we Christians respond? We argue among ourselves about which one of us is the greatest. Little has changed.

"What were you arguing about on the way?" Jesus asks us. How do we answer? We too may find ourselves bowing our heads in silence and shame before him. Can we learn to let go of our pride, ego, and the need to argue so we can become one another's servants and try to serve everyone, as Jesus did?

What does Jesus say to us as we argue among ourselves? Let it all go. Let go of your ego, your pride, your pursuit of honor and fame. Let go of your selfish demands upon others that they must serve you. Let go of control and domination over others. Let go of your problems, ambitions, career, greed, and need for achievement and accomplishment. Instead, serve one another. Serve the poor and the disenfranchised. Serve the hungry, the homeless, the sick, the imprisoned, the young, the elderly, the dying. Let go of your need to argue and follow me through humble, loving, unconditional service of suffering humanity.

> Who then is the faithful and prudent steward whom the master will put in charge of his servants to distribute the food allowance at the proper time?
>
> (LUKE 12:42)

Jesus wants faithful disciples who will carry on his work of love and justice. He struggled throughout his life to form disciples who understood his way of active nonviolence and compassionate love, who could remain faithful when he went home to heaven. He loved his community members and tried hard to get them to serve as he served, to obey God's commandments, and to live in his spirit.

"Be like servants who await their master's return from a wedding," Jesus tells his disciples, "ready to open immediately when he comes and knocks. Blessed are those servants whom the master finds vigilant on his arrival. Amen, I say to you, he will gird himself, have them recline at table, and proceed to wait on them. And should he come in the second or third watch and find them prepared in this way, blessed are those servants. You must be prepared, for at an hour you do not expect, the Son of Humanity will come" (Luke 12:36–48).

Although these beatitudes exult the true disciple, Peter balks. "Lord, is this parable meant for us or for everyone?" he asks, confused by all this talk of eternal service and perpetual vigilance.

"Who then is the faithful and prudent steward whom the master will put in charge of his servants to distribute the food allowance at the proper time?" Jesus asks Peter in response. "Blessed is that servant whom his master on arrival finds doing so. Truly I say to you, he will put him in charge of all his property."

The Gospel uses two adjectives to describe the type of disciple Jesus is looking for: "faithful" and "prudent." To be faithful means to keep the faith; to maintain constant, consistent allegiance; to be reliable, true, conscientious, dutiful, and loyal, come what may. Jesus wants servants who will remain obedient their entire lives, who will never give up, who will never abandon him, and who will love him until their last breath. To be prudent is to exercise sound judgment in practical matters, especially concerning one's interests; to be cautious and discreet in conduct, not rash, but circumspect. Jesus also wants servants who are wise, who are careful to do what is right, who live unselfish lives in pursuit of God's reign of justice and peace.

Who is the most faithful and prudent servant of God the Creator who ever lived? Surely, Jesus of Nazareth! But the Gospel asks us today, "Who among you is the faithful and prudent servant?" If we reflect on the people we have met, we probably can count several ordinary, everyday saints we have known—relatives, friends, or coworkers.

We all know the shining examples of faithful and prudent servants like Mahatma Gandhi, Dorothy Day, Oscar Romero, Ita Ford, Philip Berrigan, Jean Donovan, and Thomas Merton.

Jesus' cumbersome question leads us to reflect on our own desires and spiritual goals. Do we want to be faithful and prudent servants of Jesus our master? Do we want to be found faithful when he appears before us? If so, then we have another set of questions to address. Do we need to change our direction and spirit in any way so that we fit more faithfully into Jesus' gospel? How can we persevere in this long-haul Gospel life so that, when we die, we leave behind a committed life and find ourselves before Christ, radiating faith and devotion?

We all respect Jesus, certainly, and it is worth the energy to end up in his company. That is reason enough to strive to be his faithful and prudent servants, so that when we finally meet him, he smiles and says to each one of us, "Here is my faithful and prudent servant, my friend. Welcome."

Why are you testing me?

(MARK 12:15; MATTHEW 22:18)

One would think that if some holy person miraculously healed the sick, raised the dead, walked on water, inspired hope, and pointed us toward God, we would all rejoice and welcome this person with open arms. Instead, Jesus was met time and time again with resistance, harassment, doubt, and rejection. People challenged him, ridiculed him, questioned him, objected to him, mocked him, threatened him, and eventually killed him.

When the Pharisees and Herodians came after Jesus "to ensnare him in his speech" and "trap him" with their loaded question about paying taxes, Mark writes, "Knowing their hypocrisy, Jesus asked, 'Why are you testing me?' " Matthew's version takes a slightly different twist: "Knowing their malice, Jesus asked, 'Why are you testing me, you hypocrites?' "

The authorities tested Jesus because they were full of malice, jealousy, and violence. Because they did not believe a word he said, they wanted to do away with him, either by exposing him as a fraud or assassinating him. Jesus saw all this coming and knew where it would lead: to crucifixion. Nonetheless, he asked them, as he asks us, "Why are you testing me?"

According to the Book of Deuteronomy, Moses instructed the Hebrew people to serve God alone. "You shall not follow other gods, such as those of the surrounding nations." Then he continued, "You shall not put the Lord your God to the test, as you did at Massah, but keep the commandments of the Lord your God, and the ordinances and statutes God has enjoined on you. Do what is right and good in the sight of the Lord, that you may, according to God's word, prosper and enter in and possess the good land which the Lord has promised" (Deuteronomy 7:13–18).

Centuries later, while fasting in the desert, Jesus was tempted by Satan, who led him to the parapet of the Temple and said, "If you are the Son of God, throw yourself down." Jesus quoted Deuteronomy, saying, "It is written, 'You shall not put the Lord your God to the test'" (Matthew 4:5–7).

The gospel teaches that we should not test God, and therefore we should not test the nonviolent Jesus. He does not deserve such unjust treatment from us. Unfortunately, however, each one of us breaks this commandment and at some point starts testing God. We test Jesus saying, "If you are the Son of God, prove it!" We resist him, doubt him, and reject him. In our worst moments, we too do not believe Jesus.

Why do we test Jesus? Because we doubt him. We despair. We are afraid. We are unhappy, lonely, sad, and miserable. We are impatient for love, happiness, and God, and we do not know where we are headed, except into the great unknown, the mystery of death. If Jesus is, as he claims to be, the Son of God, we should test him—or so the world tells us.

But instead of testing Jesus, the Gospel calls us to believe him, love him, accept him, affirm him, support him, defend him, and trust him. If we are his obedient servants, we have no need to test him. In fact, we have no right to question him. Rather, our duty is to help him with his work of nonviolent transformation, to do what he wants us to do.

Faith in Jesus summons us to love Jesus with all our hearts. That love leads us to put our hope in God, and faith, hope, and love for Jesus give us the freedom to live in perfect trust. We no longer need to test Jesus or God. Rather, we can do what he says, even if we do not fully understand it, knowing that it must be right. From now on, we walk in his footsteps, not testing God but obeying the commandments, doing what is right, and trusting God, every step on the way, right into the Promised Land.

> Is it not written: My house shall be called
> a house of prayer for all peoples?
>
> (MARK 11:17)

M any of us would probably prefer if Jesus were more like Buddha: sitting in the lotus position, telling us that God loves us, and leaving it at that. But Jesus went further. He served the poor in Galilee, then embarked on a walking campaign of creative nonviolence to Jerusalem, where he confronted the ultimate institution of religious and imperial injustice: the Temple.

The Temple was a huge building, like the Pentagon, the U.S. Capitol, the White House, and the National Cathedral all rolled into one. The authorities told the very poor that God lived in the Temple and everyone was expected to come to Jerusalem once a year at Passover to offer sacrifice to God, or they would not be offering God true worship.

These corrupt religious authorities considered the poor to be unclean, even subhuman, so they set up a hypocritical, unjust system which taught that in order to worship God the impoverished masses had to pay a hefty fee to buy the appropriate lamb or at least a dove for an authentic sacrifice acceptable to God.

The Pharisees and scribes, working with the empire, made a fortune. Each year at Passover, the population of Jerusalem jumped from 50,000 to 180,000. The very poor could only afford to buy doves, but they were taught that their offering made them clean and able to worship.

The only hitch in this vast, corrupt, unholy business was that the Roman coins used by the people, and needed to purchase the doves, portrayed the face of Caesar on them. Caesar claimed to be divine, and technically these idolatrous coins were not allowed in the sanctuary. So the Pharisees created a bank in the sanctuary alongside the slaughterhouse, so that the idolatrous Roman money could be changed into "holy" Temple money. Of course, a large tax was taken in the process—again to support the corrupt ruling, religious officials. They had a very profitable system, which brought them not only riches but power and prestige.

After three years on his journey to Jerusalem, Jesus entered the Temple, saw this unjust scheme—the collaboration with the empire, the oppression of the poor, and the abuse of God's house—and took immediate action. According to Mark, he "drove out those selling and buying, he turned over the tables of the money changers and the seats of those who were selling doves, and he did not permit anyone to carry anything through the Temple area" (11:15).

Jesus would not tolerate injustice, especially in the name of God. He would not allow unjust structures to rob the poor in the name of his beloved God, so he disrupted the whole operation. He did not want to merely lower prices for the poor; he was not trying to help the poor get a good deal on doves. He did not try to reform the Temple. Rather, he called for an end to the entire cultic system.

This action in the Temple is the boldest political statement in the entire Bible, the culmination of Jesus' lifelong obedience to God and civil disobedience to imperial and religious injustice. This dramatic event is recorded in all four Gospels. (Only the miracle of the loaves and the fishes and the Crucifixion also appear in all four Gospels.) According to Matthew, Mark, and Luke, Jesus' action resulted in his arrest, trial, torture, and execution.

It is important to note that Jesus does not hurt anyone, strike anyone, whip anyone, kill anyone, or bomb anyone. He is not violent, but he is not passive either. He shuts down business as usual. Only John's account says he took a whip, but the actual Greek word refers to a cord typical of the times, used for cattle. If there were cattle in the sanctuary, Jesus would have let them go, using the cord that the cattle owners brought with them.

Jesus' nonviolent direct action offers a model for activists and heroes of justice. Mahatma Gandhi walked calmly to the sea, picked up the illegal salt, broke the salt laws, and was arrested, and it was he who ultimately brought down the British Empire and its unjust rule over India. Dr. King walked peacefully through the park in Birmingham, broke the segregation laws, and was arrested and jailed, and he ultimately brought down Jim Crow segregation. Daniel and Philip Berrigan entered the military headquarters in Catonsville, Maryland, on May 19, 1968, with seven others, took draft files, burned them with homemade napalm in the parking lot, and were arrested and imprisoned, and they ultimately helped end the unjust Vietnam War.

As Jesus turned over the tables, he asked, "Is it not written: 'My house shall be called a house of prayer for all peoples?' Yes, the prophet Isaiah wrote that God's house is open to all" (Isaiah 56:7). "But you have made it a den of thieves," Jesus said, quoting Jeremiah (7:11). "The chief priest and the scribes came to hear of it and were seeking a way to put him to death," Mark concludes.

If Jesus is so zealous for God, God's house, and God's justice, if he is so disturbed about injustice in the Temple and gives his life to confront unjust structures that oppress the poor, what does that mean for us his followers? We too have to resist injustice, seek justice, and confront the structures of institutionalized violence. Our churches must become houses of prayer and quiet contemplation, not places of business where there is buying, selling, and profit-making. Our churches must be places, where everyone is welcome—people of every race, language, gender, class, and religion; the elderly, the disabled, the immigrants, the homeless, the hungry, the gays, the lesbians, even our enemies. God freely welcomes everyone, and from now on, Jesus insists, we will too.

SIXTEEN

DISCIPLESHIP

Will you lay down your life for me?
(JOHN 13:38)

Anne Lamott tells a story in her book *Bird by Bird* about an eight-year-old boy with a younger sister who was dying of leukemia and who needed a blood transfusion in order to live. The parents asked the boy if they could have his blood tested. He agreed, and it was discovered that his blood and his sister's blood matched. When asked if he would donate his blood to his sister, the boy said he would have to think about it overnight.

The next morning the boy told his parents that he was willing to donate his blood. In the hospital the boy was put in a bed next to his sister, and both children were hooked up to IVs. After the nurse took a pint of blood from the boy and put it into the girl's IV, the boy lay there in silence, watching his blood drip into his sister. She became much better, and later that morning, when the doctor came in to see how the children were doing, the boy opened his eyes and asked, "How soon now until I die?"

Jesus invites us all to that kind of great love: to lay down our lives for him and for one another. After he washed his disciples' feet during the Last Supper, he announced that one of them would betray him. Then he said, "Where I go, you cannot come. I give you a new commandment: love one another. As I have loved you, so you also should love one another" (John 13:34).

"Where are you going?" Simon Peter asked him.

"Where I am going, you cannot follow me now, though you will follow later," Jesus answered.

"Master, why can't I follow you now?" Simon Peter asked. "I will lay down my life for you!" he declared.

"Will you lay down your life for me?" Jesus asked Simon Peter.

The question marks the dramatic climax in the long, tense crescendo of the Gospel. In this, one of his most challenging and haunting questions, we hear Jesus express a mixture of sadness, love, hope, and pathos. He asks Peter to lay down his life for him, but he also hints at Peter's inability to do that. "Amen, amen, I say to you, the cock will not crow before you deny me three times," Jesus answered. And later that night he told his disciples, "No one has greater love than this, to lay down one's life for one's friends. You are my friends if you do what I command you. This I command you: love one another" (John 15:13–17). A few hours later the soldiers arrested Jesus, the disciples abandoned him, and Peter denied him. The next day Jesus was tortured and executed. He laid down his life for his friends, which included the whole human race.

This question stands at the heart of the Gospel. We might prefer to skip all this talk of suffering, but the Gospel summons us to deny ourselves, to take up the cross, and to follow Jesus—even to the point of laying down our lives for him, for one another, and for all humanity. Few have achieved the noble death of nonviolent suffering love, but martyrdom remains the greatest gift one can offer humanity.

"Will you lay down your life for me?" Jesus asks us today. And from us this question requires quiet, peaceful meditation over a long period of time. If we can get beyond our fears, worries, despair, and low expectations, so that we can hear the love in this question, we may receive the grace to enter that "greater love" that Jesus demonstrated on the cross.

On July 30, 1941, when a prisoner escaped from Auschwitz, the Nazi guards picked ten prisoners at random to be locked up and starved to death as punishment, in an attempt to deter further escape attempts. One of those selected begged to be spared in the hope that one day he might see his wife and children again. Maximilian Kolbe, a Polish Catholic priest, stepped forward and volunteered to take that prisoner's place. The guards agreed, and Kolbe was locked in the cell with the other poor men. After most of the others had died, Kolbe was injected with carbolic acid and died on August 14, 1941. Today his life and martyrdom epitomize that "greater love" that Jesus teaches. He laid down his life for others, just like Jesus.

Jean Donovan also said yes to Jesus. In early 1980, while the United States was funding El Salvador's brutal death squads, which killed thousands of helpless peasants and church workers, several North American churchwomen debated whether they should quit their ministry among the poor and return home to safety. Jean Donovan was a twenty-seven-year-old accountant from Cleveland who had joined the Maryknoll Lay Mission program to serve suffering Salvadoran children. "The Peace Corps left today and my heart sank low," she wrote in October 1980. "The danger is extreme and they were right to leave.... Now I must assess my own position, because I am not up for suicide. Several times I have decided to leave El Salvador. I almost could except for the children, the poor, bruised victims of this insanity. Who would care for them? Whose heart could be so staunch as to favor the reasonable thing in a sea of their tears and loneliness? Not mine, dear friend, not mine."

Jean Donovan stayed in El Salvador to serve the victims of the U.S. war. She feared death and hoped she would survive, but she decided to stand by her friends no matter what. On December 2, 1980, with Sisters Ita Ford, Dorothy Kazel, and Maura Clarke, she was raped and killed by U.S.-backed, Salvadoran death squad soldiers. Her death shocked the world and drew attention to U.S. militarism throughout Central America. She, too, showed that "greater love" and laid down her life for Christ in the suffering children of Central America.

In the early 1980s I befriended Jean's parents, Pat and Ray Donovan, and arranged public speaking engagements for them around the country. We became close and remained close until their deaths in the late 1990s. Pat and Ray grieved Jean's death every single day of their lives. They never recovered. Their lives were irrevocably changed. Jean was present to them constantly, but so was the price of her love. There was nothing easy, romantic, or idealistic about her martyrdom. The cross was a concrete reality in their daily lives. They knew Jean gave her life for Jesus, as they told me on several occasions, but the enormity of that gift was a terrible burden for them. It was also a great grace, and over time they too learned to give their lives to Jesus present in the suffering people of Central America. They too became martyrs of love.

As I hear this question of Jesus, I want to answer yes. Years of work among the poor, in their struggle for justice and peace, have led me to desire an even greater surrender to God. And yet, and yet, I know that Simon Peter lives within me. I too could shortly deny Christ, despite all my pronouncements to the contrary about dying for him in some glorious act of love. I know how weak and unfaithful I am.

Later on Peter began to speak out in the name of the risen Jesus. He emerged as a faithful follower and even miraculously healed suffering people in Jesus' name. Eventually he was arrested and crucified for speaking about Jesus. He too laid down his life for his friend Jesus. I am encouraged by Peter. Perhaps one day I too can lay down my life for my Lord and friend Jesus. If it is not a dramatic assassination because of my pursuit of justice, I will be grateful if my death is the culmination of a daily dying on behalf of Jesus' reign of nonviolence. That will be a great gift, a tremendous blessing.

Each one of us can say yes to Jesus. After all, we are going to die; it's inevitable. Meditation will lead us to ask ourselves, "What kind of death do I want? How do I want to die? What is the most helpful death I can undergo, a death that will be a gift to others, a death that is given for Jesus?" Each one of us can ask for the grace to surrender ourselves completely to Jesus. Perhaps, like Peter, we too will start to follow Jesus and one day lay down our lives in nonviolent love for him.

Can you drink the cup that I am going to drink?

(MATTHEW 20:22; MARK 10:38)

I still remember the day a few years ago, when the story in which Jesus raises that question was read during the Eucharist," notes Henri Nouwen in his book titled *Can You Drink the Cup?* "It was 8:30 in the morning, and about twenty members of the Daybreak community were gathered in the little basement chapel. Suddenly the words 'Can you drink the cup?' pierced my heart like the sharp spear of a hunter. I knew at that moment—as with a flash of insight—that taking this question seriously would radically change our lives. It is the question that has the power to crack open a hardened heart and lay bare the tendons of the spiritual life. 'Can you drink the cup? Can you empty it to the dregs? Can you taste all the sorrows and joys? Can you live your life to the full whatever it will bring?' I realized these were our questions."

Jesus' piercing question came in response to the selfish, egotistic request of the brothers James and John. "Teacher, we want you to do for us whatever we ask of you," they say to Jesus. But he does not chastise them. Rather, he simply asks them what they want. "Grant that in your glory we may sit one at your right and the other at your left," they demanded.

"You do not know what you are asking," Jesus replies. "Can you drink the cup that I am going to drink?" he asks. Mark's version adds, "Can you drink the cup that I drink or be baptized with the baptism with which I am baptized?"

"We can," they answer.

But Jesus continues: "The cup that I drink, you will drink, and the baptism with which I am baptized, you will be baptized, but to sit at my right or at my left is not mine to give but is for those for whom it has been prepared."

What is the cup that Jesus will drink? It is the cup of pain and suffering, the cup of love and peace, the cup of nonviolence and resistance, the cup of blood and death. "This is the cup of my blood," Jesus says at the Last Supper, "drink it," demanding of his followers no more than he was willing to do himself. Jesus drank his cup to the bottom. He resisted the empire and the idols of death, remained faithful to the living God, and eventually gave his life in love for humanity. By drinking the cup, he taught us not to shed the blood of others but to shed our own blood for others, to give our lives as martyrs for humanity, just as he did on the cross. The cup of Jesus, in other words, is the cup of martyrdom.

James and John said yes to Jesus, and so can we. Drinking the cup of Jesus is not easy. Few books, sermons, priests, or spiritual directors will urge us to drink the cup of blood, to take up the cross, but that is precisely what Jesus invites us to do, and, like James and John, we must and can summon our courage, say yes to Jesus, and drink up.

Later, when the other disciples hear what James and John demanded, they become indignant, according to Mark. So Jesus calls them together and says, "You know that those who are recognized rulers over the Gentiles lord it over them, and their great ones make their authority over them felt. But it shall not be so among you. Rather, whoever wishes to be great among you will be your servant; whoever wishes to be first among you will be the slave of all. For the

Son of Humanity did not come to be served but to serve and to give his life as a ransom for many" (Mark 10:45).

As we drink the cup, we become, like Jesus, servants of one another. We lift the cup, toast Jesus, drink the Gospel all the way to the bottom, and give away our lives in love for the whole human race.

Eventually we will join with the psalmist who wrote, "How shall I make a return to the Lord for all the good God has done for me? I will take up the cup of salvation and call upon the name of the Lord. My vows to the Lord I will pay in the presence of all God's people" (Psalm 116:12–14).

Do you also want to leave?

(JOHN 6:67)

At one point, after a heated confrontation with the Pharisees, many of Jesus' disciples have had enough. They suddenly realize that he is deadly serious. They think his teachings are outlandish, his politics revolutionary, his life far too challenging. His only outcome, they know, will be disastrous. They can no longer believe him, so they walk away and go back home. Jesus turns to the remaining, original twelve disciples and asks, "Do you also want to leave?" It is one of the most touching, heartbreaking, and haunting questions of his life.

Peter, of course, speaks up. "Well, do you have any better ideas about whom we should follow?" It is not exactly a ringing endorsement of support. But he goes on to state that he believes Jesus is the "Holy One of God," implying that they will not leave him. Not long afterward, at that tragic, climactic moment when Jesus is arrested in the Garden of Gethsemane, they will in fact all leave him to his death. Only later, after his resurrection, do they return. And once they are filled with his spirit at Pentecost, they never leave him again.

But the question continues to hang in the air with a sense of sadness, a searching spirit, a wounded heart, a desire for friendship, and an expectation of disappointment. Jesus faces rejection time and time again. He invites everyone to share his life, follow him, and practice his way of love, but most people cannot handle his steadfast nonviolence or profound faith. He is rejected not only by the religious establishment, the political authorities, and the crowd, but by his own family and closest friends as well. People walk away from him all the time.

As we listen to this question, we hear the pain in Jesus' voice and his love for us. Jesus does not want us to leave him. Rather, he wants us to be with him, and he wants to be with us.

But we have many reasons for leaving Jesus and his Gospel. Let's face it: Practicing faith while living in our culture of doubt is difficult. Creative nonviolence in a world of total nuclear violence is formidable, if not frustrating and painful. Hope in the face of widespread despair is exhausting. Unconditional love, even for our enemies, in a culture that glorifies the bombing of innocent civilians is lonely and tough. Living peacefully while our country wages war is seemingly impossible. In this culture, who can do the things that Jesus asks? Who can put the Gospel into practice with authenticity? Who is willing to suffer for the sake of truth and love? Who can endure persecution, rejection, arrest, imprisonment, or even martyrdom, as the Gospel requires? Once we understand the radical commitment that discipleship to Jesus demands, why would anyone stay with Jesus?

We have all known relatives and friends who turned and walked away from Jesus and rejected God. But as we begin to understand just how serious Jesus is in his call to radical discipleship, we too are faced with the question. Probably at some point each one of us has walked away from Jesus. There is still a part of us that rejects his difficult message and urges us to leave him.

But the astonishing promise of the Gospel is that no matter how many disciples walk away from Jesus, no matter how tempted we are to chuck the whole project and walk away from him, no matter how many times we have rejected God throughout our lives, no matter what we do or fail to do, no matter how unfaithful we are, God never leaves us. Jesus never gives up on us. Jesus never walks away from us.

And so there lies deep down a stronger part of us that never wants to leave Jesus, that wants to stay with him forever. We know he is right. We know he is the greatest, kindest, most loving and sincere person who ever lived.

His question invites us to reflect how we stay close to Jesus, how we can walk with Jesus every day for the rest of our lives. Such fidelity requires a regular, intimate relationship with Jesus that can only come through daily meditation. Each morning we can sit with Jesus in quiet, intimate prayer, share our burdens with him, and let him share his peace with us. During the day we can imagine Jesus standing right next to us. In the evening we can return to him, reflect on the day, and thank him for his companionship. Toward the end of our lives, we can look back and see that we actually lived every day of our lives with Jesus and never left him.

As we read his story, feel his loving presence, accept his resurrection gift of peace, open our hearts to the truth of his Gospel, and serve him in the poor and needy, we are transformed and fall in love with Jesus. We cannot leave him. We ask for the grace to remain faithful to him for the rest of our lives. We try to be his companion and friend. Like those first disciples, we too take up his message—and his cross—and follow in his footsteps, because we have discovered that, more than anything else in the world or in our lives, we want to be with Jesus. We want to support him, serve him, and do what he wants. We want to spend eternity in the company of Jesus.

Did I not choose you twelve?

(JOHN 6:70)

When Jesus asked the original twelve apostles if they too want to leave him, Peter speaks up. "Master, to whom shall we go? You have the words of eternal life. We have come to believe and are convinced that you are the Holy One of God."

"Did I not choose you twelve?" Jesus replies. "Yet one of you is a devil."

The question sounds odd at first glance, given the context. Jesus had, indeed, deliberately chosen those original ragamuffin disciples.

But Peter's affirmation seems to confirm that Jesus made a good choice. Peter speaks with confidence, "We believe!" Even though they doubted, betrayed, abandoned, and denied him, the eleven eventually stand up and give their lives for Jesus. He chose good people who eventually become great, humble apostles. The Gospels even imply that the choice of Judas was providential, that his betrayal was inevitable, that the Scriptures had to be fulfilled so that Jesus could redeem humanity through the cross of suffering love.

But perhaps the twelve, led by Peter, were beginning to get full of themselves. Maybe they thought they knew what they were doing, that they were in charge, that they were his equals, that they were the ones who were holy. Peter's answer is full of typical male bravado. "We believe! We are convinced! Trust us, Jesus!" But Jesus never trusts such loud, egotistic assertions. He can see the cracks in Peter's faith and the inevitable abandonment and denials.

The Gospels and letters of St. Paul repeatedly testify that Jesus does all the choosing, not the disciples. Jesus is in charge. Jesus chooses them, calls them. He knows what he is doing all along. He knows his disciples inside and out and has confidence in them. While the question seems simple enough, while the answer should be obvious—"Yes, Jesus, you choose the twelve"—the question remains unanswered. The proud, egocentric, male disciples believe they have chosen Jesus. They think they are in charge, not Jesus. "Whom shall we choose to follow?" Peter basically asks. "We have chosen you." Jesus' question reduces them to silence.

Just as Jesus called the original twelve apostles, he calls each one of us. But we can easily get caught in the same trap as Peter. We begin to think that we have chosen to be disciples of Jesus, that we are in charge of our lives, that we know what we are doing, that we have decided to pursue the spiritual life, that we chose Jesus—but at most we choose to be chosen. And like those original twelve disciples, we can accept the call and choice of Jesus. We can cooperate with Jesus. But the initiative always begins and remains with Jesus. Jesus is in charge, not us. Jesus chooses us. We do not choose Jesus. Jesus is the one who calls us to discipleship. The action starts with him.

This basic insight seems obvious, yet most of us who profess interest and faith in Jesus act like Peter. We are under the illusion that we are in charge of our lives. "We have confidence in you," we say to God, unaware of the cracks in our faith which will surely break the moment the next crisis comes.

Instead of boldly asserting our own authority, we might try humility before Jesus. "Yes, Lord, we want to stay with you," we might say to Jesus in our prayer. "We want to be your disciples. You are the one who chooses whomever you like. Choose us. Call us. Keep on choosing us, despite our failings, brokenness, pride, arrogance, sins, doubt, infidelities, denials, and abandonment. Please call us again and again to be your disciples. Even though we are poor, weak ragamuffins, bless us by choosing us. The choice is yours."

> When I sent you forth without a money bag
> or a sack or sandals, were you in need of
> anything?
>
> (LUKE 22:36)

During the Last Supper, as the hour for his arrest approaches, Jesus asks the disciples, "When I sent you forth without a money bag or a sack or sandals, were you in need of anything?"

"No, nothing," they reply.

"But now one who has a money bag should take it," Jesus says, "and likewise a sack, and one who does not have a sword should sell his cloak and buy one. For I tell you that this Scripture must be fulfilled in me, namely, 'He was counted among the wicked'; and indeed what is written about me is coming to fulfillment."

"Lord, look," the disciples say to him, "there are two swords here."

"It is enough!" he replies. Then he leads them out to the Garden of Gethsemane. When the soldiers arrive a few hours later, Peter strikes the high priest's servant with a sword and cuts off his right ear. "Stop, no more of this!" Jesus shouts (Luke 22:50). He touches the wound, heals the ear, and is arrested.

The question comes as a stark contrast to two earlier episodes in Luke, when Jesus sends his disciples out in complete poverty to announce the coming of God's reign. "Take nothing for the journey," Jesus says, "neither walking stick, nor sack, nor food, nor money and let no one take a second tunic. Whatever house you enter stay there and leave from there" (Luke 9:3).

Later Jesus sends seventy-two disciples out in pairs ahead of him to every town he intends to visit. "Go on your way," he says. "Behold, I am sending you like lambs among wolves. Carry no money bag, no sack, no sandals, and greet no one along the way. Into whatever house you enter, first say, 'Peace to this household.' If a peaceful person lives there, your peace will rest on him or her, but if not, it will return to you. Whatever town you enter and they welcome you, eat what is set before you, cure the sick in it, and say to them, 'The reign of God is at hand for you' " (Luke 10:3–7).

Now, however, at the hour of arrest, Jesus changes his tone. He still sends his disciples out, but this time he sends them out more like exiles in flight, underground fugitives, running from the law. Luke is clearly addressing the persecuted Christian communities of his day. At the end of that first century, Christians were regularly hunted down, rounded up, arrested, and executed by Roman soldiers. Luke's Jesus speaks with poetic, figurative language, urging his disciples to take cover and be on guard. But the disciples misunderstand Jesus, and for two thousand years, so has everyone else.

Jesus' whole life calls for unconditional, nonviolent love, even toward our enemies and persecutors. His active nonviolence forbids taking up the sword. So when he speaks in dramatic language, calling the disciples to flee to the hills, take their money bags and buy a sword, he describes people in flight, persecuted for their stand against the idolatrous empire. But the disciples take him literally and say, "Look, Lord, here are two swords." They miss the point of Jesus' dramatic call for nonviolent vigilance. When Jesus says, "It is enough!" he is exasperated by the disciples and says in effect, "Oh forget it! That's enough of that. You have missed the entire point." He does not call anyone to kill with a sword or wage war or threaten with nuclear weapons. Hours later, the Evangelists make this abundantly clear, when Jesus tells Peter pointedly, "Put your sword back into its sheath, for all who take up the sword will perish by the sword" (Matthew 26:52; John 18:11).

The question invites reflection on how the Gospel of Jesus continues to send us into the world, like those first disciples, as missionaries of peace and nonviolence. We are to go forth as pilgrims, without money, sack, or shoes, to announce God's reign, learn dependence on God, and plumb the depths of faith and trust. Jesus pushes us out to practice his way of voluntary poverty, unconditional love, creative nonviolence, and prophetic truth-telling. St. Francis, Dorothy Day, and many others have taken up this challenge through the ages, and it remains a noble calling for any disciple of Jesus today. Each time I cross the line in an act of civil disobedience to war and nuclear weapons and land in jail, I taste the flavor of this command and find all my needs met.

This pilgrimage, missionary life sounds crazy at first, but it is extremely liberating. For the first time, we feel completely free. We announce the Gospel not only by word but by example.

"When I sent you forth without a money bag or a sack or sandals, were you in need of anything?" Jesus asks us. If we dare to experiment with the Gospel, and go forth as missionaries of nonviolent love into the world as Jesus commands, all our needs will be met by God. Miracles will happen. Food, clothing, and money will be provided. Marvelous people will welcome us into their homes, and we will be asked to announce the Gospel of peace. God will be present at every turn, in every corner, from the glorious sky to the smallest hovel. Life will explode with grace and peace. Jesus knows this because he lived it first.

Do you realize what I have done for you?

(JOHN 13:12)

I t will take a lifetime of daily meditation to begin to understand what Jesus has done for us. Perhaps only when we die and go to heaven, when we hear his own story and see all that he endured for humanity, will we realize what he has done for us personally and collectively. And we will spend eternity thanking him.

Jesus imagined us, created us, and breathed life into us. He loves us, protects us, and redeems us. He gave his life for us, rose from the dead for us, sent his Holy Spirit upon us, and welcomes us into his reign of peace as his beloved sisters and brothers.

If we look back carefully over our lives, from childhood to the present moment, from the perspective of God's abiding love, we catch a glimpse of God's presence and realize that Jesus walks with us and helps us every step of the way. Even when we are most alone and in greatest need, Jesus supports us. He is always there for us.

This question arises in John's Gospel, during the Last Supper, when Jesus shocks his disciples by bending over and washing their feet. When he is finished, he asks them, "Do you realize what I have done for you?"

In those days, no one ever had their feet washed except the emperor and his henchmen, the rulers and the rich, who put their feet up to be washed by their slaves. But here, the Creator of the fifteen-billion-year-old universe gets down on his hands and knees and washes our feet with humility and love. I will never forget Henri Nouwen preaching about this passage, announcing in his thick Dutch accent that we have "a bent-over God" who invites us to bend over and serve one another with humble love.

By rights, we should serve Jesus. He is, after all, our lord and master, the Son of God, the word of God, the lamb of God. We should wash his feet, meet his needs, and give our lives for him. Instead, he serves us. "I have given you a model to follow," he tells the disciples. "You too should wash one another's feet. As I have done for you, you should do for one another. Blessed are you if you do it" (John 13:15–17).

From now on, we are expected to serve one another without desire for reciprocation. In other words, we do not seek service in return. Rather, we selflessly meet each other's needs, to the point of washing each other's dirty feet and giving our lives for one another.

But this symbolic action is more than a call to service. Jesus was inspired to wash his disciples' feet by a woman who a few days earlier had bent down, poured oil on his feet, and washed them with her tears (see John 12:1–9). She did this to prepare Jesus for his death on the cross. While everyone else discouraged Jesus from going to Jerusalem and risking the cross, this one person encouraged him and blessed him by anointing him. Jesus decided to do the same thing for his followers. He anointed them to prepare them to die on the cross as well.

The Gospel invites us to serve one another with humble love and to prepare each other for our own deaths on the cross. This famous foot-washing scene is not only about service but about martyrdom. We anoint one another for the journey ahead to our own suffering and death, our own cross and resurrection. We help one another face death with the same faith, hope, and love that Jesus showed on the cross.

"Do you realize what I have done for you?" Jesus asks each one of us personally. Perhaps the best response is an honest, prayerful confession: No, Lord, I simply cannot grasp all that you have done for me and the human race. But I thank you and praise you nonetheless, and I beg for the wisdom to learn, understand, and know what you have done for me and all of us. I ask you to help me imitate you by humbly serving others, selflessly loving others, and gently preparing others to meet their deaths gracefully. Help me to give my life in service for suffering humanity, like you did. Grant that I may spend eternity thanking you for what you have done for me. Let us all grow in awareness of your infinite gift and praise you forever with grateful hearts.

If there were not [many dwelling places in my Father's house], would I have told you that I am going to prepare a place for you?

(JOHN 14:2)

D o not let your hearts be troubled," Jesus tells his friends at the Last Supper. "You have faith in God. Have faith also in me. In my Father's house, there are many dwelling places. If there were not, would I have told you that I am going to prepare a place for you?"

The disciples do not answer him. Although they know he always speaks the truth, they cannot grasp his impending doom, his subsequent resurrection, his supernatural ascension, or his talk about dwelling places in heaven.

"If I go and prepare a place for you, I will come back again and take you to myself, so that where I am you also may be" (John 14:3).

Jesus always keeps a long perspective on eternal life. He does not let the immediate political crises or the dead-end reality of death deter him from his true destination, his eternal home with his beloved God, whom he calls *Abba*, Father. Rather, he knows where he is headed: He is going home, into his reign of love, peace, and nonviolence.

But the shocking truth of his question leaves his disciples speechless, because not only does he announce that he is headed home to an eternal paradise of peace, he goes to prepare a place for his friends "so that where he is, we also may be."

Do we believe this? Would he have told us if it was not true? Yes, there are many dwelling places in God's house (or as older translations put it, "many mansions in God's reign"). Jesus goes to prepare a place for his disciples, for us. He is at work getting God's house ready for his friends. When we die, we too shall rise, ascend, and enter his reign. We will become our true selves, will be transformed into perfect, unconditional love, and will live in the presence of Jesus forever.

I find this one of the most consoling verses in the entire Gospel. In the midst of the world's insane violence, greed, and wars, as I try to follow the nonviolent Jesus and live in peace, I hear his question and realize anew that I am his friend, that he has a place ready for me and my friends, and that one new day, after the long, dark night is over, I shall enter God's house, be welcomed by my brother, my savior, and my beloved Lord Jesus, and actually dwell in his presence. I will feel his peace, see him smile, hear him laugh, receive his greeting, and spend eternity there at his side. After a lifetime of struggles, defeats, failures, pain, solidarity with the poor, resistance to imperial war-making, and daily apostolic activity, there is nothing I want more. For me, the heart of Christianity is living in intimate relationship with Jesus, becoming his friend and companion. If this is the core of my spiritual existence—and I hope it is—then there is nothing more I could ask for than to live in the presence of the truest, most loving, noblest person who ever lived, not only for me, but for my family and friends as well—indeed, for the whole human race.

"If there were not [many dwelling places in my Father's house], would I have told you that I am going to prepare a place for you?" Jesus asks. He would not tell us that he is preparing a place for us in paradise if it were not true. Therefore the only task left is to get ready for our return home to Jesus. As St. Paul said, we keep our eyes on the prize, keep running the race, and keep preparing for the beginning of our lives in heaven. We do good works, serve the needy, repent of sin, love our enemies, forgive everyone, pray for our persecutors, make peace, and seek God's reign of justice. As we carry on with the Gospel life and follow in the footsteps of Jesus on the path of nonviolence, we do not let our hearts be troubled. In fact, nothing can trouble us anymore. Like Jesus, we now know where we are headed. We have faith in Jesus. Our hearts burn with a secret joy. We glimpse the resurrection and go forward one day at a time, one step at a time, trusting in Jesus, headed toward home, looking forward to that great reunion and reconciliation in paradise, so that wherever he is, we also may be.

Could you not keep watch with me for one hour?

(MARK 14:37; MATTHEW 26:40)

After the Last Supper, Jesus leads the disciples to the Garden of Gethsemane, where he takes Peter, James, and John and goes off to pray. "My soul is sorrowful even to death," he tells them. "Remain here and keep watch." He walks forward a little, falls to the ground, and begs God to let him live. "Abba, all things are possible to you. Take this cup away from me, but not what I will, but what you will."

When Jesus returns, he finds his three friends sound asleep. "Simon, are you asleep? Can you not keep watch for one hour?" he asks. "Watch and pray that you may not undergo the test. The spirit is willing but the flesh is weak" (Mark 14:32–38). After waking them up, he leaves again to pray alone in agony for the strength to accept God's will.

Over and over again, Mark's Jesus urges the disciples to "keep watch." "Be watchful! Be alert!" he tells them as the end draws near. "You do not know when the time will come. Watch therefore. What I say to you, I say to all: Watch!" (Mark 13:33–37).

This call to keep watch with Christ is one of the Gospel's most urgent commands. The disciples are not able to do it, so Jesus continues to urge them on. Likewise, he presses us to keep watch with him. That means that we are called to be contemplatives, to look out for his coming, to remain alert, to open our eyes and be ready for his coming. Can we do this? Can we become contemplatives on the lookout, prayerfully keeping watch at our post for Christ?

"Can you not keep watch with me for one hour?" Jesus will ask us. If we take Jesus seriously and try to keep watch with him, we live as if we are fully alert. We remain awake, like sentries guarding the city through the long night, or watchmen and watchwomen alone in the fire tower looking out into the wilderness in case of fire, or air traffic controllers alert to the coming of the next plane. We become entirely focused on God's coming, ready for God's surprise and imminent arrival.

When I was imprisoned for an antinuclear disarmament action, this text became a metaphor for life. Sitting in jail for speaking out for peace meant keeping watch with Christ in Gethsemane. Now, living and working among the poor in the New Mexico desert, I find myself still keeping watch with Christ, on the lookout, ready and waiting for his arrival.

Jesus asks specifically, "Can you not keep watch for one hour?" Many saints and mystics hear this question as a call to spend at least one hour a day in prayer with Christ. That prayer can take many forms—from thirty minutes of silent meditation, to fifteen minutes of reading the Gospel or other spiritual writings, to attending daily Mass or some communal prayer service. In the long run, one hour of prayer each day is not that much, but it can mean the difference between life and death. It transforms our day and, over time, our entire lives.

As we sit and keep watch in silent contemplation with Christ, we enter a sacred space of solitude, love, and inner peace. With time, we will wonder how we survived without prayer. Prayer becomes the air we breathe. We need it to live in peace.

More and more, this holy hour with Christ can lead us to surrender our hearts and lives more and more to him, until at last we join his prayer of acceptance—that God's will, not our will, be done.

Are you still sleeping and taking your rest?

(MARK 14:41; MATTHEW 26:45)

Buddha's name means "Awakened One." Buddhism is the practice of an ever-growing awareness of reality into full enlightenment. All major religions speak of waking up, coming alive, and becoming enlightened. Jesus was fully conscious, wide awake in the present moment. Until his last breath, his wide-awake spirit enabled him to love everyone at every moment with perfect inner peace, compassion, forgiveness, and nonviolence. He lived in communion with the God of peace, in relationship with his beloved God, listening for God, attentive to God's presence everywhere.

At this climactic moment of arrest, abandonment, and execution, Jesus begs his friends to wake up, stop sleeping, and quit resting. When he returns a second time to find Peter, James, and John snoring, he wakes them again and asks, "Are you still sleeping and taking your rest?" They are speechless. They probably wonder how he can still be awake after so many days without sleep. That week alone, Jesus wept over Jerusalem, turned over the tables in the Temple, offered his friends his body and blood, and was now awaiting arrest and execution. After a week like that, and a lifetime of nonviolent action, maybe there was no way he could get to sleep. If it were our last night on earth, and we suspected it, we no doubt would stay awake and pray too.

In the late 1990s a friend and I got up early one summer morning and drove from New York City to the Vermont countryside to spend a quiet afternoon with the great Buddhist master and author Thich Nhat Hanh. He was not feeling well that day and was resting when we arrived. So my friend and I went for a walk, found a tree overlooking the green hills, lay down on the green grass, and promptly fell sound asleep, exhausted from the trip.

I remember waking slowly from a daze when someone gently tapped me on the shoulder. I turned around to find Nhat Hanh sitting there in the full lotus position, in his brown robes, smiling at me, delighted to have caught me napping. We spent that afternoon sharing our stories, our journeys, our reflections on mindfulness, nonviolence, Christ, Buddha, our friends, and the peace movement. It was literally "an awakening" to be in his presence. Sitting with the great Buddhist teacher for hours that day, and on other occasions, I learned again about life in the present moment, about waking up to the peace of the present moment. When you wake up to reality, everything is transformed. Beauty surrounds you, and peace flows from within you, around you, and back through you.

Nhat Hanh has spent his life trying to remain awake. He calls this awakening "mindfulness," living mindfully in the present moment. "Our true home is in the present moment," he writes. "To live in the present moment is a miracle. The miracle is not to walk on water. The miracle is to walk on the green earth in the present moment, to appreciate the peace and beauty that are available now. Peace is all around us—in the world and in nature—and within us—in our bodies and our spirits. Once we learn to touch this peace, we will be healed and transformed. It is not a matter of faith; it is a matter of practice. We need only to find ways to bring our body and mind back to the present moment so we can touch what is refreshing, healing, and wondrous."

Jesus wants us to wake up and keep watch with him. But his call is not just a summons to live fully alive every moment. It is a practical warning as well. Jesus and his gang are hunted fugitives of the law. Soldiers roam the hills looking for them. Perhaps Jesus wants his friends to look out for the soldiers. He had eluded their grasp before; I think he wants to avoid arrest again, which is why he prays so fervently in the garden.

The Christian life of active nonviolence—in its earliest form in the first three centuries to present-day persecutions in El Salvador, Palestine, and Haiti—leads to clashes with the law and its imperial authorities. Arrest, imprisonment, even martyrdom are scary realities in Third World repressive war zones. People have to be on alert.

That night in Gethsemane, Jesus wanted his disciples awake, keeping permanent watch for him. For some, this has become a way of life.

Why are you sleeping?

(LUKE 22:46)

In the Garden of Gethsemane, Jesus prayed in such agony, according to Luke, that "his sweat became like drops of blood falling on the ground." For a third time, he returned to find Peter, James, and John, only to find them sound asleep. "Why are you sleeping?" he asked them. "Get up and pray that you may not undergo the test." And at that moment, Judas and the soldiers arrived to arrest Jesus.

Jesus could not understand why his disciples slept when his hour was at hand. He did not scold them or punish them, but he simply asked "Why?" He never found an answer because minutes later they all ran and abandoned him.

"Why are you sleeping?" Jesus asks us. Like the disciples, we are tired—tired of life, tired of struggling, tired of confrontation, tired of being overworked and underpaid, tired of health problems and family divisions, tired of worrying about the future, tired of resentment and misunderstanding, tired of failure and fear, tired of war, violence, and poverty.

Apparently each of us, on average, spends over seven years of life asleep. But biblically speaking, sleep represents more than the important physical need for rest. Spiritually speaking, we are sound asleep. We have grown lazy, comfortable, lethargic. We see no need to wake up to the life of prayer, the presence of God, the needs of the poor, the demands of justice and peace, the reality of death. We are too tired for all that. We prefer to take the attitude of "Wake me when it's over!"

If we were to wake up to the reality of our world and see its thirty-five wars, tens of thousands of nuclear weapons, executions, widespread starvation, systemic injustice, and ongoing destruction of the earth, we would realize that Christ is crucified every day. The whole world has become Gethsemane, and our brother Jesus is in agony all over again, praying that God's will for peace and justice become reality, that we wake up and join his work to disarm and transform the world.

Why do we fail to keep watch with Christ in Gethsemane, or to seek justice and make peace, or to announce God's reign, or to love and serve everyone? Why do we snore our lives away, roll over and go back to sleep when we hear God rumbling, turn off the spiritual alarm clock or hang up when God sends us a wake-up call?

Jesus, it seems, rarely slept. The Gospels record only one incident when Jesus slept, while he and the disciples crossed the Sea of Galilee and a violent squall nearly capsized the ship. Throughout this terrifying storm, Jesus slept on a cushion in the stern. Just as the boat was about to sink, the disciples woke him and demanded that he save them. Jesus has such trust in God that he has nothing to fear. Even in his sleep, Jesus teaches us about faith, trust, and love. Though he became physically alert and calmed the storm, the disciples remained spiritually asleep.

The hour of his arrest and crucifixion, however, is different. It is the culmination of his active nonviolence, his campaign toward Jerusalem, his confrontation with the authorities. He knows that his arrest and execution are imminent, that the forces of evil seek to crush him. It is not a time to sleep but a time to remain alert in prayer to God.

How can we, like Jesus, wake up and remain awake?

I think of my friend Philip Berrigan, the antiwar, antinuclear activist who gained international fame when he, his brother Daniel, and others poured homemade napalm over draft records in Catonsville, Maryland, on May 19, 1968, and later hammered on nuclear weapon nosecones in the first of several disarmament actions in King of Prussia, Pennsylvania, on September 9, 1980. When Philip died on December 6, 2002, he had spent over eleven years of his life behind bars for nonviolent antiwar demonstrations. When he was not in prison, he lived in Baltimore, Maryland, at Jonah House, the peace community that he and his wife, Elizabeth, founded to serve the local poor and speak out against war and injustice.

Spiritually speaking, Phil never slept. He kept permanent vigil with Christ in Gethsemane. He spent every waking minute fully alive, opposing nuclear weapons, speaking out against war, and praying for the coming of God's reign of peace. As our friend, actor Martin Sheen, said at his funeral, Phil "took the Gospel personally. He acted as if Christ's words were intended for him."

Between 1993 and 1994, I spent eight months with Philip in a tiny North Carolina jail cell after hammering on an F-15e nuclear-capable fighter bomber at the Seymour Johnson Air Force Base in Greensboro, North Carolina. We were trying to enact Isaiah's prophecy, that someday "They will beat their swords into plow-shares." Throughout our confinement, Phil remained in good spirits, meditated regularly, wrote countless letters, read the Gospels, and issued prophetic statements inviting Christians to join the struggle for disarmament. He resembled Christ in Gethsemane, praying in agony for peace, taking up his cross, and suffering in love for God's reign of peace.

Compared to most Americans, Phil was not only countercultural, he was from another world. He simply could not tolerate war or sit by quietly while the U.S. war machine rolled over the world's poor. Phil decided that he did not want to sleep through life. He wanted to wake up, as Peter, James, and John did, and like them, give his life for God's reign of peace.

The government, the war-makers, and the culture of violence need us to sleep soundly while they pillage the world, but Jesus wants us to wake up. He will keep shaking us awake and asking us why we sleep, until at last we come to our senses and join him as he confronts injustice and disarms the planet.

SEVENTEEN

ARREST AND TRIAL

Whom are you looking for?

(JOHN 18:4,7)

W e are now back where we started. At the beginning of John's
Gospel, Jesus asked the people following him, "What are
you looking for?" When he was twelve years old and his parents
found him in the Jerusalem Temple, he asked them, "Why are you
looking for me?" Now, at the end of the story, when Judas, the Roman soldiers, the guards, the chief priests, and the Pharisees surround
the Garden of Gethsemane to arrest him with "lanterns, torches and
weapons," Jesus asks, "Whom are you looking for?"

"Jesus of Nazareth," they answer.

"I am," he says. Jesus uses the name first spoken from the burning bush to Abraham. The soldiers "turned away and fell to the ground," John writes (18:6).

In one of the only incidents mentioned in all four Gospels, Jesus repeats his question, "Whom are you looking for?" When they answer again "Jesus of Nazareth," he replies, "I told you that I am. So if you are looking for me, let these men go." With that, Simon Peter strikes the high priest's slave with a sword and cuts off his right ear. "Put your sword back into its scabbard," Jesus orders Simon Peter.

At this moment of his betrayal and arrest, on the night before his execution, Jesus' simple question inquires after the soldiers and the religious authorities as human beings. He could be inviting them into the new life of discipleship, just as he invited his disciples. Compared to their confusion, darkness, and violence, Jesus is in charge. He is the one who questions them. As John will soon make clear, Jesus is the real authority, the true judge.

He also tries to protect his disciples so they will not be arrested or hurt. He is a good shepherd who looks after his flocks and, at this hour of darkness, gives his life for them.

We may need to listen to his question for a while before jumping to our own answer. Eventually we may answer, "We too are looking for Jesus of Nazareth."

But we need to reflect on our answer. Why are we looking for Jesus? Are we spiritually greedy, intending to use Jesus to get whatever benefits we can from him, even though our hearts and lives are far from him? Will we too eventually reject him, betray him, and crucify him again in the world's poor? How sincere and pure are our intentions? How important is Jesus to us? Do we truly want to follow him? If so, dare we risk betrayal, arrest, and the cross of martyrdom as well, and be faithful to him on his way of love, no matter what the future brings?

Over time, we may want to pray: Jesus, we are looking for you. We want to be with you, to grow in faith, hope, love, and peace, to listen to your words, to take your Gospel to heart, to love God and neighbor as you do, to serve you and follow you, to be your friend and companion, to live in your presence. We have had enough of the world's lies and illusions, its violence and greed, its darkness and betrayal, its glitter and pomp, its death and destruction, its emptiness and meaninglessness, its idols and false gods. We have tried them and found them all wanting. We are looking for you. Help us find you and remain with you. Show yourself to us. Take us to be with you, to stand by your side, to dwell in the light of your peace, now and forever.

Shall I not drink the cup that God gave me?

(JOHN 18:11)

"Put your sword back into its scabbard," Jesus orders Simon Peter after he cuts off the ear of the high priest's servant. "Shall I not drink the cup that God gave me?"

Earlier, when Jesus spoke about his impending torture and crucifixion, Simon Peter exploded with shock and horror. "God forbid something should happen to you," he said to Jesus. But Jesus responded, "Get behind me, Satan, for you are thinking as people do, not as God does. If you want to be my disciple, you must deny yourself, take up your cross, and follow me."

Simon Peter and the other disciples did not want Jesus to be arrested or killed. Rather, they hoped he would be the long-promised military Messiah, like Norman Schwarzkopf, or better, Arnold Schwarzenegger in the film *The Terminator*. They wanted Jesus to storm Jerusalem, overthrow the empire, and install Israel as an eternal, sovereign power. Simon Peter offered no answer to Jesus, but he surely was thinking, "No, Jesus, you should not drink the cup God gave you."

How did Simon Peter respond to this question and Jesus' prohibition of violence? He and the others ran away. And most of us today would do the same thing. Few of us accept the cross of Christ and instead advocate violent self-defense and war. Like Simon Peter, we take up the sword, not the cross, and strike our opponent. (And also like Peter, we usually miss our targets—the ruling authorities—and hurt the innocent poor.) We would not sit by while a beloved friend disrupts the culture, risks his life, and gets hauled away. Nor would we let ourselves be carried off as martyrs for some unreachable "kingdom of heaven." Rather, we reach for a gun, retaliate with bombing raids, or drop nuclear weapons. We prefer human violence to divine nonviolence.

Jesus, on the other hand, always responds nonviolently. He will not hurt, kill, or bomb anyone, even to protect his own life. He drinks the cup God gave him, the cup of suffering love, the cup of martyrdom, the cup of the cross. And he invites us to drink with him. He commands his followers to walk in his footsteps on the path of suffering love, infinite compassion, never-ending forgiveness, constant truth-telling, and deep faith. Even though it seems that only a few saints and martyrs have adopted his nonviolence, nonetheless Jesus calls us all to put down the sword and drink from the cup.

What would have happened if Jesus had not drunk from the cup of God? Perhaps, Simon Peter would have kept swinging and injured more soldiers. Perhaps those hundreds of armed soldiers would have struck back, stabbing and killing Jesus and all the disciples right there on the spot. They were, after all, a far greater military force than the ragtag disciples with their one or two swords. And *that* would have been the end of the story. There would have been no luminous example of nonviolent love shining from the cross. Humanity would not have been redeemed and saved. We would not know that God wants us to practice perfect truth, love, justice, compassion, and forgiveness. There would have been no resurrection, no Pentecost, no church, no Gospel, no Eucharist, and no saints and martyrs. Everything would have collapsed, and Jesus would have been immediately forgotten as just another violent terrorist or revolutionary. The world might have long ago gone up in flames. Instead Jesus' insistence on nonviolence literally saves us all. Yet, we still have no idea of the power of nonviolent love, the ramifications of his selfless gift throughout history.

The world says there are two options in the face of violence: We can fight back or run away. Jesus gives us a third option: creative, active nonviolent resistance to injustice. We refuse to run away, but we do not resort to the violent methods of our opponents. Instead we trust in God, reach out in love, insist on the truth of justice, and if possible disarm our opponents through a human, loving exchange, such as the questions of Jesus or even humor. But under no circumstances are we allowed to hurt or kill other human beings, however noble the cause.

If there ever was a historical moment when violence was justified, it is precisely at this hour of darkness. Simon Peter was right, given his understanding of life, to strike back. That is what the Scriptures taught. But now, in Christ, violence is forever outlawed. If Jesus is not to be defended with violence, no one is. From now on, we defend one another nonviolently. Instead of striking, killing, and bombing others, we are willing to face death in a nonviolent struggle for justice. Instead of inflicting violence on others, we accept and undergo suffering without even the desire to retaliate, in pursuit of justice and peace for all people.

"The way of violence leads to bitterness in the survivors and brutality in the destroyers," Martin Luther King Jr. writes in his first book, *Stride Toward Freedom*. "But the way of nonviolence leads to redemption and the creation of the beloved community. True nonviolent resistance is not unrealistic submission to evil power. It is rather a courageous confrontation of evil by the power of love, in the faith that it is better to be the recipient of violence than the inflictor of it, since the latter only multiplies the existence of violence and bitterness in the universe, while the former may develop a sense of shame in the opponent, and thereby bring about a transformation and change of heart. Nonviolent resistance does call for love, but it is not a sentimental love. It is a very stern love that would organize itself into collective action to right a wrong by taking on suffering itself."

Jesus asks us, "Shall I not drink the cup that God gives me?" Deep down, we know that he should drink the cup of suffering, that his forgiving love and cross have redeemed us all. His perfect innocence, steadfast compassion, insistence on truth, demand for justice, complete forgiveness but refusal to retaliate draws the whole human race to him.

Eventually everyone will turn toward Jesus. One new day, we will all confess that he was right. We will repent of our violence, beat our swords into plowshares, accept his way of divine nonviolence, and spend eternity thanking him for drinking the cup of nonviolence.

> Judas, are you betraying the Son of Humanity with a kiss?

(LUKE 22:48)

Jesus was no different in appearance from any of the other ragtag disciples. The ruling authorities and chief priests could not recognize him. That is why Judas needed a signal to let the soldiers know which of the guerrilla revolutionaries to arrest.

But why a kiss? Scholars speculate that this was the affectionate trademark of the Jesus community. Whenever Jesus and the other disciples greeted one another, they kissed each other, as most Mediterranean and Middle Eastern men still do today. Jesus had created a community of love, friendship, and affection. He taught them to welcome each other with this sign of peace. He was training them to fulfill his greatest commandment, issued only an hour before: Love one another.

As Judas approaches to kiss him, Jesus asks, "Judas, are you betraying the Son of Humanity with a kiss?" Judas does not answer. Instead Simon Peter strikes with a sword, the disciples run away, and Jesus is hauled off to his death. It is a cruel irony that this intimate act of affection is used to betray and kill the holy Christ of God. Judas the kisser wanders off and hangs himself.

This question leads us to contemplate the horror and reality of betrayal. The greatest sin of all, according to the Gospels, is the betrayal of Judas. He may have been Jesus' best friend and most trusted confidant, as the Scriptures hint. Betrayal, we now realize, does not come from outside the community but from within it. It does not come from the fringe of the community, but from its heart.

For the past two thousand years, church people have continued to betray one another. Priests, nuns, ministers, preachers, bishops, cardinals, and popes have betrayed humanity throughout history. As this intimate kiss suggests, we are most often betrayed not by our enemies but by those we love the most, those closest to us, our intimate friends, relatives, parents, children, even our spouses. Today, when over half of all marriages end in divorce, the kiss of betrayal is practically taken for granted.

But if we dare imagine Jesus asking us this question, we slowly begin to realize that we too have betrayed Christ. Judas lives in each one of us. At one point or another, we have all turned on Jesus, handed him over, and tried to make a buck in the process. Christ is betrayed all over the world every single day in the suffering poor and marginalized, whenever we greedily pursue money instead of active solidarity with Christ in the poor and the nonviolent struggle for justice and peace.

Do we also betray the Son of Humanity with a kiss? Do we pretend to love Jesus, admire him, even worship him with regular church attendance, yet turn against him whenever the going gets tough? In these days of right-wing Christian fundamentalism and its global, all-American pursuit of war, bigotry, and hegemony in the name of Christ, betrayal has become commonplace. We live in a culture of betrayal. Instead of following Jesus, we are followers of Judas, and we do not even know it, except that we have made far more than thirty silver pieces.

Prayerful meditation on this question will lead us ultimately to repent of our betrayals and beg the all-merciful Christ to forgive us all over again.

Have you come out as against a robber, with swords and clubs, to seize me?

(MARK 14:48; LUKE 22:52; MATTHEW 26:55)

As soon as Judas kissed Jesus, "they laid hands on him and arrested him," Mark reports. "Have you come out as against a robber, with swords and clubs, to seize me?" Jesus asked. "Day after day I was with you teaching in the temple area, yet you did not arrest me; but that the Scriptures may be fulfilled."

"All of this has come to pass that the writings of the prophets may be fulfilled," Matthew adds. With that, "they all left him and fled," Mark concludes.

With this question, Jesus condemns the whole array of brutality around him, the cowardly ambush and the empire behind it. Why all these weapons? he asks. Do they think that he will not practice the nonviolence he preaches? Do these ruthless religious authorities suspect that Jesus is a person of violence, like them, who will strike back and kill? Jesus sees through them all and, in Mark's version, holds them responsible for the violent reaction of his disciples.

When Jesus asks if they considered him a robber, he is referring to the "social bandits" who roamed the countryside stealing and killing, often in the name of revolution, like the two insurgents crucified along with him, according to first-century Roman historian Josephus.

Jesus' question reveals his disdain for state-sanctioned, religiously supported violence, enacted in the name of preventing terrorism, but which in reality is the ultimate form of terrorism. Jesus asks the authorities if they think he himself is a violent terrorist. He accuses them of justifying their massive armed response as a war on terrorism, when in reality they are acting to maintain total control over everyone and crush any rabble-rousers. His question exposes them as the real terrorists. Then he points out the simple truth: They do not have the power or the courage to arrest him in public but have to come at night, under cover.

With the events of September 11, 2001, the U.S. government's so-called war on terrorism and our invasion and occupation of Iraq, this question takes on new relevance. State-sanctioned violence continues today on a scale even greater than in the Roman Empire. We see this oppressive violence when racist, white New York police officers storm apartments in Harlem and shoot unarmed citizens like Amadou Diallo, or when armed FBI agents harass and arrest hundreds of unarmed Muslims because of their religion and nationality, or when armed INS squads hunt down and arrest unarmed Latin American immigrants. Armed people continue to seize unarmed people in the name of prevention, protection, religion, empire, and the war on terrorism.

As Jesus knows all too well, ruling authorities are the worst terrorists anywhere. The Romans invented the war on terrorism, but they became the ultimate terrorists, as Jesus' question implies. Today U.S. military forces harass, torture, and kill innocent people around the world, leaving a trail of blood from Iraq and the Philippines to Colombia and Guatemala.

In the name of ending terrorism, our nation adopted the method of terrorists and has become, as Nelson Mandela said in December 2002, the greatest terrorist on earth. We claim the high ground as the world's policeman, trying to stop terrorism, but in reality the Pentagon wants global military control, the multinational corporations want global economic control, the oil barons want global oil control, and Wall Street wants global monetary control. We do not care about the victims of terrorism. If we did, we would not harm one child on the planet. We would spend our resources cutting off the roots of terrorism and abolishing world hunger, poverty, unemployment, disease, racism, sexism, child abuse, homelessness, illiteracy, and pollution. As a nation, we do none of these things.

With our nuclear arsenal, we have far surpassed the Roman soldiers. We now hold the whole world hostage, as Philip Berrigan pointed out. We go after Christ with the nuclear sword, the nuclear club. And if we do not get our way, we threaten other nations with total annihilation. We have not sided with the unarmed Jesus but with the armed soldiers. Like those who arrested Jesus, we hunt down so-called terrorists and crush any nation that dares challenge our hegemony. This question stands as a judgment upon us all.

In the end, Jesus is determined to remain faithful to the Scriptures, especially the prophets. He accepts his calling as the suffering servant savior of humanity. He knows the Scriptures are fulfilled, which is his most important obligation, so he goes forth, trusting that he is doing what he is supposed to do, that all he need do now is remain loving, nonviolent, truthful, compassionate, forgiving, and faithful until his last breath.

> Do you think that I cannot call upon my God and he will not provide me at this moment with more than twelve legions of angels? But then how would the Scriptures be fulfilled which say that it must come to pass this way?
>
> (MATTHEW 26:53–54)

P ut your sword back into its sheath," Jesus tells Simon Peter, according to Matthew's account, "for all who take the sword will perish by the sword. Do you think that I cannot call upon my God and he will not provide me at this moment with more than twelve legions of angels? But then how would the Scriptures be fulfilled which say that it must come to pass this way?"

Jesus' question remains unanswered today. Simon Peter has seen Jesus calm a storm, walk on water, and raise the dead. He knows that Jesus can easily call upon God to send twelve legions of angels at that very moment to the Garden of Gethsemane. But he probably looks at Jesus with complete astonishment and bewilderment, because he suddenly realizes that Jesus has no intention of fighting back. Instead of answering Jesus, Simon Peter turns and runs.

Twelve legions of angels! "Legion" was the word for a battalion of thousands of Roman soldiers. Jesus uses this loaded word to refer to his own nonviolent army. If we think about it, the image is shocking. Imagine twenty-four thousand angels surrounded by glowing light suddenly appearing in the middle of the Garden of Gethsemane. If the angels had materialized from out of nowhere, not only would the soldiers have dropped their weapons, they would have passed out from fright. One angel would be enough to convert anyone. Twenty-four thousand angels would have literally disarmed that armed death squad.

So why doesn't Jesus call upon this supernatural battalion to protect himself? Why doesn't he do something dramatic to get himself out of this awful mess?

The second difficult question offers the answer. Jesus insists that he has come to fulfill the Scriptures. He is determined to be faithful to the text. He will become the martyred suffering servant Messiah, described in Isaiah 53, destined to save the human race, not through violence but through nonviolent suffering love.

In other words, Jesus refuses to resort to magic. He will not attempt the inhuman. He will not play God. In the face of systemic injustice and imperial violence, he takes action, demands justice, risks his life—but refuses to resort to worldly violence. He maintains his humanity, does what is most human, and accepts the inhuman consequences of being human in an inhuman world. That means he loves everyone, speaks the truth of justice, denounces the lie of injustice, announces God's reign of nonviolence, confronts institutionalized evil, and accepts the world's punishment for his goodness. He will go to his death with faith, hope, and forgiving love. He will not fight back or defend himself. He will not use violence or engage in spectacular acts of divinity. Rather, he will fulfill the Scriptures, come what may. In the process, he will take upon himself the sins of the world and redeem us all. He will accept his calling, including its inevitable bloody outcome.

Simon Peter could not answer these questions. Only decades later, in the first letter of Peter, do we get a hint of the deep understanding he eventually learned. "Whenever anyone bears the pain of unjust suffering because of consciousness of God, that is a grace," Peter writes shortly before his own crucifixion in Rome. "If you are patient when you suffer for doing what is good, this is a grace before God. For to this you have been called, because Christ also suffered for you, leaving you an example that you should follow in his footsteps. . . . When he was insulted, he returned no insult. When he suffered, he did not threaten; instead he handed himself over to the one who judges justly. He himself bore our sins in his body upon the cross, so that, free from sin, we might live for righteousness. By his wounds you have been healed. . . . Do not return evil for evil or insult for insult; but on the contrary, a blessing, because to this you were called, that you might inherit a blessing. For it is better to suffer for doing good, if that be the will of God, than for doing evil" (I Peter 2:19–24; 3:9, 17).

How do we answer Jesus? If we can make the jump to Gospel nonviolence and accept the logic of suffering love for justice and peace, then we can say, Of course, Jesus, you could have called upon thousands of angels to intervene on your behalf and protect you, but thank you for not calling upon them. Thank you for undergoing your martyrdom with such a glorious spirit of forgiving, nonviolent love. Thank you for fulfilling the Scriptures, redeeming us, saving us, and disarming us by your holy cross. Thank you for summoning us to be human, to stop playing God, to reject the temptation to call upon legions of angels, and to take up our cross of nonviolent resistance to evil. Thank you for challenging us also to fulfill the Scriptures as your modern-day disciples who carry on your mission of nonviolent love and risk our lives in pursuit of your reign of justice and peace.

Why ask me?

(JOHN 18:21)

Here at the end of the story, for the first time, Jesus addresses our need to question him. He knows that he is the only one with the heavenly authority to ask the questions and offer spiritual koans for our growth and salvation.

But now he is under arrest. The ruling authorities have him in their clutches. He will be dragged before the religious leaders, who have been out to kill him from the start, and eventually King Herod and the Roman procurator Pontius Pilate.

John's account of Jesus' trials begins with the high priest who "questioned Jesus about his disciples and about his doctrine" (John 18:19). Jesus has been harassed by religious authorities all his life, but this is the first time he stands trial before the high priest himself.

"I have spoken publicly to the world," Jesus tells him. "I have always taught in a synagogue or in the temple area where all the Jews gather, and in secret I have said nothing. Why ask me? Ask those who heard me what I said to them. They know what I said."

In the context of his statement before this powerful, violent religious authority, Jesus announces that he has nothing to hide, that he has never spoken in secret, that he always spoke in public. His statement exposes the hypocrisy of the high priest, who not only schemes in private but tries Jesus in secret under cover of the night.

Jesus puts forth a simple, honest question. "If you really want to know about my disciples and my teachings," Jesus says, "ask those who heard me." If the high priest is sincere, he could ask the other Pharisees because they heard Jesus speak on many occasions. But the high priest would never consent to ask anyone about Jesus, because the high priest believes he is God's one true representative who knows what to do, and Jesus is merely some troublemaking charlatan who threatens his authority. The high priest would never concede to Jesus. Rather, he wants to trap Jesus in blasphemy so that he can finally be rid of him. Up until now, he has heard only hearsay evidence against Jesus.

As the trials continue, John's Gospel presents a subtle turning of the tables. Throughout the passion narrative, Jesus is presented as the real judge, and the other shady characters, including the high priest, King Herod and Pontius Pilate, are on trial. When the unjust high priest questions him, Jesus turns the focus on the high priest. "You question me? I am the one who should question you," Jesus says, in effect.

"Why ask me?" Jesus asks us. Taking the question out of context, we can ask ourselves: Why do we ask Jesus anything? Do we want to understand the eternal mysteries? Are we trying to get him to do what we want? Are we trying to manipulate and control Jesus? Are we subtly seeking to justify ourselves and assert our egos over and above Jesus?

As we hear his question, we might say to him, We ask you questions because you have all the answers. We ask you questions because we want to know you better. We ask you questions because we are lost, stuck, deaf, dumb, blind, and we need your help. We ask you questions because, in truth, we do not know anything.

This exchange leads me to wonder if John's Gospel is urging us never to question Jesus again. His question reveals the depth of his humility and powerlessness before the worldly authorities. But the more we ponder his humility, the more we realize the power of his divine majesty. As St. Paul writes, his weakness and cross reveal that he is greater than all of us, "above every name."

Thus not one of us has the authority to question Jesus. If we do, we become a new breed of arrogant, dominating, imperial rulers and venomous, self-righteous religious authorities who think we are more powerful than God, like the high priest, King Herod, and Pontius Pilate.

This question humbles us because we realize that from now on we should not ask Jesus anything. Rather, we should simply answer his questions, take his word to heart, do what he says, and beg for his mercy.

> If I have spoken wrongly, testify to the
> wrong; but if I have spoken rightly, why do
> you strike me?
>
> (JOHN 18:23)

As soon as Jesus questions the high priest, one of the Temple guards strikes Jesus in the face. "If I have spoken wrongly, testify to the wrong," Jesus says, "but if I have spoken rightly, why do you strike me?"

Jesus appeals to reason and truth. He tries to communicate with us, to help us grasp the truth, to teach us how to live. He only speaks truth. Indeed, he embodies truth.

Jesus wants us to correct each other when we are wrong and to help each other accept the truth. He cannot understand why we are not likewise committed to truth. He knows that once we are committed to truth, we will never strike or kill another person ever again, that we will realize our calling to live at peace, that we will be nonviolent toward one another. In his profound humility, he himself is never wrong. He cannot be. So he tries to reason with the brutal, unreasonable soldier, "If what I say is wrong, show me; if it is right, then accept it. Why do you strike me?"

Mahatma Gandhi concluded that the spiritual life requires a steadfast pursuit of truth. "To find truth completely is to realize oneself and one's destiny, to become perfect," he writes. "Realizing truth means realizing that all human beings are one." Once we realize the truth of our common unity, we will never strike or hurt anyone ever again, much less kill or wage war. "Truthful people cannot long remain violent," Gandhi continues. "They will perceive in the course of their search that they have no need to be violent and they will further discover that so long as there is the slightest trace of violence within, they will fail to find the truth they are seeking. Without nonviolence, it is not possible to seek and find truth. Nonviolence and truth are so intertwined that it is practically impossible to disentangle and separate them."

When Jesus inquires about right and wrong, he inquires about violence. "Why do you strike me?" he asks the soldier. They do not answer him because they do not distinguish between right and wrong. Instead they do not know what he is talking about, because they are not committed to the truth. Their entire training and purpose is to strike and kill uppity prisoners and enemies. They can do whatever they want. Any soldier, any army anywhere has permission to strike, kill, and bomb, because the first casualty of war is truth. We no longer have any boundaries. We forget ourselves, deny our basic humanity, and become savage killing machines. Though the soldier treats Jesus as if he is not a human being, in truth the soldier long ago lost his humanity, as all soldiers are forced to do in their basic training. Striking and killing people is the most inhuman thing anyone can ever do, and yet it is the job of every soldier. Those who engage in militarism and war lose their humanity, their soul. In this case, the guards cannot even hear Jesus' question. Within a few hours, they will strike him over and over again. They will slap him, strip him, spit at him, mock him, torture him, and nail him to wood.

Why do we do violence to the Christ in one another? Why do we strike our children, spouses, neighbors, prisoners, and enemies? Why do we bomb and kill people, like the beautiful children of Iraq, the innocent people of Hiroshima, the millions of victims of our greed and wars? Why do we continue to strike Jesus? He wants to know.

The question invites us to look deeply at the violence within our own hearts and to vow, in the name of the suffering, nonviolent Christ, never to resort to violence again.

> Do you say this on your own or have others
> told you about me?
>
> (JOHN 18:34)

After Jesus is interrogated by Annas and Caiaphas, the high priest, he is brought to the praetorium, the Roman headquarters in Jerusalem, to appear before Pontius Pilate, the Roman procurator. Pilate tries and fails to dismiss the case against Jesus, so he calls Jesus in and asks him point-blank, "Are you the king of the Jews?"

"Do you say this on your own or have others told you about me?" Jesus asks Pilate in return. Jesus' question shows his desire, even at the hour of his death, to learn if someone believes in him, if someone is making the leap of faith into discipleship. It also demonstrates that Jesus, not Pilate, is the true judge. Jesus is the one who asks the questions. Pilate, like everyone else, is really the one on trial before Jesus.

"My reign does not belong to this world," Jesus explains to Pilate. "If my reign did belong to this world, my attendants would be fighting to keep me from being handed over to the Judeans. But as it is, my reign is not here."

"Then you are a king?" Pilate asks.

"You say I am a king. For this I was born and for this I came into the world, to testify to the truth. Everyone who belongs to the truth listens to my voice" (John 18:34–37).

Pilate's interrogation of Jesus yields one of his most telling statements. Yes, Jesus is a king, but no, his "kingdom" is not like the Roman Empire. Jesus reigns over an entirely new and different realm of peace, nonviolence, truth, and love. In Jesus' reign there is no violence, no fighting, no killing, and no war. Everyone is peaceful, loving, nonviolent, and kind. Therefore, his reign is not of this world. It is a completely different world.

Everyone who claims to be a follower of the nonviolent Jesus is called to be a citizen of Jesus' reign of nonviolence. As citizens of Jesus' reign, our home is not here, in the empire of violence, but with Jesus in his reign of peace. We pledge allegiance to our nonviolent king, renounce violence, refuse to fight anyone, and actually love everyone we meet. Jesus is not only our king but also our brother. We are all members of the royal family in his reign, so we will live forever in the royal household of peace, in ecstatic love with God and everyone. But here on earth, no one can comprehend this otherworldly peace. As Jesus' obedient followers, we are completely misunderstood. But as we recall how profoundly misunderstood and rejected Jesus was, we take heart and refuse to be crushed. Indeed, we expect the same trouble Jesus received. The world of violence can never understand God's reign of nonviolence, but we carry on, first and foremost, as citizens of his realm.

If we approach Jesus as Pilate did—sure of ourselves, thinking that we are superior to Jesus, but asking about his kingdom in order to justify ourselves or entrap him—Jesus will ask us the same question: "Do you say this on your own or have others told you about me?" How will we respond to Jesus?

If we say, "We have heard about you, Jesus. The whole world knows about you. Millions claim to worship you. All my relatives aspire to be with you. They all say you are a king," then Jesus will turn to us and ask, "But who do you say that I am?" He wants to know what each one of us personally thinks about him. He is looking for faith. He needs us to believe in him.

If we say, "Yes, Jesus, I say these things on my own. You are indeed the nonviolent Christ of God, the Lord and Savior, the model human being, the Way, the Truth, and the Life, the true King of Peace," he may say, "Come, follow me, that where I am, you may also be."

Like Peter and Pilate, sooner or later each one of us has to decide where we stand before Jesus. Will we oppose him, judge him, deny him, and reject him, or will we accept him, follow him, serve him, believe in him? Sooner or later, all hearts will be revealed before the nonviolent Jesus. There will be no evading the question. Jesus will eventually know where our allegiance lies.

EIGHTEEN

THE CROSS

For which of these good works are you
trying to stone me?

(JOHN 10:32)

The torture and execution of the innocent, nonviolent Jesus remains the most shocking scandal of all time and the most transforming, spiritually explosive act in human history. Why would God allow this to happen? we ask. How can Jesus be willing to suffer such a death? Why must his followers also take up their cross and risk martyrdom for social justice? Isn't there a better way to save the human race?

Jesus courageously, consistently, and nonviolently resists institutionalized injustice from the moment he emerges out of the wilderness. His life is one steady stream of good works: serving the poor, healing the sick, feeding the hungry, teaching the multitudes, empowering the powerless, and creating community. He is not passive, silent, or apathetic. Rather, he is active, outspoken, provocative, and challenging.

But from the minute he opens his mouth to proclaim God's reign, the authorities are out to get him. And the people do not welcome his message either. After his first sermon in his hometown synagogue, the crowd tries to throw him off a cliff. When he heals the man with the withered hand, the religious authorities seek counsel with the political rulers in a plot to kill him. The elite ruling class is determined to do away with him. From the start, the nonviolent Jesus is destined for martyrdom. His gift of healing love, transforming action, and creative nonviolence is repeatedly rejected.

For Jesus, this path of nonviolent resistance becomes a metaphor for life itself. The fullness of life is found in nonviolent noncooperation and confrontation with evil and the acceptance of the consequences—the world's inevitable punishment of agitators with violence and death.

The cross is the standard of discipleship. If one wishes to follow Jesus, one has to carry on his campaign against injustice, resist the forces of death, speak out against the lie of war, plumb the depths of loving nonviolence, and announce God's coming reign of peace, regardless of the response, which can only be persecution, arrest, imprisonment, torture, and even execution.

Just before they finally nail him, after healing a blind man in the Temple and explaining his gift of eternal life, Jesus declares, "My Father and I are one." Immediately the Judeans pick up rocks to stone him to death. "I have shown you many good works from my Father. For which of these good works are you trying to stone me?" he asks.

"We are not stoning you for a good work but for blasphemy," they say. "You, a man, are making yourself God." Again, Jesus tries to reason with them. When they try to arrest him, John writes, "he escaped from their power" (10:39).

Jesus' question confronts murderous intentions and tries to dig beneath the roots of violence. But the religious leaders are so threatened, they do not care about truth, justice, or good works. They want to do away with him because he challenges their authority and understanding of God. Eventually Jesus will no longer question their violence or be able to escape their grasp. He will succumb to their abuse but will remain faithful to God.

"For which of these good works are you trying to stone me?" the rejected, hunted Jesus asks us. In other words, why do we harass and punish those who do good works? Why do we crush those who offer a new vision of healing, hope, and peace? Why are we trying to kill Christ in the world today? The question exposes our hatred of goodness, our bent toward violence, our love of death. If we listen to Jesus' question, he may draw us all into his nonviolent campaign of good works, nonviolent action, and all-inclusive love. Maybe he will disarm our hearts once and for all.

Why are you trying to kill me?

(JOHN 7:19)

During the Feast of the Tabernacles, Jesus goes by himself to Jerusalem to teach in the Temple area, where he astonishes the crowds, according to John's Gospel. The authorities ask him how he could know the Scriptures without academic training.

"My teaching is not my own," Jesus replies, "but is from the One who sent me" (John 7:16). "Whoever chooses to do God's will shall know whether my teaching is from God or whether I speak on my own. Whoever speaks on his own seeks his own glory, but whoever seeks the glory of the One who sent him is truthful, and there is no wrong in him. Why are you trying to kill me?"

"You are possessed!" the crowd says to him. "Who is trying to kill you?"

John's Gospel is sometimes called the most spiritual, but it is also the most political, given the constant death threats and assassination attempts against Jesus. In this instance, he asked them point-blank:

"Why are you trying to kill me?" They deny it, and yet they were indeed trying to kill him.

To understand Jesus and his Gospel, we have to ask why he was killed. Jesus was not killed because people did not like the way he looked. He was not killed for being dumb. He was not killed by accident. Jesus was a threat to the religious, political, economic, and imperial establishments, so he was legally killed. The ruling class presumed that if Jesus continued to stir up the crowds, their control would be undermined.

A few scenes earlier in John's Gospel, the crowds wanted to make Jesus a king (6:15). Jesus called people to resist the Roman Empire, noncooperate with the imperial occupation, share their resources with one another, stop paying taxes, and accept him as their Messiah. Jesus was far more than a nonviolent revolutionary, but his teachings were revolutionary. If everyone enacted his word, then the whole world would have changed, beginning in Jerusalem and reaching all the way to Caesar's throne in Rome.

Whenever ruling authorities feel threatened, they clamp down on the population with repressive violence, mainly to snuff out their leaders. In some nations, death squads are sent out to kill troublemakers, as we have seen in El Salvador, Guatemala, and South Africa. Sometimes nations simply assassinate subversive, prophetic voices. Israel's ruling elite killed Prime Minister Rabin after he offered real hope of ending their occupation of the Palestinians. While celebrating Mass, El Salvador's Archbishop Romero was assassinated by a lone gunman hired by the right-wing ruling political party which opposed his call for an end to the war and U.S.-backed military dictatorship. Hindu extremists assassinated Mahatma Gandhi because they opposed his commitment to make peace with Pakistani Muslims. Many believe that Pentagon and CIA assassins killed President John Kennedy because of his vision of nuclear disarmament, peace with Cuba and the Soviet Union, and the withdrawal of troops from Vietnam. Recent Memphis civil hearings confirmed that the government, local police, mafia, and FBI conspired to assassinate Martin Luther King Jr.

The ruling forces of evil will not let the grassroots forces of good take control of any nation. They will use any means necessary—including repression, assassination, or full-scale warfare—to maintain their unjust military and economic control. Crucifixion was the Roman Empire's ultimate weapon of deterrence. It made an example of any unruly revolutionaries by publicly nailing them naked to trees along popular thoroughfares. Jesus grew up in one of the world's most repressive periods and regions, under the brutal thumb of the empire. Stonings and crucifixions were commonplace in his day. Although he questioned their murderous hearts and exposed their violence, he knew the consequences of such truth-telling. He could read the writing on the wall.

"Why are you trying to kill me?" It is a question that resounds throughout history. Only ten years later, when the notorious Pharisee and death-squad leader Saul was riding through the countryside in pursuit of Christians, the voice of Jesus knocked him down and called out, "Saul, Saul, why are you persecuting me?" Today, as millions die from war and the effects of war, Jesus still calls out, "Why are you trying to kill me?"

If we see Christ present in the eyes of the homeless, hungry, naked, imprisoned, sick, and dying, and most of all in the faces of our enemies, then we will discover that it is Christ we murder in the world's poor. The question summons Christians everywhere to do what the first disciples were unable to do: stand up, protest, speak out, defend, protect, and prevent the murder of Christ in the world's poor. It is the most urgent need of our time.

What should I say, "Father, save me from this hour"?

(JOHN 12:27)

As the death squads closed in on Jesus, we might wonder what he should have done. Should he have run away? Jesus had received death threats his whole life. Matthew's Gospel claims that thousands of first-born baby boys were slaughtered at the news of the Messiah's birth, and that his parents fled with him to Egypt as refugees to protect him. But Jesus knew what he was doing. His life was deliberate, focused, and centered. He was determined to live well and die well, knowing that death does not get the last word. After eluding the authorities for so long, we can conclude, Jesus chose the time and place for his climactic hour.

As the Passover neared, some Greeks approached the disciples with the request, "Sir, we would like to see Jesus." When Jesus heard this, he said, "The hour has come for the Son of Humanity to be glorified." It seems that once he knew his fame had spread to far-off Gentiles, he was ready to let go of his life. "Unless a grain of wheat falls to the ground and dies, it remains just a grain of wheat," he continued. "But if it dies, it produces much fruit. Whoever loves his life loses it, and whoever hates her life in this world will preserve it for eternal life. Whoever serves me must follow me, and where I am, there also will my servant be. The Father will honor whoever serves me. I am troubled now. Yet what should I say, 'Father save me from this hour?' But it was for this purpose that I came to this hour" (John 12:23–28).

We could argue the reasons why Jesus should have prayed for God to save him from this hour. He could have done so much more good. He could have healed many more people, taught other great lessons, called still more followers to discipleship. But Jesus knew the dynamics of martyrdom. He knew that when the grain of wheat falls and dies, it bears much fruit. He knew that he was born to live, love, serve, and die, and that this hour would bear much fruit for the whole human race.

Remember Benigno Aquino. He was a popular political leader of the Philippines who lived in exile during the ruthless Ferdinand Marcos dictatorship. Over time he concluded that Gandhi and King were right, and he committed himself to nonviolence. He knew that if he returned home, he would be assassinated. But after years of the Marcos dictatorship, corruption, and death-squad murders, he decided to return and offer his life for justice and peace. He knew the probable outcome, but he also knew the dynamics of the cross—that his hour could bear good fruit and give birth to justice, liberation, and peace for millions of suffering Filipinos.

Aquino flew home. I remember hearing about his decision and watching the interview he gave on the plane to Manila. As the plane landed at the airport, Marcos's soldiers stormed the cockpit and assassinated him instantly. He never even set foot on the ground. Although his death outraged the world, Marcos appeared to grow stronger. President Reagan continued to support the dictator, and the repression clamped down harder. But two years later, in February 1986, the People Power revolution nonviolently overthrew Marcos. For three days, millions of unarmed citizens marched through the streets. After countless hours of nonviolence training, hundreds of nuns and other religious leaders sat down in front of the tanks in downtown Manila, calling for an end to the dictatorship. Suddenly Marcos fled to Hawaii, and Cory Aquino, Benigno's widow, became the first president of a democratic Philippines. Although enormous problems persist and the struggle for justice continues, it was nonetheless a breakthrough for peace that could have come only from the gift of Benigno Aquino's life and selfless death. He was a true follower of the nonviolent Jesus. His courageous death sheds light on the gift of Christ and his choice to stay and face the cross. If we ponder this question, we too might find the courage to offer our lives in love for suffering humanity.

> At that time people will say to the mountains, "Fall upon us!" and to the hills, "Cover us!" for if these things are done when the wood is green, what will happen when it is dry?
>
> (LUKE 23:30–31)

When Jesus is brought before Herod, he does not say anything, leaving Herod baffled and angry. When Jesus is hauled before Pilate, according to Mark, he says very little. Yet Pilate releases the violent rebel Barabbas and hands Jesus over to be tortured and executed. Although each Gospel portrays Jesus' crucifixion, we are not told much, either because it was so horrific or because everyone in those days knew the horrors of the Roman death penalty.

In Luke's account, as Jesus is led out to his death carrying the cross, the soldiers force someone named "Simon, a Cyrenian" to help carry the cross. A large crowd follows Jesus, "including many women who mourned and lamented for Jesus." Jesus turns and says to them, "Daughters of Jerusalem, do not weep for me. Weep instead for yourselves and for your children, for indeed, the days are coming when people will say, 'Blessed are the barren, the wombs that never bore and the breasts that never nursed.' At that time people will say to the mountains, 'Fall upon us!' and to the hills, 'Cover us!' for if these things are done when the wood is green, what will happen when it is dry?" Moments later, the tortured Jesus is stripped and crucified.

Luke invokes the prophet Hosea, who writes that someday Israel will be punished for its idolatry and violence, and the people will "cry out to the mountains, 'Cover us!' and to the hills, 'Fall upon us!'" (10:8). But Luke adds the image of the green and dry wood. If the presence of Christ is the time of the green wood, and this is how we treat the Holy One of God, what will become of humanity when he is no longer around? What will we do to the Christ in one another?

Today we live in the time of the dry wood, the time of global crucifixion. We could answer Jesus' question with a list of names: Hiroshima, Nagasaki, Auschwitz, Dresden, Tokyo, Vietnam, El Salvador, Sarajevo, Rwanda, Afghanistan, and Iraq. It is the time of genocide, environmental catastrophe, and nuclear war. As Dr. King said the night before he died, unless we adopt the wisdom of nonviolence, we are doomed to global self-destruction.

At the turn of the millennium, on December 31, 1999, Philip Berrigan wrote a reflection on this question from his Maryland prison cell. Phil was in his late seventies, with less than two years to live, and had already spent many years in prison for nonviolent actions against nuclear weapons. "The twentieth century has been dubbed the bloodiest of centuries, with over 200 million dead from war," Phil wrote that night. "How many more are crippled physically, psychologically, and spiritually by war? 400 million? How many more have been victimized and destroyed by the spirit of war—genocides, tortures, disappearances, gulags, pogroms, economic sanctions? Incalculable! How many are alive today who have not been scarred in some way by war? The harvest of death and destruction from war is appalling.

"If we executed the Lord of Life in the green wood, what will we do in the dry wood?" Phil asks. "The twentieth century's wars reveal a dramatic shift from the number of soldiers killed in war to a huge increase in the number of civilians killed in war; as well as the introduction of nuclear weapons, more efficient weaponry, and the development of entire economies, like the U.S., based on war. Unless these trends are checked and reversed, the bloody twentieth century will become a template for the twenty-first.

"What does the general silence over war from pulpits, Congress, the media, campuses, and business communities indicate except a sullen insistence that we have the right to kill one another? As I have asked these questions during this past year, I watched the U.S. use 'depleted uranium' with its special bomber, the A-10 Warthog, in Iraq and Yugoslavia.

"The New Testament sums up 'the law and the prophets' with the simple commandment: 'Love your neighbor as yourself.' If that's how we are to worship God, if that's how we build justice and peace in the world, then how do we regard this latest weapon, depleted uranium, except with horror? A depleted uranium shell, fired from an A-10, strikes a tank or personnel carrier, quickly penetrates the armor and burns the crew alive. Meanwhile, it aerosolizes radioactive heavy-metal particles, scattering them up to twenty-five miles, to be breathed or ingested. These dustlike particles are not only carcinogenic, they are genetically destructive. Hence, the chronically ill or deformed children of Desert Storm veterans and Iraqis.

"Depleted uranium has a half-life of over four billion years. It is only slightly less radioactive than raw uranium. It joins other nuclear efforts of the past fifty-five years, most of them led by the U.S., to put the world's people on a virtual death row—mining and processing uranium, exposed uranium tailings, nuclear weapons testing, nuclear weapons fabrication, and nuclear power generation.

"Nuclear war or global irradiation: which is our fate? The Russians and ourselves have thousands of nuclear weapons on hairtrigger alert. Nuclear war could start from a mad, official decision. It could begin by accident or by technical failure. But the United States has chosen a softer approach to nuclear war, with its new depleted uranium weapons. The U.S. gives depleted uranium free of charge to weapons manufacturers, and ships it to dozens of 'friendly' nations, openly inviting them to make their own nuclear weapons, fight their own nuclear wars, and irradiate the planet further.

"If they do these things in the green wood, what will they do in the dry?

"Long before the development of depleted uranium, Thomas Merton speculated that nuclear weapons prepared Christ for a second crucifixion, this time in the human family. The power-mongers from corporate, military, and political life have imposed this lunatic burden of nuclear war on everyone, and put us all on a kind of nuclear death row.

"Where do we look for hope, as the world sinks deeper into social psychosis? To the people alone, particularly to people of faith. In the past, the people alone have checked the mad ambitions of pharaohs. Today, those who try to follow Jesus through their lives and actions can do the same. If we wake up, and live out the nonviolent resistance exemplified by Jesus, we can discard the biblical metaphors of the green and dry wood and let Jesus live again."

My God, my God, why have you forsaken me?

(MARK 15:34; MATTHEW 27:46)

The last question uttered by Jesus before his death is the hardest question of all, the question of Job, the question of Dachau, the question of Rwanda, the question of death row, the question of the world's starving masses.

"At noon darkness came over the whole land until three in the afternoon," Mark writes. "And at three o'clock Jesus cried out in a loud voice, 'Eloi, Eloi, lema sabachthani?' which is translated, 'My God, my God, why have you forsaken me?' Then Jesus gave out a loud cry and breathed his last" (Mark 15:33–37). Mark emphasizes the question by giving the Aramaic version, while Matthew mixes in Hebrew.

Jesus feels totally abandoned, completely rejected, and spiritually isolated. The question reveals his bitter sense of God's absence just when he needs God the most.

But Jesus does not renounce God. He does not say, "I was wrong. God does not exist. God is a myth, a lie, a ghost." He does not reject God. Rather, Jesus remains in complete relationship with God. He addresses God—and that is the clue to his extraordinary faith and forgiving love.

Any first-century Jew would recognize this question as the first line of Psalm 22, a prayer of lament and desolation. Rabbis often invoked an entire psalm by citing its first line. Psalm 22 moves from anguish and abandonment to sorrow and grief to hope and redemption to exultation and joy. Because first-century Christians would know this psalm and its jubilant outcome by heart, the Evangelists offer this psalm as a key to the mind and heart of Jesus at the moment of his death. Like the psalmist, Jesus turned from despair to hope, from doubt to faith, from sadness to joy:

> My God, my God, why have you forsaken me, far from my prayer, from the words of my cry? O my God, I cry out by day, and you answer not; by night, and there is no relief for me. . . . But I am a worm, not a man, the scorn of men, despised by the people. All who see me scoff at me; they mock me with parted lips, they wag their heads, "He relied on the Lord; let God deliver him, let God rescue him, if God loves him." . . . A pack of evildoers closes in upon me. They have pierced my hands and my feet. I can count all my bones. But you, O Lord, be not far from

me. O my help, hasten to aid me. . . . I will proclaim your name to my brothers and sisters. I will praise you in the midst of the assembly. I will fulfill my vows. . . . All the ends of the earth shall remember and turn to the Lord. For dominion is the Lord's and God rules the nations. To God alone shall bow down all who sleep in the earth. Before God shall bend all who go down into the dust. To God my soul shall live.

This bitter question invites us to contemplate the crucified Christ and to meditate on his heart and attitude. It leads us to ask, "How have we abandoned Christ? How do we forsake Christ in the world today? Do we serve Christ in those who suffer around us—from the sick and homebound, to the hungry and homeless, to the imprisoned and dying? Do we help Christ in the crucified peoples of the world, or do we turn our backs on them, mock them, walk by them, and ignore their cry?"

The question is critical because sooner or later, when our hour comes, at that moment of death, we too may feel abandoned by God. If we share in the life and death of Jesus, we, too, may share in the feeling of God's absence, precisely when we most desire God's presence. But like Jesus, we too can dare to move through Psalm 22 and place our faith, hope, and trust in the God of Life. This is the spiritual journey, finally, to surrender ourselves to God, to say with the crucified Christ, "Into your hands, I commend my spirit."

NINETEEN

THE
RESURRECTION

Woman, why are you weeping? Whom are
you looking for?

(JOHN 20:15)

This question brings us to the heart of the good news of Jesus
Christ: The story does not end at the cross. Death does not get
the last word. Life is stronger than death. Love is stronger than fear.
Truth is stronger than lies. Nonviolence is stronger than violence.
Peace, justice, and compassion are stronger than all the forces of war,
injustice, and hate. God is stronger than the war-making empire.

Jesus is alive! He is not dead. He has been raised. This is the
shocking, breathtaking afterword to the Gospel. The story continues.

The discipleship journey goes on—and the questions do not end. Jesus rises from the dead and starts questioning us all over again!

On Sunday morning, the first day of the week, Mary Magdalene goes to the tomb to anoint the body of Jesus but finds the tomb empty. According to John's account, she runs, finds the disciples, tells them, and returns with them. After they leave, she stays outside the tomb, weeping. When she looks into the tomb, she sees two angels in white. "Woman, why are you weeping?" they ask her. "They have taken my Lord," she answers, "and I don't know where they have laid him."

Turning around, she sees Jesus but does not recognize him. "Woman, why are you weeping?" Jesus asks her. "Whom are you looking for?"

Mary thinks he is the gardener, so she asks him where he has taken the body of Jesus. "Mary," he says to her. "Rabbouni!" she cries out. "Do not cling to me," he says, "for I have not yet ascended to the Father. But go to my brothers and tell them I am going to my Father and your Father, to my God and your God." So Mary goes and tells the disciples, "I have seen the Lord!" (John 20:1–18).

At his first encounter with this faithful disciple, the risen Jesus asks two profound questions. First, why are you weeping? Mary's tears are to be expected, but the risen Jesus sounds perplexed. He expected the disciples to believe him when he announced that he would rise on the third day. He wants us to recognize him and rejoice with him. We have heard the second question before. As the discipleship journey began and ended, Jesus asked, "Whom are you looking for?" Now he asks it a third time, only now Mary gives the answer he has been looking for. She addresses him as "my Lord." With that, he calls her by name, she recognizes and worships him, and he sends her forth as an apostle to announce the good news of Resurrection.

The risen Jesus continues to question us. "Why are you weeping? Whom are you looking for?" If we answer like Mary—that we weep because of his crucifixion and for today's crucified peoples, and that we are looking for him and for his resurrection among the poor and the marginalized—he will call us by name, we will see him, and he will send us out with a new mission to announce the new life of Resurrection.

The Resurrection means our survival is guaranteed. Like Jesus, we too can give our lives to resisting the forces of death, to practicing creative nonviolence, to speaking out against war, and to trusting in God, knowing that, even if the worst happens, we too shall rise to new life in God's house of peace. The Resurrection summons us to take up where Jesus left off, to enter the discipleship story, to risk our lives on behalf of suffering humanity, to renounce violence and take on suffering in the struggle for justice and disarmament, to forgive those who hurt us, and to have faith in the God of Resurrection.

We need weep no more. We need only recognize the risen Christ in our midst and hear him send us forth to announce the good news of Resurrection peace.

> Concerning the resurrection of the dead,
> have you not read what was said to you by
> God, "I am the God of Abraham, the God
> of Isaac, and the God of Jacob"?
>
> (MATTHEW 22:31–32)

The Sadducees, who did not believe in the Resurrection, questioned Jesus about the meaning of Resurrection shortly before he was arrested. He told them that they were misled because they knew neither the Scriptures nor the power of God. "Concerning the resurrection of the dead, have you not read what was said to you by God, 'I am the God of Abraham, the God of Isaac, and the God of Jacob'? God is not the God of the dead but the God of the living" (Matthew 22:29–32).

The Resurrection changes everything, including the meaning of life, our purpose on earth, our attitude toward the world, our understanding of God. God is not dead but alive, not the God of the dead but the God of the living, not the God of Crucifixion but the God of Resurrection. To explain the Resurrection, Jesus recalls God's announcement that God is the God of our holy ancestors, Abraham, Isaac, and Jacob, who are alive and well at home with the living God in the promised land of the living.

If we translate the question using contemporary saints, I think Jesus would name God as the God of Dorothy Day, the God of Martin Luther King Jr., the God of Mother Teresa, the God of Mahatma Gandhi, the God of Jean Donovan, the God of Oscar Romero.

Have we not read that God says, "God is the God of Abraham, Isaac, and Jacob"? We may indeed have read this before, but if we listen to his question again, we realize that God is alive, that the saints are alive, and that God is a living God of living saints. Following the logic of the question, we know that our deceased relatives, friends, loved ones, and heroes have not vanished but are alive. All the earth's poor and oppressed live on in paradise, happy and at peace. They live on in the new life of resurrection.

We can pretend we have not read these words, but if so we deny the reality of death and the existence of God. But then we fool ourselves, because we will still die and will still encounter the living God. We delude ourselves by pretending that we are not going to die. Deep down we may be mystified or terrified by this great upcoming event. When will we die? How will we die? What will happen when we die?

Jesus tells us that the holy ones of God live on in God's reign of perfect peace and love. They are in a better place, restored to health, perfectly whole in the fullness of life. Then God raises Jesus from the dead, vindicating him and his way of nonviolence, and Jesus reveals the Resurrection to us. So we are going to die, but if we are baptized and spend our lives in loving service as Christ's disciples, we too shall rise. We will be welcomed into that paradise. We will meet Abraham, Isaac, and Jacob, as well as Dorothy Day, Mother Teresa, and Martin Luther King Jr. We will laugh with our relatives and friends once more, share an eternal wedding banquet party together, and rejoice with our beloved, risen Lord. We will discover that we are more alive than ever and that our beloved God is indeed the God of the living.

> I am the Resurrection and the life; whoever believes in me, even if he dies, will live, and everyone who lives and believes in me will never die; do you believe this?

(JOHN 11:26)

Do we believe in Resurrection? Do we believe that Jesus is the Resurrection and the life? Do we believe that after we die, like Jesus, we too shall rise and live on in God's paradise of peace? These are the ultimate questions of the Gospel.

When Jesus is summoned to Bethany to heal his dear friend Lazarus, who is sick, he does not leave immediately. According to John's Gospel, when he finally arrives, Lazarus has already been dead for four days. Tradition held that after four days the soul was gone. It was too late. Nothing could be done. Martha, his sister, reprimands Jesus: "Lord, if you had been here, my brother would not have died. But even now, I know that whatever you ask of God, God will give you."

"Your brother will rise," Jesus tells Martha.

"I know he will rise, in the Resurrection on the last day," Martha replies.

"I am the Resurrection and the life; whoever believes in me, even if he dies, will live, and everyone who lives and believes in me will never die; do you believe this?"

Martha has just confessed her faith in Resurrection, but Jesus pushes her further. "Yes, Lord," she answers. "I have come to believe that you are the Messiah, the Son of God, the one who is coming into the world." And with that expression of faith, Jesus approaches the tomb and commands the crowds to take away the stone.

Suddenly Martha changes her tune. "Lord, by now there will be a stench! He has been dead for four days!"

Martha was probably one of Jesus' closest friends and most devout disciples, given her declaration of faith. (In fact, one could ask, Why did Jesus not award Martha "the keys to the kingdom," as he did to Peter for making a similar statement of faith?)

Martha professes her faith in Jesus and in the Resurrection, but at the moment of his confrontation with death, she resisted Jesus and protests his action on behalf of life. When it comes to the moment of truth, Martha, like all of us, tries to stop the Resurrection of Lazarus.

Why does Martha try to prevent Jesus from raising Lazarus from the dead? Because she does not want Resurrection! She does not want the trouble, the mess, the scandal, and the political implications. She cannot accept that much hope, that much freedom, that much shocking faith. Despite her tears and grief, like the professional mourners hanging around the tomb, she has grown comfortable with death. She is at peace with the culture, the empire, the reality of death. Despite her words of faith, deep down Martha knows that death does get the last word. There is nothing that can be done in the face of death. Lazarus is dead. Our loved ones die. Famine, war, disease leave a trail of death—and that's life. Death is the living end.

Jesus asks his question because he knows Martha's love and faith, but he needs to hear her articulate it publicly. He also knows that she and everyone else believes ultimately not in the God of life but in the power of death.

Martha tries to stop Jesus from raising Lazarus because she knows instinctively that if Jesus raises Lazarus, everything is up for grabs. If he raises her brother, there can be no doubt that their friend Jesus is the God of life, standing in their midst. She knows that reality is not as it appears. Martha knows that if Jesus brings life back to her brother, she will have to move from merely professing words of faith in Jesus to enacting deeds of faith by following the life-giving Jesus as he confronts death, undergoes death, and enters the new life of Resurrection.

When the people take away the stone, Jesus offers a prayer of gratitude and calls Lazarus to come out of the tomb. But Lazarus is still bound hand and foot by burial clothes, so Jesus commands them, "Unbind him and let him go free." We are never told whether or not they obey his command. Lazarus could still be there. If Lazarus represents the human race, oppressed by the culture of death, as some scholars suggest, then the God of life still waits for us to unbind humanity from the trappings of death and set it free.

Do we believe in Jesus and the Resurrection? If we really believe in Jesus, his Resurrection, and the truth of Resurrection, then we too should stop opposing Resurrection and start welcoming it. Instead of condemning those who oppose war, the death penalty, nuclear weapons, and the forces of death, or those who support life and bring life, we should join the nonviolent campaign against death, roll away the stone of death in our culture, and let each other go free to live life to the full.

This is what Martha learns when she says, "Yes, Lord" to the great question of Jesus. It is the lesson that awaits us all.

What are you discussing as you walk along?
What things?

(LUKE 24:17, 19)

I often think that if I were betrayed, denied, and abandoned by close friends, then brutally tortured and capitally executed by the government, and then asked by God to rise from the dead, I would not want to go back. I would feel deeply hurt, angry, and resentful. I would nurse a bitter grudge for several thousand years before I would ever consider returning to the horrible world. So I would beg God, "Please, do not send me back there. I don't want to see those awful people ever again!" But if God said, "No, Son, you must go back there," my first instinct upon returning would be to yell at everyone for letting me down, abandoning me, hurting me, and killing me.

Jesus does nothing of the sort. He rises from the dead and greets his friends with perfect peace, gentleness, loving kindness, and, most of all, forgiveness. No mean words. No anger. No resentment. No grudge. No bitterness. He does not say, "Why did you let me down? Why did you deny me and abandon me? Why did you let them kill me?" Rather, Jesus appears to his friends, who hide in fear behind locked doors, and greets them with the loving words, "Peace be with you." He shows them his wounds, then repeats his greeting, "Peace be with you." Finally, he breathes on them and says, "Receive the Holy Spirit. As God sent me, so I send you."

Years ago I celebrated Easter Sunday with a small liturgy and picnic in a New York park with my Jesuit friends Daniel Berrigan and Bob Keck. After reading the Gospel account of the Resurrection, I confessed to my friends my inner violence and resentment and my sheer wonder and awe at Jesus' nonviolence and forgiveness, revealed in all its glory in the very fact of his Resurrection, that he would even be willing to return, much less offer forgiveness and love.

After some silence, Daniel replied, "Jesus didn't have a mean bone in his body."

When I entered the Jesuits in 1982, the novice master sent us out in groups of twos and threes for a thirty-minute walk each day for what St. Ignatius called "spiritual conversation." This tradition started over four hundred years ago. We could talk only about Jesus, God, the Scriptures, the saints, and prayer.

On one of my first walks, the other novices and I spoke about the risen Jesus' appearance to the disciples on the road to Emmaus. According to Luke, it was the first day of the week, and the two dejected disciples were walking on the road from Jerusalem to the little village of Emmaus. The risen Jesus starts to walk alongside them, but they do not recognize him.

"What are you discussing as you walk along?" Jesus asks them. They stop in their tracks, looking downcast, Luke reports. One of them says, "Are you the only visitor to Jerusalem who does not know of the things that have taken place there in these days?"

"What things?" Jesus asks.

As we walked along that day, my friend Joe Sands said this was the most amazing question in the entire Gospel. He shook his head with astonishment at the humility, modesty, and patience of the risen Christ.

"Imagine!" Joe said. "Jesus has just been betrayed, denied, abandoned, arrested, tried, tortured, and executed. He dies, rises from the dead, returns to Jerusalem, and meets his friends once again. If it were me, I would shout, 'You wouldn't believe what just happened to me! I died and now I've risen from the dead! I went to heaven and now I'm back and it was totally amazing!' I would be doing all the talking."

But Jesus is completely different. Instead of talking about himself, he asks about them. "What are you discussing as you walk along?" He draws them out, lets them speak, and hears their story. Jesus remains first and foremost a listener.

When they ask him why he does not know about the things that have happened, he simply asks in return, "What things?" It is one of the most understated questions of the Gospel, if not of all literature. Jesus is detached, free, loving. He has no need to assert himself, prove himself, justify himself, or accomplish anything. He is the embodiment of peace, patience, and mindfulness.

Jesus knows that in telling our stories, we find his resurrected presence, enter his Gospel story, feel our hearts burn within us, and run to share the good news with others.

The questions are instructive. We are full of stories, excitements, sorrows, and despair. God walks beside us through life, but we do not recognize God in our midst. God wants to hear our stories. God is eager to listen to us. But God has an even better story to tell.

What will we tell the risen Christ as he asks about us and walks with us? What do we discuss as we walk through our lives? Like the dejected disciples, what "things" have happened in the world that fill us with despair, doubt, and sorrow?

These questions reveal the heart and spirit of the risen Jesus. They invite us to tell him our story. Eventually they may lead him to reveal himself to us and tell us his story.

Was it not necessary that the Messiah should suffer these things and enter into his glory?

(LUKE 24:26)

After listening to the two downcast disciples on that road to Emmaus, the risen Jesus asks them pointedly, "Was it not necessary that the Messiah should suffer these things and enter into his glory?"

From the standpoint of the Evangelists, this question cuts to the chase. It is the climax of the Gospel. It puts the cross in our face and demands our response. Do we or do we not support Jesus and his way of the cross? Do we or do we not agree that his way of loving nonviolence, creative resistance to evil, and selfless martyrdom are the path to God? If we do support Jesus, and if we do agree that peaceful, nonviolent living is the path of God, will we follow him on his course of pain and glory?

The answer in our hearts is loud and clear: No! It was not necessary for the Messiah to suffer these things in order to enter into his glory. There had to be a better way. Jesus did not deserve such a terrible outcome. He was such a good, decent, noble, kind, loving, gentle, truthful, wise person. He could have lived until old age, like the Buddha, and died peacefully, and then could have risen to new life. He could have avoided that scene in the Jerusalem Temple, in the first place, when the only possible outcome was arrest, torture, and execution. He could have kept Peter from defending him with the sword at his hour of arrest. He could have spoken up to the authorities and convinced them of his innocence and Godliness. He could have avoided torture, and he could have avoided such a horrible death.

Apparently God's ways are not our ways. Jesus was determined from an early age to embody divine nonviolence. He would not be passive, he would not be violent, he would not be silent, he would not defend himself, he would not run away from trouble, he would not shrink from death. Jesus sought God and God's reign first and foremost, and he knew that meant running headlong into trouble and clashing with the world. He knew that God's way of truthful, suffering love would disarm humanity and save the human race.

Jesus was convinced, from his study of the Scriptures, his observation of the world, and his experience of God, that suffering love is the only way to change the world. His suffering and death on the cross—undergone in a spirit of perfect love, profound nonviolence, boundless compassion, and infinite forgiveness—have drawn the sympathy of the whole human race, more than any other human life or death. Nearly every human being knows about him, his teachings, his life, his death. Nearly every human being has considered his claim of divinity. Nearly every human being knows of the announcement of his Resurrection. Indeed, his suffering has turned him into the world's greatest, and only, nonviolent, loving Messiah. Few people have come close to his perfect nonviolence.

"How foolish you are! How slow of heart to believe all the prophets spoke," Jesus tells the despairing, Emmaus-bound disciples. Having entered the new life of Resurrection, Jesus now sees the redemption he has gained for the world. "Beginning with Moses and all the prophets," Luke writes, "he interpreted to them what referred to him in all the scriptures." When they near their town, they beg him to join them for dinner. "And it happened," Luke tells, "while he was with them at table, he took bread, said the blessings, broke it, and gave it to them. With that their eyes were opened and they recognized him but he vanished from their sight. They said to each other, 'Were not our hearts burning within us while he spoke to us on the way as he opened the Scriptures to us?' So they turned around and headed back to Jerusalem, full of hope" (Luke 24:25–35).

The risen Christ asks each one of us this difficult question: "Was it not necessary . . . ?" And sooner or later, we all have to face this ultimate question. We can dismiss the cross as pious idealism. We can ignore his life and death and go about our business. But we do so to our loss and the loss of the world. Instead, we are summoned to carry on his work, to join him and participate with him in his redemption of humanity and disarmament of the world.

If we ponder the cruelty of Jesus' death, the ongoing crucifixion of humanity, the witness of history's martyrs, and the transforming power of creative nonviolence, there is no ignoring the fact that suffering love for the sake of truth and justice is not only the high road, the way to peace and justice, and the path to God, but it is also the only practical way to resolve violence and injustice. It is the way to become human and thus share in the divine. It is the way of God, the way of salvation, the way of the Messiah.

This question will make our hearts burn with the fire of love. The more we ponder it, and the more we accept his truth, the more we will find ourselves like the Emmaus disciples: turning around from our journey to despair and taking up the road to hope. We will discover the strength to accept the cross of Christ, to renounce violence and war, and to adopt his life of creative nonviolent resistance to evil. We may find ourselves as his partners in the cosmic work of salvation, redemption, and disarmament. We might even be willing to accept the pain of Gospel peacemaking in order to participate in the Messiah's nonviolent transformation of the world and enter the glory of his company.

Why are you troubled? Why do questions arise in your hearts?

(LUKE 24:38)

Although the risen Jesus appeared before his disciples that first Easter Sunday evening, with greetings of peace, the disciples were startled and terrified. They thought they were seeing a ghost, Luke reports. This could not be their friend who was just tortured and executed, could it? "Why are you troubled?" he asks them. "Why do questions arise in your hearts?"

Here, in this ultimate act of divine revelation and action in the world—the Resurrection of the peacemaking Messiah—the disciples are not only troubled, but they are also suddenly full of questions. "How can you be alive?" they ask. "Weren't you just executed? How did you get in here? Who are you? What's going on?"

The Resurrection is first of all deeply troubling. The more we ponder the Resurrection of Jesus, the more disturbed we feel. As we meditate over the mystery of the Resurrection, questions begin to rise within us. Like those first disciples, we wonder how Jesus can be alive when he was so thoroughly killed. Like the troubled disciples, we too begin to make the terrifying connection between the cross and the Resurrection. If Jesus is God and he was martyred on the cross but has now been raised from the dead, then all his discipleship talk about taking up the cross and following him is not only true but it is intended for us, right now, today, this very moment.

Jesus' Resurrection means that we too will rise from the dead, that our survival is guaranteed, that we will live on like Jesus in perfect peace, that we will enter God's realm, that we will share eternal life, and that—O my God!—we too will have to risk the cross and martyrdom!

No wonder the disciples were troubled!

The Resurrection of Jesus means we have no more excuses. We can no longer avoid the cross. Everything Jesus said is true: God is trustworthy. God will take care of us, and we will be happy forever. All that is required is that we too lay down our lives, as he did, for suffering humanity. We need to take up our own crosses and offer our lives for God and for the struggle for justice and peace.

This prospect is terrifying. The disciples were troubled because they were afraid, and so are we. And, like the disciples, we too are suddenly full of questions. What does all this mean? we ask one another. Why does God make us suffer? Why do some children die? Why does evil prosper? Why do we have to give our lives? Why can't God just make everything better with the blink of an eye?

Precisely at this moment of confusion, the one who asks the real questions questions our questions. But he does not leave us hanging. The risen Christ offers a clue to the answer. "Look at my hands and my feet, that it is I myself," he tells us, as he told the first disciples. "Touch me and see, because a ghost does not have flesh and bones as you can see I have." And Luke concludes, "As he said this, he showed them his hands and his feet."

The answer is there. We need not be troubled. We need not raise questions in our hearts. All we need do is contemplate the hands and feet of the crucified, risen one. As we see the reality of his wounds and accept the truth that he is alive and well, we begin to welcome and receive the peace he offers. We let go of our troubles and our questions, celebrate his Resurrection, and accept his invitation to new life. Like those first disciples, we too are filled with hope. We go forward following his footsteps, trusting his words, continuing his work, living in peace.

Have you anything here to eat?

(LUKE 24:41)

The Jewish culture of first-century Palestine revolved around the synagogue and the dinner table. The Gospels typically place Jesus in the context of food. From his fasting in the desert and his temptation to turn stones into bread, to his first appearance at the wedding feast at Cana, where he and his disciples polished off the wine, to his miraculous multiplications of loaves and fishes, to his discourses on the "bread of life," to his final dramatic act at the Last Supper, where he offered bread as his own body, Jesus speaks again and again about food. He centers himself on the meal as a holy encounter with God and the locus for human community.

On the road to Emmaus on that Easter Sunday, the disciples only recognized Jesus when he took bread, blessed it, broke it, and gave it to them. He had apparently done this so many times before that they suddenly realized it was Jesus.

Later, when Jesus appeared to the disciples on that evening and asked about their doubts and questions, they became "incredulous for joy and were amazed," according to Luke. Then, just at that moment, Jesus made a simple request: "Have you anything here to eat?"

Jesus was hungry! Luke's Gospel begins with Jesus hungering for food in the desert. Now, as the Gospel closes, he is still hungering for food. In response, "they gave him a piece of baked fish," Luke writes, "and he took it and ate it in front of them."

"These are my words that I spoke to you while I was still with you, that everything written about me in the law of Moses and in the prophets and psalms must be fulfilled," Jesus said. "Then he opened their minds to understand the Scriptures. 'Thus it is written that the Messiah would suffer and rise from the dead on the third day, and that repentance for the forgiveness of sins would be preached in his name to all the nations, beginning from Jerusalem. You are witnesses of these things' " (Luke 24:44–48).

We may think that this simple question does not require consideration. But like any of Jesus' questions, it can lead us deeper into the mind and heart of Christ. A similar question appears in John's Resurrection account, so the Evangelists are trying to say something to us about the risen Christ, his hunger, the Eucharist, and serving him in the world's hungry.

Over fifteen hundred years ago, St. Benedict wrote that Christ comes to us disguised in every stranger knocking at the door asking for help, hospitality, and food. The duty of the Christian, he taught, is to welcome Christ in the world's hungry and needy, to feed him and serve him. Then he will open our minds to understand the Scriptures.

The disciples fed the hungry risen Jesus, but only after he asked for food. Today the hungry Christ continues to cry out for food in the world's starving masses. Over eight hundred million people are chronically malnourished. As Mother Teresa and Dorothy Day write, they are Jesus, asking, "Have you anything here to eat?" Our answer will be the test of our faith.

"Have you anything here to eat?" This question can lead us to volunteer at soup kitchens and homeless shelters to serve the hungry and needy in our local community, but it will also push us to advocate on behalf of the starving masses for an end to hunger itself. If our government can send people to walk on the moon, we can certainly end world hunger. There is plenty of food on earth for everyone. But the richer nations must stop hoarding the food and resources of the poorer nations. The Gospel demands that we share our excess with all those in need. Analysts insist that if the First World nations stop spending billions of dollars on war and weapons of mass destruction and instead spend those funds for long-term programs to address starvation and its related diseases, we could end world hunger in two weeks.

Not one child on the planet should ever go to sleep hungry. This should be our highest national and international priority. Christians everywhere have a holy obligation to feed the hungry Christ. His question remains.

Have you come to believe because you
have seen me?

(JOHN 20:29)

The apostle Thomas was absent that Easter Sunday night when
the risen Jesus appeared. "We have seen the Lord!" the disciples
tell him. But Thomas refuses to believe that Jesus is alive. "Unless I
see the mark of the nails in his hands and put my finger into his side,
I will not believe."

A week later, when Jesus appears again, he says to Thomas, "Put
your finger here and see my hands, and bring your hand and put it
into my side, and do not be unbelieving, but believe." Thomas answers, "My Lord and my God!" Jesus' next question must have
haunted Thomas for the rest of his life. "Have you come to believe
because you have seen me? Blessed are those who have not seen and
have belief."

This climactic question calls for reflection on two aspects of our
relationship to Christ: seeing him and believing in him. Where have
we seen Christ, and do we really believe in him anyway? Thomas saw
the risen Jesus and became a believer. But Jesus especially blesses those
who believe in him but have not seen him. That's us.

Even though we may not actually see the bodily Jesus with our
own physical eyes, as Thomas did, if we look through the eyes of
faith, we will see Christ present in the world today.

When we see the hungry and the homeless, we see Christ.

When we see the sick and the dying, we see Christ.

When we see the imprisoned, we see Christ.

When we see the suffering poor and oppressed and their work
for liberation and restoration, we see Christ. When we see those
struggling for justice, working for peace, and speaking the truth, we
see Christ. When we see the wounds of the broken, crucified peoples
of the earth, we see Christ. When we look upon another human being as a sister or a brother, we see Christ. Christ is everywhere around
us, if we dare open our eyes and look for him.

To see Christ in one another, though, we have to believe, which gets to the heart of the question. Do we really believe in Jesus? If we do not, we will not see him. We will just go through the motions. But if we believe in him with all our hearts, we will not only see him, but we will change our lives and start acting more and more like him. Indeed, we will give our lives for his reign of peace and justice, just as he did.

When Thomas finally came around to believing, he addressed Jesus as "my Lord and my God." Unfortunately, we have lost the original power of those words. In the last decade of the first century, the Roman emperor Diocletian ordered that he was to be addressed as "my Lord and my God." The law stated that he was god and the empire would not tolerate any other gods. If someone refused to address the emperor by his divine title, or worse, named someone else with this divine title, that person would be immediately executed. So when Thomas called Jesus "my Lord and my God," second-century readers of John's Gospel would have gasped, realizing that Thomas disobeyed the emperor and faced execution. During the first three centuries of the church's history, Christians were routinely martyred for refusing to worship the emperor and obey the empire's laws and for calling Jesus "my Lord and my God." They had not known Jesus in person before his crucifixion, but they would have believed in him, suffered and died for him, and been, as John's Gospel declares, blessed.

If we believe as Thomas learned to believe, we too will declare that Jesus is "our Lord and our God." But that declaration of faith will hold social and political consequences. We too will have to disobey the laws that violate God's law. Since we obey our Lord and God Jesus, we will love our enemies and refuse to support our government's wars or its idolatrous nuclear weapons. We will not place our security in our government or its weapons of mass destruction but in the risen Jesus. We will practice divine obedience to Jesus and civil disobedience against the false gods of war and systemic injustice. We will pay the price for our faith and discover what it means to be blessed.

Children, have you caught anything to eat?
(JOHN 21:5)

Everything appears to come to an end for Jesus at the Last Supper, but Jesus turns the law of nature upside down by rising from the dead and surprising us by offering the First Breakfast. This touching scene symbolizes the dawn of new life, the promise of Resurrection.

John's Gospel reports that Simon Peter and several other disciples are out fishing on the Sea of Galilee, several weeks after the Resurrection. They have been out in the boat all night and have caught nothing. "And morning came, and Jesus was standing on the shore," John writes. This idyllic scene portrays the risen Jesus standing by the beautiful sea at the break of day, radiating peace and joy. Betrayal, abandonment, pain, torture, and death are all behind him now. He now embodies the God of life.

Jesus calls out to the fishermen: "Children, have you caught anything to eat?" "No," they answer, not recognizing him. "Cast the net over the right side of the boat and you will find something," Jesus then instructs. When they do, they are not able to pull in the net because there are so many fish. "It is the Lord," the beloved disciple tells Peter, who jumps into the sea and swims toward Jesus.

When they arrive on shore, they see "a charcoal fire with fish on it and bread." "Bring some of the fish you just caught," Jesus tells them. "Come, have breakfast."

This scene offers a new unfolding, a deeper revelation of the life and gentle spirit of the risen Christ. I am amazed that, after rising from the dead, Jesus inquires if his friends have had anything to eat and then proceeds to make breakfast for them. If I had loved perfectly and practiced steadfast nonviolence only to be betrayed, denied, abandoned, condemned, tortured, and executed, I would not want to return, much less make breakfast for anyone. I might be angry, judgmental, resentful, and bitter. But Jesus shows none of that. As the God of peace, the God of life, the God of infinite compassion, he is without any trace of anger, judgment, resentment, or bitterness. He is way beyond such worldly failings. The risen Jesus is not some mean, unreachable divinity. Rather, in this intimate human scene, we see a gentle, caring friend.

Jesus calls the disciples "children." John is making it clear that this figure standing by the shore is more than meets the eye; he is not just a simple Galilean who knows how to catch fish. Rather, here is the Creator, our heavenly parent, who addresses us lovingly as his beloved children.

Earlier, John took pains to point out in detail that when Peter three times denied knowing Jesus, Peter was warming himself around "a charcoal fire" in the courtyard of the Roman Empire. Peter was making himself comfortable in the house of death, while Jesus was inside being interrogated and tortured. Now, by contrast, Jesus invites Simon Peter to warm himself and feed himself in the house of life, around his own charcoal fire, in the paradise of a beautiful new day by the shining Sea of Galilee. Jesus restores Peter to his friendship and reveals the intimate, loving care that marks God's realm of peace and eternal life.

As we ponder the question "Children, have you caught anything to eat?" we can first imagine Jesus standing there in perfect peace as the sun rises over the Sea of Galilee. That contemplative image alone can heal us, disarm us, and console us. As we hear ourselves addressed as "children," we may find, contrary to our all-American independent individualism, that we like it. We may feel freer to be who we really are, children of a benevolent, loving Creator-Parent. Finally, we may be heartened by his concern for our welfare. Every parent is mindful of their child, especially if children are hungry. Like any doting parent, God-in-Jesus is trying to take care of us. Even though he has just risen from the dead, in the greatest event in human history, his focus is not on himself but on his friends, on us. He wants to make sure we are all right. His care is astonishing, and it will draw us closer to him in intimate love, as well as inspire us to show the same care, concern, and intimate love to one another and meet one another's needs. The question and our imitation of the questioner will lead us, in others, to practice resurrection.

> Simon, son of John, do you love me more
> than these? Do you love me? Do you love
> me?

(JOHN 21:15–17)

The conclusion of John's Gospel offers the most intimate, touching, beautiful question of all. Throughout our lives, we look to heaven and ask God, "Do you love me?" Here God turns the question on us and asks, not once but three times, if we love God.

Sitting by the charcoal fire after that intimate breakfast by the Sea of Galilee, Jesus turns to Peter, addressing him by his prediscipleship name, Simon, and asks him point-blank, "Simon, son of John, do you love me more than these?" In the original Greek, the Evangelist uses the word *agape*, meaning unconditional, sacrificial, nonviolent love, the love that leads one to lay down one's life for one's friends. Peter cannot profess such love. "Yes, Lord, you know I love you," he responds, using the Greek word *philia*, referring to the ordinary love between brothers and sisters and friends, not the all-inclusive, suffering love of God. Jesus accepts his answer, though, and missions him, saying "Feed my lambs." The Greek word for lambs poetically refers to "martyrs."

A second time Jesus asks, "Simon, son of John, do you love me?" Peter answers, "Yes, Lord, you know that I love you." "Tend my sheep," Jesus tells him.

Finally, Jesus asks a third time, "Simon, son of John, do you love me?" "Lord, you know everything," Peter answers, "you know that I love you." "Feed my sheep," Jesus commands. "Amen, amen, I say to you, when you were younger, you used to dress yourself and go where you wanted; but when you grow old, you will stretch out your hands and someone will lead you where you would rather not go. Follow me" (John 21:15–20).

In this intimate exchange, the risen Jesus gives Peter three opportunities to reconcile with him, reversing his three statements of denial with three expressions of *agape* and fidelity. It is an act of forgiveness and reconciliation on Jesus' part, and it exemplifies the new life in God's realm of Resurrection.

But even more poignantly, this climactic exchange reveals a vulnerable Jesus in need of love and affirmation. He wants to know if Peter—and by extension, all of us—loves him. Jesus does not come across as a proud, tough, arrogant, dominating male. Instead he is open, humble, needy. He reveals God's desire for our love.

This moving invitation suggests that, in the end, all we have to do is let God love us and tell God how much we love God. If we can do that, everything else will be taken care of. The point of the spiritual life is to live rooted and grounded in this intimate, loving relationship with Jesus and our Creator. From this intimate relationship, all things will be resolved. All questions will be answered. All things will be possible. All will be well. Indeed, this life of divine love foreshadows life in the reign of God, where all people will live in an eternal, loving relationship with our beloved God. Jesus simply does not want us to wait until we die before we repent and are reconciled. Rather, he invites us to live in that realm of *agape* and Resurrection, here and now, by sharing his life of *agape*.

As we tell Jesus that we love him, he missions us to carry on his work of disarming, healing, and reconciling love. Love leads us to reach out in loving care for suffering humanity. The spiritual life then is not just a vertical relationship between us "down here" and God "up there," but a horizontal relationship among all of us, a relationship of *agape* toward every human being treating each one as our very sister or brother. Like Peter, we begin to feed and tend one another, meaning we care for one another, meet one another's needs, guide one another to peaceful pastures, and defend the weak and helpless from the forces of violence and death. This great life of *agape* will motivate us to give ourselves away on behalf of the suffering poor and oppressed peoples of the planet. It will embolden us to protect them through creative nonviolent resistance and give our lives for them, just as Jesus, as the Good Shepherd, gave his life for us.

Just as Jesus called Peter to follow him on the way of the cross, so too Jesus will call us to walk in his footsteps and lay down our lives with unconditional, sacrificial, nonviolent love for the poor and oppressed. As we demonstrate our love for Jesus by giving our lives for him in suffering humanity, we join his redemptive work of global transformation and begin to share with him in the new life of Resurrection. This will fill us with joy, just as he promised, because finally we have learned to love Jesus and to be with the One we love. We will dwell from now on in the peace of the risen Christ.

CONCLUSION

I t is hard to find words to describe the extraordinary life of Jesus of
Nazareth. Thousands of books have been written about him, yet
John's Gospel concludes that there is not enough room on the planet
to contain all the books that could be written about him.

One clumsy way to describe him is simply as a genius with a bril-
liant mind and a rare, luminous intelligence. We need to read his story
in the four Gospels every day if we want to understand his creative life,
his astonishing teachings, his miraculous works, his steadfast resistance to injustice, his courageous suffering and death, and his way out
of the world's violent madness. More, if we curtail the endless questions we ask God and listen to the questions Jesus asks us, we might
begin to enter his mind, learn how he thinks, find out what matters
most to him, and discover through his life the answers to life itself.

Regular contemplation of his unusual questions can lead us closer to his transforming spirit and can transform us, free us, and heal us. The questions may seem strange, dated, or even irrelevant at first, but returning to them, they come alive, melt our hearts, open our spirits, and enlighten our minds. They do not harangue; rather, they invite. They do not challenge; rather, they summon. They do not condemn; rather, they welcome us to the truth. If we sit with his questions, and don't rush to assert our own answers, we will receive the gift of wisdom.

In this age of despair, death, and destruction, we are terribly lost and confused. We do not know what to do. We ask our questions, then look to the media, the government, the military, the religious establishment, and the rich and famous for answers, but we find little relief, little hope, little truth. More and more, we realize our need for wisdom. If we are to survive individually and as a race, we need wisdom, the wisdom of God.

The questions of Jesus can open our minds to receive God's wisdom. As we ponder the mind of Christ, even put on the mind of Christ, as St. Paul urges, we begin to live wisely. We think of God, ponder the truth, see Christ in one another, and find new ways to heal our personal brokenness and our broken world. The Holy Wisdom of Christ teaches us God's way of nonviolence, compassion, justice, and peace. His wisdom and truth are the last hope for us all.

"A person is known better by his questions than his answers," Thomas Merton once wrote. The questions of Jesus can lead us on the journey to wisdom. They do not require immediate answers but, rather, attentive listening. If we listen to his questions, we may enter the spirit behind them and feel the love and presence within the questions themselves. If we dare live with these questions, our own inner rumblings, confusion, and questions may subside. We may find ourselves drawn into his healing, loving presence. We will begin to breathe again his Resurrection gift of peace. We will live in his spirit of truth, which he promised to send us, and discover the living word of God.

The disciples were constantly questioning Jesus, but really, they thought they knew all the answers. In reality, Jesus is the one who asks the right questions and the only one with authentic, truthful answers.

The night before he was killed, he told his disciples that they would weep, mourn, and grieve, but soon they would see him again and be filled with a joy that no one would ever take away. "On that day," Jesus told his friends, "you will not ask me any more questions" (John 16:22–23).

That day is here. We need not question Jesus anymore. All we have to do is listen to his questions, live with his questions, and let them lead us to the house of wisdom where we will find ourselves welcomed, at home, at last in the presence of the Great Answer.

APPENDIX

What are you looking for?   (1:38)

Do you believe because I told you I saw you under the fig tree?
   (1:50)

Woman, how does your concern affect me?   (2:4)

You are teachers of Israel and you do not understand this?   (3:10)

If I tell you about earthly things and you do not believe, how will
   you believe if I tell you about heavenly things?   (3:12)

Do you not say, "In four months the harvest will be here"?   (4:35)

Do you want to be well?   (5:6)

How can you believe, when you accept praise from one another and
   do not seek the praise that comes from the only God?   (5:44)

But if you do not believe the writings of Moses, how will you
   believe my words?   (5:47)

Where can we buy enough food for them to eat?   (6:5)

Does this shock you?   (6:61)

What if you were to see the Son of Humanity ascending to where
   he was before?   (6:62)

Do you also want to leave?   (6:67)

Did I not choose you twelve?   (6:70)

Is not one of you a devil?   (6:70)

Did not Moses give you the law?   (7:19)

Why are you trying to kill me?   (7:19)

If a man can receive circumcision on a Sabbath so that the law of
   Moses may not be broken, are you angry with me because I made
   a whole person well on a Sabbath?   (7:23)

Woman, where are they?   (8:10)

Has no one condemned you?   (8:10)

Why do you not understand what I am saying?   (8:43)

Can any of you charge me with sin?   (8:46)

If I am telling the truth, why do you not believe me?   (8:46)

Do you believe in the Son of Humanity?   (9:35)

For which of these good works are you trying to stone me?   (10:32)

Is it not written in your law, "I said, 'You are gods' "?   (10:34)

If it calls them gods to whom the word of God came, and scripture
   cannot be set aside, can you say that the one whom the Father has
   consecrated and sent into the world blasphemes because I said, "I
   am the Son of God"?   (10:36)

Are there not twelve hours in a day?   (11:9)

I am the resurrection and the life; whoever believes in me, even if he
   dies, will live and everyone who lives and believes in me will never
   die. Do you believe this?   (11:26)

Where have you laid him?   (11:34)

Did I not tell you that if you believe you will see the glory of God?
   (11:40)

What should I say? "Father, save me from this hour"?   (12:27)

Do you realize what I have done for you?   (13:12)

Will you lay down your life for me? (13:38)

If there were not many dwelling places in my Father's house, would I have told you that I am going to prepare a place for you? (14:2)

Have I been with you for so long a time and you still do not know me? (14:9)

How can you say, "Show us the Father"? (14:9)

Do you not believe that I am in the Father and the Father is in me? (14:10)

Are you discussing with one another what I said, "A little while and you will not see me, and again a little while and you will see me"? (16:19)

Do you believe now? (16:31)

Whom are you looking for? Whom are you looking for? (18:4,7)

Shall I not drink the cup that God gave me? (18:11)

Why ask me? (18:21)

If I have spoken wrongly, testify to the wrong; but if I have spoken rightly, why do you strike me? (18:23)

Do you say this on your own or have others told you about me? (18:34)

Woman, why are you weeping? Whom are you looking for? (20:15)

Have you come to believe because you have seen me? (20:29)

Children, have you caught anything to eat? (21:5)

Simon, son of John, do you love me more than these? Do you love me? Do you love me? (21:15–17)

What if I want him to remain until I come? What concern is it of yours? (21:22)

The Questions of Jesus in the Gospel of Mark

Why are you thinking such things in your hearts? (2:8)

Which is easier, to say to the paralytic, "Your sins are forgiven," or to say, "Rise, pick up your mat and walk"? (2:9)

Can the wedding guests fast while the bridegroom is with them? (2:19)

Have you never read what David did when he was in need and he
and his companions were hungry?

How he went into the house of God when Abiathar was high priest
and ate the bread of offering that only the priests could lawfully
eat, and shared it with his companions?   (2:25–26)

Is it lawful to do good on the Sabbath rather than to do evil, to save
life rather than to destroy it?   (3:4)

How can Satan drive out Satan?   (3:23)

Who are my mother and my brothers?   (3:33)

Do you not understand this parable? Then how will you understand
any of the parables?   (4:13)

Is a lamp brought in to be placed under a bushel basket or under a
bed and not to be placed on a lamp stand?   (4:21)

To what shall we compare the kingdom of God, or what parable can
we use for it?   (4:30)

Why are you terrified?   (4:40)

Do you not yet have faith?   (4:40)

What is your name?   (5:9)

Who has touched my clothes?   (5:30)

Why this commotion and weeping?   (5:39)

How many loaves do you have?   (6:38)

Are even you likewise without understanding? Do you not realize
that everything that goes into a person from outside cannot defile,
since it enters not the heart but the stomach and passes out into
the latrine?   (7:18)

How many loaves do you have?   (8:5)

Why does this generation seek a sign?   (8:12)

Why do you conclude that it is because you have no bread? Do you
not yet understand or comprehend? Are your hearts hardened? Do
you have eyes and not see, ears and not hear? And do you not
remember, when I broke the five loaves for the five thousand, how
many wicker baskets full of fragments you picked up? When I
broke the seven loaves for the four thousand, how many full
baskets of fragments did you pick up? Do you still not
understand?   (8:17–21)

Do you see anything?   (8:23)

Who do people say that I am?   (8:27)

But who do you say that I am?   (8:29)

What profit is there for one to gain the whole world and forfeit his life?   (8:36)

What could one give in exchange for his life?   (8:37)

Elijah will indeed come first and restore all things, yet how is it written regarding the Son of Humanity that he must suffer greatly and be treated with contempt?   (9:12)

What are you arguing about with them?   (9:16)

O faithless generation, how long will I be with you? How long will I endure you?   (9:19)

How long has this been happening to him?   (9:21)

What were you arguing about on the way?   (9:33)

Salt is good, but if salt becomes insipid, with what will you restore its flavor?   (9:50)

What did Moses command you?   (10:3)

Why do you call me good?   (10:18)

What do you wish me to do for you?   (10:36)

Can you drink the cup that I drink or be baptized with the baptism with which I am baptized?   (10:38)

What do you want me to do for you?   (10:51)

Is it not written: "My house shall be called a house of prayer for all peoples"?   (11:17)

Was John's baptism of heavenly or of human origin?   (11:30)

What will the owner of the vineyard do?   (12:9)

Have you not read this scripture passage: "The stone that the builders rejected has become the cornerstone; by the Lord has this been done, and it is wonderful in our eyes"?   (12:10–11)

Why are you testing me?   (12:15)

Whose image and inscription is this?   (12:16)

Are you not misled because you do not know the Scriptures or the power of God?   (12:24)

As for the dead being raised, have you not read in the Book of Moses, in the passage about the bush, how God told him, "I am the God of Abraham, the God of Isaac, and the God of Jacob"? (12:26)

How do the scribes claim that the Messiah is the son of David? (12:35)

David himself calls him "Lord," so how is he his son? (12:37)

Do you see these great buildings? (1:2)

Why do you make trouble for her? (14:6)

Simon, are you asleep? Could you not keep watch for one hour? (14:37)

Are you still sleeping and taking your rest? (14:41)

Have you come out as against a robber, with swords and clubs, to seize me? (14:48)

My God, my God, why have you forsaken me? (15:34)

The Questions of Jesus in the Gospel of Luke

Why are you looking for me? (2:49)

Did you not know that I must be in my Father's house? (2:49)

What are you thinking in your hearts? (5:22)

Which is easier, to say, "Your sins are forgiven" or to say, "Rise and walk"? (5:23)

Can you make the wedding guests fast while the bridegroom is with them? (5:34)

Have you not read what David did when he and those who were with him were hungry? (6:3)

I ask you, is it lawful to do good on the Sabbath rather than to do evil, to save life rather than to destroy it? (6:9)

If you love those [only] who love you, what credit is that to you? And if you do good [only] to those who do good to you, what credit is that to you? If you lend money to those from whom you expect repayment, what credit is that to you? (6:32–34)

Can a blind person guide a blind person? Will not both fall into a pit? (6:39)

Why do you notice the splinter in your brother's eye, but do not
   perceive the wooden beam in your own? How can you say to your
   brother, "Brother, let me remove that splinter in your eye," when
   you do not even notice the wooden beam in your own eye?
   (6:41–42)

Why do you call me, "Lord, Lord," but do not do what I command?
   (6:46)

What did you go out to the desert to see—a reed swayed by the
   wind? Then what did you go out to see? Someone dressed in fine
   garments? Then what did you go out to see? A prophet?
   (7:24–26)

Then to what shall I compare the people of this generation? What
   are they like?   (7:31)

Which of them will love more?   (7:42)

Do you see this woman?   (7:44)

Where is your faith?   (8:25)

What is your name?   (8:30)

Who touched me?   (8:45)

Who do the crowds say that I am?   (9:18)

But who do you say that I am?   (9:20)

What profit is there for one to gain the whole world yet lose or
   forfeit himself?   (9:25)

O faithless and perverse generation, how long will I be with you and
   endure you?   (9:41)

And as for you, Capernaum, "Will you be exalted to heaven?"
   (10:15)

What is written in the law? How do you read it?   (10:26)

Which one of these three, in your opinion, was neighbor to the
   robbers' victim?   (10:36)

What father among you would hand his son a snake when he asks
   for a fish? Or hand him a scorpion when he asks for an egg? If
   you then, who are wicked, know how to give good gifts to your
   children, how much more will the Father in heaven give the Holy
   Spirit to those who ask him?   (11:11–13)

If Satan is divided against himself, how will his kingdom stand? If I, then drive out demons by Beelzebub, by whom do your own people drive them out? (11:18–19)

Did not the maker of the outside also make the inside? (11:40)

Are not five sparrows sold for two small coins? (12:6)

Friend, who appointed me as your judge and arbitrator? (12:14)

Can any of you by worrying add a moment to your life span? If even the smallest things are beyond your control, why are you anxious about the rest? (12:26)

If God so clothes the grass in the field that grows today and is thrown into the oven tomorrow, will God not much more provide for you, O you of little faith? (12:28)

Who then is the faithful and prudent steward whom the master will put in charge of his servants to distribute the food allowance at the proper time? (12:42)

Do you think that I have come to establish peace on the earth? (12:51)

You know how to interpret the appearance of the earth and the sky; why do you not know how to interpret the present time? (12:56)

Why do you not judge for yourselves what is right? (12:57)

Do you think that because these Galileans suffered in this way they were greater sinners than all other Galileans? Or those eighteen people who were killed when the tower at Siloam fell on them— do you think they were more guilty than everyone else who lived in Jerusalem? (13:2, 4)

Why should it exhaust the soil? (13:7)

Does not each one of you on the Sabbath untie his ox or his ass from the manger and lead it out for watering? This daughter of Abraham, whom Satan has bound for eighteen years now, ought she not to have been set free on the Sabbath day from this bondage? (13:15–16)

What is the kingdom of God like? To what can I compare it? . . . To what shall I compare the Kingdom of God? (13:18, 20)

Is it lawful to cure on the Sabbath or not? (14:3)

Who among you, if your son or ox falls into a cistern, would not immediately pull him out on the Sabbath day?   (14:3, 5)

Which of you wishing to construct a tower does not first sit down and calculate the cost to see if there is enough for its completion? . . . Or what king marching into battle would not first sit down and decide whether with ten thousand troops he can successfully oppose another king advancing upon him with twenty thousand troops?   (14:28, 31)

What man among you having a hundred sheep and losing one of them would not leave the ninety-nine in the desert and go after the lost one until he finds it? . . . Or what woman having ten coins and losing one would not light a lamp and sweep the house, searching carefully until she finds it?   (15:4, 8)

If you are not trustworthy with dishonest wealth, who will trust you with true wealth? If you are not trustworthy with what belongs to another, who will give you what is yours?   (15:11–12)

Who among you would say to your servant who has just come in from plowing or tending sheep in the field, "Come here immediately and take your place at table?" Would he not rather say to him, "Prepare something for me to eat; put on your apron and wait on me while I eat and drink; you may eat and drink when I am finished"? Is he grateful to that servant because he did what was commanded?   (17:7–9)

Ten were cleansed, were they not? Where are the other nine? Has none but this foreigner returned to give thanks to God?   (17:17–18)

Will not God secure the rights of God's chosen ones who call out to God day and night?

Will God be slow to answer them?   (18:7)

When the Son of Humanity comes, will he find faith on earth?   (18:8)

Why do you call me good?   (18:19)

What do you want me to do for you?   (18:41)

Tell me, was John's baptism of heavenly or of human origins?   (20:4)

What then does this Scripture passage mean: "The stone which the
builders rejected has become the cornerstone"?   (20:17)

Show me a denarius; whose image and name does it bear?   (20:24)

How do they claim that the Messiah is the Son of David? . . . Now if
David calls him "Lord," how can he be his son?   (20:41, 44)

Who is greater, the one seated at table or the one who serves? Is it
not the one seated at table?   (22:27)

When I sent you forth without a money bag or a sack or sandals,
were you in need of anything?   (22:35)

Why are you sleeping?   (22:46)

Judas, are you betraying the Son of Humanity with a kiss?   (22:48)

Have you come out as against a robber, with swords and clubs?
(22:52)

At that time people will say to the mountains, "Fall upon us!" and
to the hills, "Cover us!" for if these things are done when the
wood is green, what will happen when it is dry?   (23:30–31)

What are you discussing as you walk along?   (24:17)

What things?   (24:19)

Was it not necessary that the Messiah should suffer these things and
enter into his glory?   (24:26)

Why are you troubled? And why do questions arise in your hearts?
(24:38)

Have you anything here to eat?   (24:41)

The Questions of Jesus in the Gospel of Matthew

You are the salt of the earth, but if salt loses its taste, with what can
it be seasoned?   (5:13)

If you love [only] those who love you, what recompense will you
have? Do not the tax collectors do the same? And if you greet
your brothers only, what is unusual about that? Do not the pagans
do the same?   (5:46–47)

Is not life more than food and the body more than clothing?
(6:25)

Are you not more important than the birds of the sky? (6:26)

Can any of you by worrying add a single moment to your life span? (6:27)

Why are you anxious about clothes? (6:28)

If God so clothes the grass of the field, which grows today and is thrown into the oven tomorrow, will he not much more provide for you, O you of little faith? (6:30)

Why do you notice the splinter in your brother's eye, but do not perceive the wooden beam in your own eye? How can you say to your brother, "Let me remove that splinter from your eye," while the wooden beam is in your eye? (7:3–4)

Which one of you would hand his son a stone when he asks for a loaf of bread, or a snake when he asks for a fish? (7:9–10)

Do people pick grapes from thorn bushes or figs from thistles? (7:16)

Why are you terrified, O you of little faith? (8:26)

Why do you harbor evil thoughts? (9:4)

Which is easier, to say, "Your sins are forgiven," or to say, "Rise and walk"? (9:5)

Can the wedding guests mourn as long as the bridegroom is with them? (9:15)

Do you believe that I can do this? (9:28)

Are not two sparrows sold for a small coin? (10:29)

What did you go out to the desert to see? A reed swayed by the wind? Then what did you go out to see? Someone dressed in fine clothing? . . . Then why did you go out? To see a prophet? (11:7–9)

To what shall I compare this generation? (11:16)

As for you, Capernaum, will you be exalted to heaven? (11:23)

Have you not read what David did when he and his companions were hungry, how he went into the house of God and ate the bread of offering, which neither he nor his companions but only the priests could lawfully eat? Or have you not read in the law that on the Sabbath the priests serving in the temple violate the Sabbath and are innocent? (12:3–5)

Which one of you who has a sheep that falls into a pit on the
Sabbath will not take hold of it and lift it out?   (12:11)

If Satan drives out Satan, he is divided against himself; how, then,
will his kingdom stand?   (12:26)

How can anyone enter a strong man's house and steal his property,
unless he first ties up the strong man?   (12:29)

Who is my mother? Who are my brothers and sisters?   (13:48)

Do you understand all these things?   (13:51)

O you of little faith, why did you doubt?   (14:31)

Why do you break the commandment of God for the sake of your
tradition?   (15:3)

Are even you still without understanding? Do you not realize that
everything that enters the mouth passes into the stomach and is
expelled into the latrine?   (15:16–17)

How many loaves do you have?   (15:34)

You of little faith, why do you conclude among yourselves that it is
because you have no bread? Do you not yet understand, and do
you not remember the five loaves for the five thousand, and how
many wicker baskets you took up? Or the seven loaves for the four
thousand, and how many baskets you took up? How do you not
comprehend that I was not speaking to you about bread?
(16:8–11)

Who do people say that the Son of Humanity is?   (16:13)

Who do you say that I am?   (16:15)

What profit would there be for one to gain the whole world and
forfeit his life? Or what can one give in exchange for his life?
(16:26)

O faithless and perverse generation, how long will I be with you?
How long will I endure you?   (17:17)

What is your opinion, Simon? From whom do the kings of the
earth take tolls or census tax? From their subjects or from
foreigners?   (17:25)

What is your opinion? If a man has a hundred sheep and one of
them goes astray, will he not leave the ninety-nine in the hills and
go in search of the stray?   (18:12)

Have you not read that from the beginning, the Creator "made them male and female" and said, "For this reason a husband shall leave his father and mother and be joined to his wife and the two shall become one flesh"? (19:5)

Why do you ask me about what is good? (19:17)

What do you wish? (20:21)

Can you drink the cup that I am going to drink? (20:22)

What do you want me to do for you? (20:32)

Yes, and have you never read the text, "Out of the mouths of infants and nurslings you have brought forth praise"? (21:16)

Where was John's baptism from? Was it of heavenly or of human origin? (21:25)

What is your opinion? . . . Which of the two did his father's will? (21:28–31)

What will the owner of the vineyard do to those tenants when he comes? (21:40)

Did you never read in the Scriptures: "The stone that the builders rejected has become the cornerstone; by the Lord has this been done, and it is wonderful in our eyes"? (21:42)

Why are you testing me, you hypocrites? (22:18)

Whose image is this and whose inscription? (22:20)

And concerning the resurrection of the dead, have you not read what was said to you by God, "I am the God of Abraham, the God of Isaac, and the God of Jacob"? (22:31–32)

What is your opinion about the Messiah? Whose son is he? (22:42)

How does David, inspired by the Spirit, call the Messiah "Lord," saying: "The Lord said to my Lord, 'sit at my right hand until I place your enemies under your feet' "? If David calls him "Lord," how can he be his son?" (22:43–45)

Blind fools, which is greater, the gold, or the temple that made the gold sacred? . . . You blind ones, which is greater, the gift, or the altar that makes the gift sacred? (23:17–18)

You serpents, you brood of vipers, how can you flee from the judgment of Gehenna? (23:33)

You see all these things, do you not? (24:2)

Who then is the faithful and prudent servant, whom the master has put in charge of his household to distribute to them their food at the proper time?   (24:45)

Lord, when did we see you hungry and feed you, or thirsty and give you drink? When did we see you a stranger and welcome you, or naked and clothe you? When did we see you ill or in prison, and visit you? . . . Lord, when did we see you hungry or thirsty or a stranger or naked or ill or in prison, and not minister to your needs?   (25:37–39, 44)

Why do you make trouble for the woman?   (26:10)

So you could not keep watch with me for one hour?   (26:40)

Are you still sleeping and taking your rest?   (26:45)

Do you think that I cannot call upon my Father and he will not provide me at this moment with more than twelve legions of angels? But then how would the Scriptures be fulfilled which say that it must come to pass this way?   (26:53–54)

Have you come out as against a robber, with swords and clubs to seize me?   (26:55)

My God, my God, why have you forsaken me?   (27:46)

John Dear is a priest, retreat leader, author, and peace activist. He has served as the executive director of the Fellowship of Reconciliation, an interfaith peace organization, and as a Red Cross coordinator of chaplains at the Family Assistance Center in New York City after the September 11, 2001, attacks. He has traveled to the world's war zones on missions of peace, has been imprisoned repeatedly for civil disobedience against war, and has been featured in the *New York Times*, the *Washington Post*, NPR's *All Things Considered*, *USA Today*, and the *National Catholic Reporter*. He lives in northeastern New Mexico. For further information, see *www.johndear.org*